To
Diana Howe Etheridge
class of 1962
with respect and admiration

Allen D. Breck

FROM THE ROCKIES TO THE WORLD

(A companion to the History of the University of Denver, 1864–1997)

Second Edition

by
Allen D. Breck
Professor Emeritus of History
and
University of Denver Historian

The University of Denver
Denver, Colorado
1997

The Seal of the University of Denver

Designed by Frank L. Phillips, a University of Denver art instructor, the seal was created under the direction of Anne Evans, daughter of University founder John Evans. The mountains in the background represent Mount Evans. Anne Evans took great interest in Native American culture and art and wanted a Native American design above the mountains—the swirl. It has been said the swirl is a symbol of good luck and long life, but such meaning has not been substantiated. The motto on the seal, "Pro Scientia et Religione," means *for knowledge and faith.* This seal was adopted April 26, 1933. The words, "Colorado Seminary" were added to the seal in 1976, and the University began using it for business and legal matters.

School Colors

The University colors had been gold and crimson, but in 1931, by order of the board of trustees, the official colors adopted were lemon yellow and alizarin red. On June 10, 1956, the hues and meanings were defined more exactly. Crimson symbolized Colorado, which means "red" in Spanish (from the preponderance of the color of the earth in some parts of the state); gold was selected to represent the metal mined from Colorado's mountains and panned from its streams, the search for which was the chief reason for the pioneers' settling in this territory.

1st Edition printed at the Hirschfeld Press, Denver
2nd Edition printed at Edwards Brothers, Michigan
Copyright 1997 by the University of Denver (Colorado Seminary)
Library of Congress Catalog Card Number LD 1563.B744b 1996
ISBN No. 0-9648871-0-X

Contents

V. The University in the Second World War and Aftermath 131

VI. The University Enters the Widest World, 1953–89 155

VII. Reinvigoration and Expansion, 1989–97 211

By Way of Introduction

Dear reader, you have in your hand a narrative that surveys a single aspect in the history of a major institution of the Rocky Mountain West—its developing role in relation to the people and ideas around it. It is a "companion" in the sense that it answers a number of important questions, but it omits many that would find their place in more leisurely paced volumes. Such works will have to depend on many more written materials. Here then is a proposal that each of the many units of the University (colleges, schools, departments, programs) assemble and publish its own history. How much richer we would be with a full-scale account of, say, the College of Law, the Denver Research Institute, the High Altitude Laboratory, the Department of History! We need personal reminiscences. The target publication date could be well before the sesquicentennial celebration of the founding in 2014.

That the University is a school completely different from the struggling seminary that began its life in 1864 at the corner of 14th and Arapahoe is abundantly clear. Yet among all the vicissitudes of its life, the structure—the charter, trustees, a teaching body, students, commitment to service—remained in place. Our purpose, then, is to show how such an institution, over time, has been both the agenda of the times and the clay molded and influenced by the enlarging world around it.

The events of 133 years crowd in—so many personalities, crucial turning points, opportunities seized or missed, programs initiated and developed or abandoned, relationships secured, hopes fulfilled, bright promises tarnished. Combining all these elements in a short narrative is impossible, so we shall be guided by a single theme—the enlargement of the role this University has played in relation to the great world beyond, first in its origins, then in the frontier environment in which it was born, then in its extension throughout the West and across America, and its present position with world-wide interests and concerns. It is a story of dreams, visions, frustrations, and accomplishments.

Heartfelt thanks go to the countless people who have searched for and furnished materials and who have shared their reminiscences. In the preparation of this volume, special thanks go to Dr. Robert E. Roeder, who tirelessly and with thoughtful and painstaking care saw the manuscript through the press. Steven Fisher and Nancy Metzger in Archives and Special Collections ferreted out endless sources. Robert Runnels in graphics, and Tom Cherrey, University photographer, made unique contributions. Further thanks go to Randolph P. McDonough for his fund of memories, and to my wife, Salome, for her constant support, which included many proofreadings.

Thanks also go to the Gamma of Colorado Chapter of Phi Beta Kappa for an initial grant for supplies, and to members of the University's Board of Governors for funds for publication. I am pleased to offer the research and writing of this history as a gift to my alma mater.

Allen D. Breck
Preface to the First Edition

Eight years would seem too short a time in which to expect another edition of this work. Happily, so much has happened since 1989—a new chancellor, vast plans for programs, people, buildings in process of being put to use on campus drastically different in purpose and appearance—that the story needs to be told here and now.

We need to remember that this account is of necessity incomplete. Much is left out: Changes are going on with surprising frequency. Eventually a complete history will be possible, constructed from special histories of all the individual colleges, departments, and administrative units, as well as biographies and memoirs.

Meanwhile, it should be possible to publish each year a summary of the previous year's activities in a format that could be added to this volume.

My deepest thanks go to all those people who responded to telephone calls and memos and participated in interviews with a prompt supply of data and materials of all sorts. Further thanks go to all who read the manuscript but who are in no way responsible for any errors that appear in the final text. For production of this book, my appreciation goes to Provost Bill Zaranka, Charlotte Million, Rebecca Brant, Steve Fisher, and all those who saw this book through the press.

Allen D. Breck
December 1997

I. The Founding of the University: Colorado Seminary and Its Origins

The crowd that gathered at the Tremont House in Auraria, Denver City, Colorado Territory, the evening of May 16, 1862, had come to see their newly appointed governor, fresh from Washington at the bidding of President Abraham Lincoln. It was a large and expectant group, eager to hear the man who had succeeded the first governor, so abruptly removed by presidential order. They were not disappointed. The man, then 48, who appeared on the balcony above them, was cast in a large mold. At 180 pounds, almost six feet tall, Dr. John Evans was every inch a leader. With black hair brushed back over the nape of his neck, his chin covered with a short beard, his face lined, his eyes dark and snapping, he commanded attention not only with his striking appearance, but with the power of his words—his ideas just the ones the crowd wanted to hear.

It was a short, crisp speech, directed to the heart of his listeners' concerns. After apologizing for his reluctance to have a formal reception, he commented on a "pleasant and agreeable" trip across the plains. Such an understatement augured well for his powers of endurance. He continued by commenting that the land before him, which had been reported as a "barren waste, sterile and unproductive," would surely, in the quickest time, become fertile and prosperous. But balanced against such optimism, he saw the grim reality of scarce and expensive provender. Food was being sold at ruinous "prices that in the most flourishing and promising cities of the east would inspire terror and gloomy apprehension." All this was the result of the overwhelming and relentless desire of men to dig, to strike a bonanza, and either return to the East or remain and rise rapidly in society. Who in such excitement could stop to grow produce for the market?

Evans' Vision and Denver's Reality, 1862

But the remedy for these and other ills was clear in Evans' mind—the projection of the railroad west through Iowa and Nebraska, across Kansas into Denver, then to splay out north, west, and south. Transportation, the mines, the soil—all spoke to a glorious future.

As the band played popular airs on that cool spring evening and citizens pressed forward to introduce themselves, one man departed for his office in the *Rocky Mountain News* building, then perched on stilts in the middle of bone-dry Cherry Creek. As editor and owner, William Newton Byers had come to report. By the time he left, he was entranced. Byers, surely the most irrepressible booster Colorado has ever had, came away convinced he had heard just the man the hour and the place needed, a man of "plain, practical, sound sense." He entitled his editorial "Thank Heaven Colorado Has at Last Got a Governor!" Evans and Byers became firm friends, each finding in the other a vision for the future of Denver and a relentless intent to make it glorious.

The village Evans saw before him that evening was called "Denver City," more for advertising purposes than for any accurate description of population. At most there were some 3,000 people, nearly all men. The number varied erratically, as discouraged and disillusioned miners came down from the mountains to return east or move farther west, only to be replaced by newcomers lured by fantastic stories of new discoveries. They came on foot, on horseback, in wagon trains—resolute to gain great wealth and return home.

Denver was a town of log, frame, and adobe buildings, with here and there a brick structure. Almost all were unpainted and unplastered. East Denver, where Evans built his first house and donated the land for the Colorado Seminary building two years later, consisted of 11 unpaved streets laid out and named, extending from Cherry Creek east and north. Cross streets were lettered E (now 14th), F (now 15th), and G (now 16th). Beyond stretched the treeless and shrubless prairie, dotted with a few houses. When one got as far as California Street, it was "almost as isolated from town and neighbors as if on a ranch."

Lower down, along the west bank of Cherry Creek, was West Denver, formerly the town of Auraria. Here people saw greater prospects for homes, the planting of trees, and even some boardwalks.

In East Denver, the business section extended only to Arapahoe on the east and 16th (G Street) on the south. Here, in the absence of government offices, were the post office and all the busy apparatus of an entrepreneurial center for a rapidly developing mountain hinterland. Day and night, men jostled one another along the boardwalks and dirt streets. The boarding houses, saloons, gambling places, and bordellos enjoyed a thriving seven-day-a-week business. Beside them, the banking and minting companies, supply stores, and commission houses were equally active. Immense ox-drawn freight wagons filled the busy streets, and the stage lumbered in from the east and out toward Mormon territory to the west. Prosperity—the hope of personal, corporate, and public wealth—was in the air, accompanied always by the nagging doubt that it would not last. Even the most sanguine were concerned by their experiences with almost regular alternations of boom and bust on a national scale.

John Evans (1814–1897)

The mood of the day was impermanence: Could a decent civilization be built on such an unstable foundation? There were those (Evans and Byers among them) who believed it could. All it needed was business enterprise (of which there was plenty), religious enthusiasm and organization (surely sporadic on the frontier, but nevertheless present), and opportunity for educational training and culture. Physical vigor, boundless enthusiasm, and careful planning by the right leaders would take care of the rest. In the life of John Evans, these ingredients came together. Evans, known first as a canny businessman, was an upright and devout member of the Methodist church, filled with practical vision for the future of many a difficult enterprise. An incredibly hard-working man, he settled comfortably on the newest frontiers—both of geography and the mind.

The Background of a Frontier Capitalist

The descendant of a Welsh family that had migrated to Philadelphia in the 18th century, Evans was born, appropriately, in a frontier log cabin near Waynesville, Ohio in 1814. His grandfather had moved to South Carolina, marrying a woman who brought him into the Quaker fold. Their departure from the South, motivated by an intense dislike of slavery, brought them to the farming land of the Ohio frontier. They carried with them their Quaker faith, inventive genius, and sturdy independence. John's father, David Evans, became wealthy through extensive farming and business enterprises.

Young John, determined not to continue in the family business, worked on the farm, attended the nearest district school, and for a while attended Clermont Academy in Philadelphia. Despite his father's fervent wishes for John to follow in his footsteps, he attended a private medical school in Cincinnati. After two years' study of four months each (standard throughout the country at the time), he graduated as a doctor of medicine in 1838. After practicing medicine among the pioneer settlers along the Illinois River, he married the daughter of a well-known physician in Ohio and moved to Attica, Indiana. There he not only created a successful practice but became known as a successful financier. Nevertheless, public philanthropy was still his chief goal.

As a result of his planning, consultation with experts, and the drive necessary to get a tax bill through the state legislature, a substantial Hospital for the Insane was built in Indianapolis. Evans became its first superintendent. But the thought of teaching medicine in some larger sphere, and combining that profession with business enterprise, led him to join the faculty of Rush Medical College in Chicago in 1845 where he stayed for 11 years. These years were, as always for Evans, highly productive: a seminal monograph on cholera, the editorship of the *Northwestern Medical and Surgical Journal,* some significant inventions of medical apparatus, and becoming a founding father of the Illinois General Hospital of the Lakes.

Religion and education came together in Evans' thinking. Although he had been a practicing Quaker in his youth, he became impressed with the "practical idealism" of the Rev. Matthew Simpson, the first president of Indiana Asbury University at Greencastle (later DePauw). John and Hannah Evans joined the little Methodist church in Attica in 1842. The year before, he had been inspired by Simpson's lecture, by now famous in the Midwest, "On Education." Young Matthew Simpson, then 28, had arrived in 1839 with his family to take over the new school.

The town of Greencastle consisted of some 500 people, clustered in log cabins or story-and-a-half frame houses. The university, like almost all on the frontier, was only a preparatory school, housed in a two-story building with two rooms below, one above. Simpson took charge of the upper room, where he "heard his classes." Then four years into his ministry, he plunged into the development of his tiny frontier school with all the force and vigor that made him and his views on higher education famous and led to his appointment as bishop in 1852.

His inaugural sermon at the first commencement lasted two hours, following a line of reasoning that appealed to college builders and donors alike. People, the analysis ran, are the creatures of their education. They are continually receiving it, their character is directly dependent on the kind of instruction they have received, there is a national character, directly dependent on the intellectually nourished individual. The address contained great praise for colleges as precursors of the improvement, indeed the determination, of the progress of humanity. Parts of the speech appeared in his lectures in various towns all over the region.

It was heady stuff. Evans confessed his head was awhirl with the vistas opened up by education—education as the civilizing element in society, the Christian faith at its heart as the driving force, Methodist principles at work in the raw but redeemable world of the frontier.

Small wonder, then, that Evans took on a teaching position at Rush Medical School and threw himself into "Christian endeavor." He directed the development of the Methodist Book Concern, aided the Northwestern Christian Advocate greatly, promoted the Methodist Church Block in downtown Chicago, served on the city council, and helped establish the first high school. Meanwhile, he was laying the foundations of a fortune in real estate and transportation.

He saw "the city," whether Chicago, or later Denver, as the essential hub of a network of railways, stretching out into the hinterland and beyond to ports and other commercial centers. In pursuit of this vast endeavor, he helped inaugurate the Chicago and Fort Wayne Railroad, securing rights of way into the city, and as its managing director, building depots, freight yards, and storage facilities. All these activities aided both civic and personal prosperity.

Educational Theory and the Creation of Northwestern University

But the pull of higher education and the need to build an institution to secure its future were ever present. He later summed up his conviction in a succinct statement:

> There is no other use to which you can more profitably lend your influence, your labor, and your means, than of Christian education by aiding in founding a university. We may do good by improving the country, by defending it in a righteous cause, by serving it in the councils of legislation on the bench or in the forum, but these labors are more or less transient, and the impress we make is temporary. But when we found an institution to mold minds and characters for good, that will continue its operations and accumulate influence from generation to generation through all coming time, we have done the very highest and noblest service, to our country and our race, of which we are capable.

In countless speeches to church and civic groups, he returned to this theme with great effect, the thrust best shown in a speech to the Denver Board of Trade in 1873, when he was thinking of a school to be shared by several churches:

> A well-founded university lives as long as the country in which it is founded lives. It lives for ages. Its influence runs through all time. . . . Why, there is nothing in all a man's lifetime that he can do that will be so permanent in its beneficial results as founding an institution of learning that will live on, and work, year after year, age after age, after he is laid in the grave.

By 1850 Evans was ready to propose a great Christian university for Chicago. Believing Illinois the most important state in the Old Northwest (Illinois, Michigan, Indiana, Ohio), he felt the university should be located somewhere in that state and named "The Northwestern University." From the beginning it was to rival eastern schools and be financially independent. His role in the foundation of the school and in its history was summed up by a later Northwestern president, Walter Dill Scott: "From 1851 to 1894, Dr. Evans served not merely as the president of the Board of Trustees of Northwestern University. In reality, for that period, he was the university's chief educational leader and financial benefactor."

A first meeting of nine friends (three of whom were Methodist ministers) favorable to the creation of a university in or near Chicago came together May 31, 1850, and drew up a resolution:

Whereas the interests of sanctified learning require the immediate establishment of a university in the Northwest, under the patronage of the Methodist Episcopal Church, therefore be it resolved that a committee of five prepare a draft of a charter to incorporate a literary university to be located at Chicago, to be under the patronage and control of the Methodist Episcopal Church, to be submitted to the next General Assembly of the State of Illinois.

There would be a board of 28 prominent citizens, 24 of whom would be elected by the various nearby Methodist Conferences of Rock River, as well as Wisconsin, Michigan, Northern Indiana, Illinois, and Iowa.

But Evans could not leave it to ecclesiastical jurisdictions (whose members were more apt to promise than to pay) to fund as large an establishment as he had in mind. In 1851 he consequently purchased 16 lots at what is now the corner of Jackson and LaSalle streets in Chicago, for $8,000 and, as the property appreciated, sold lots to the university for a preparatory school location. Together with Matthew Simpson, he wrote the text of a bill for the legislature that would perpetually exempt university property from all taxation, both state and local. In this he was successful, with Section 4 of the legislative act of February 14, 1855, providing "that all property of whatsoever kind or description belonging to or owned by said corporation shall be forever free from taxation for any and all purposes."

This exemption was challenged in 1874 by the tax officials of Cook County, and the case was taken to the Illinois Supreme Court, which decided against the university. The trustees of the school took their case to the Supreme Court of the United States, which reversed the Illinois decision. An attempt to tax income-producing property in Chicago was decided in Northwestern's favor by the state court on December 16, 1903.

The discovery of a piece of high, dry land on the shore of Lake Michigan, 12 miles north of Chicago, was made by Orrington Lunt, a member of the board. He persuaded the trustees to authorize payment of $71 per acre for 379 acres of prime land, a total of some $25,000. The trade was closed by Evans, who took the property in his own name and gave back a mortgage for it. The town created around the university was named "Evanston" in his honor. In writing of Evanston in 1891, Frances E. Willard, famous for her leadership of the temperance movement, called it a "classic town":

Count half a dozen blocks of stores, half a score of smaller churches, four spacious public school buildings and a fine high school, and fill in the rest with comfortable and often palatial homes for about twelve thousand people, and you have a faint outline of the picture that Evanstonians enjoy.

Evans himself saw to it that one quarter of every block was reserved from sale for the endowment of the school. His generosity to Northwestern continued through his lifetime. At one time, he endowed chairs of Latin and of mental and moral philosophy with $50,000, later increasing the amount to $100,000. The Garrett Biblical Institute was located on the campus, and nearby stood the Northwestern Female College, of which Frances Willard was later president.

Bright prospects indeed, but the earliest days were filled with deepest gloom as revenues failed to come in. The university's survival was a tribute to the self-sacrifice, wise foresight, and sublime faith of the trustees and most of the faculty that their plans would be successful. Evans led them all in the exuberant pursuit of these new vistas.

The Move to Colorado

The school was started with an incoming class in November 1855, Evans' railroad was in operation, and real estate was paying well. But one dimension of life John Evans had not yet savored: the strong brew of politics. Addressing that area with his customary energy and enthusiasm, Evans became a member of the state Republican convention at Decatur, Illinois, at which time the convention named Abraham Lincoln their choice for president. Although Lincoln was well aware of Evans as a civic leader and most capable businessman, it was only through the direct intervention of Bishop Simpson that Evans was considered for political appointment, specifically as one of the territorial governors, whose jobs were given (and taken back as quickly, on occasion) by presidential order. The appointment to Nebraska went to someone else, and Washington Territory was later available, but Evans deemed it too far away from his other interests. Finally, Colorado Territory became available with the removal of William Gilpin, and Evans applied indirectly for the position. This time, Lincoln, recalling promises to Bishop Simpson, nominated Evans for a four-year term. On the confirmation by the Senate, Lincoln signed the commission on March 26, 1862. That April, Evans took the oath of office in Washington, was successful in his nomination of Samuel Hitt Elbert as territorial secretary, and prepared for his trip back home, then on to Denver. He made the journey alone, leaving his second wife, Margaret Gray Evans, and two children behind in Evanston.

Surely, in the crowd around the Tremont House in the remote village of Denver City that night of May 16, there were some who wondered why a man of such background, already prosperous, well-educated, and settled, would come here, not to seek immediate wealth, not intending to return East at the first opportunity, but apparently to grow up with the country. But for Evans there were compelling reasons.

Here was work to be done—glorious work—and he was here, if not at the beginning at least at the most opportune moment. The force of the push into the mountains had become less insistent and the opportunity of settling down and "building up the country" had arrived, giving him the chance to put resources to work in creating civic as well as personal wealth. The future looked splendid to him, much as it did to Byers and a handful of others, the present almost an unwritten slate on which could be inscribed the organizations, the lines of communications, the banks, churches, and educational institutions of a stable and enduring society. While the progress was indeed spiritual, the measuring stick was that of the advancement of industrial civilization.

Of course there were dangers and disappointments. The Gold Rush had subsided, and the energies of the federal government seemed all directed to the prosecution of the war that spring. Grant was on the move along the Mississippi, and McClellan was inching his way toward Richmond. Shiloh was fought April 6, and New Orleans fell to Farragut on April 25. The costs of the war were enormous, and the end seemed farther away than ever to Westerners. But there were other battles to be fought nearer at hand, among them the struggle for some sort of formal education.

Education (if Any) on the Frontier

Here, the educational picture was almost empty. In the absence of public schools, various attempts were made by individuals to offer schooling, the more successful including O.J. Goldrick and Lydia Maria Ring. Finally in December 1862, two public schools were established, one on each side of Cherry Creek. Although there was no scarcity of children of school age in the 1860s, a general indifference to education held by the people who considered themselves only temporary residents of the district worked against the development of any system of public education. What education was available in these schools, housed as they were in temporary quarters, was meager at best in the absence of books, other than those brought by settlers, and without adequate supplies of any sort.

It was not surprising that the new governor took the problems of education seriously. In his first message to the legislature July 18, 1862, he pointed out that as more people sought permanent homes, provision must be made for the proper education of youth. Some law, he assured them, could be framed that would make a claim for schools on all newly discovered lodes of gold or silver. Old mineral and farm land, he was afraid, would not be available, since they were always occupied before surveys could be made. Since the champions of higher education would have to wait even longer, well-to-do residents procured private tutors and sent their college-age children back to "the States" to finishing schools and colleges. Byers, who had only the rudiments of a formal education but possessed a magical gift for words, lavished many column inches in the *News* on his hopes. He shared good news on July 22, when the paper reported that a proposal would be introduced in the legislature, then meeting in the courtroom on Ferry Street in Auraria, "to enable trustees of colleges, academies, and universities to become bodies corporate," a necessary first step toward formal higher education.

Meanwhile, Evans was busy with the project of establishing a school, something more than sporadic, uncoordinated products of the minds of independent individuals, but necessarily less than a full-fledged university or college. The term "seminary" appealed to him. Originally used in horticulture for a seed-bed or nursery plot from which plants could be transferred, the term was used to describe such places as Westminster School in London as early as the 17th century. In colonial America, the term was used for boys' schools, but by the 19th century it more often appeared in the title of organizations for schooling women. The label "female seminary" also always carried the connotation of spiritually uplifting and ladylike accomplishment in the arts and literatures, free from the rigors of hard subjects more fitted to masculine needs and abilities. It was only the solid work of people like Mary Lyon and her Mount Holyoke Seminary in the 1830s that redressed the balance and introduced science, mathematics, and history into the seminary curriculum. Thus, by the 1860s, the term no longer defined a restricted offering or one directed solely to women's education. The further narrowing of the definition describing a school for the training of priests led to its common use today.

Evans' own experience with academies and similar schools in the Midwest had taught him several things: (1) they were almost always founded by religious groups; (2) they rested on shaky foundations of a transient and not always enthusiastic population in areas of economic scarcity; (3) a single fire or other disaster consequently could wipe out the entire investment of time, talent, and treasure; and (4) despite all hazards, they set out to form character, provide opportunities for personal advancement, and aid community growth.

In the states of the old Northwest, 43 universities, academies, colleges, institutes, or seminaries were still operating by 1850. There were 16 in Ohio, seven in Indiana, five each in Missouri and Michigan, four in Illinois, and three each in Wisconsin and Iowa. Of this number, only eight were officially non-sectarian, the rest having some tie, not necessarily financial, with some church body. Of the latter, the Methodists led with nine, followed by the Baptists with four, and the Presbyterians and Congregationalists, sometimes together, with eight. Roman Catholics had founded four schools, Episcopalians, Lutherans, the Friends, and United Brethren had established one each, and there were two interdenominational schools. It is no exaggeration to say of the college of the Middle West that it is the child of the church. It is equally safe to say that until the Civil War, most of them (including the universities) were, on the whole, preparatory schools offering a classical curriculum, housed in a single building, the chief officer being the man who raised the funds, taught the classes with the aid of tutors, and had a wife who ran the boarding establishment and nurtured the students.

A dozen or so Methodist conferences used the term "seminary," including the Amenia Seminary of the New York Conference (1853) and the Wesleyan Seminary in Maine (1821). There were the Worthington Female Seminary (1839), Blendon Young Men's Seminary, and Canton Female Seminary, all in Ohio. New Jersey Methodists had Pennington Male Seminary (1839), and there were others. The founders all assumed the absolute necessity of education and the equally pressing need for that education to be founded on religious principles for the purpose of character training and civic improvement. All the apparatus of research, laboratories, faculty publication, seminars, and libraries lay in the post–Civil War future, and then only for the largest and most progressive universities.

Colorado Seminary in Embryo

As a participating Methodist in 1862, Evans knew he could turn to his fellow churchmen for moral and, perhaps, financial support. First he would need a capable fiscal agent who would perform the same functions Orrington Lunt had so capably carried out in the development of Northwestern. His opportunity came soon, on the resignation of the Rev. John M. Chivington from the position of presiding elder of the Kansas Conference of the Methodist Episcopal Church. When the First Regiment of Colorado Volunteers was organized, Chivington was offered a chaplaincy, but he declined and requested a "fighting position," which he then received.

On Evans' recommendation, the conference called the Rev. Oliver A. Willard to come to Denver in October 1862 to take charge of the small Methodist Church, to build it up, and to take a hand in whatever educational opportunities there were to be developed. A brilliant young man, the brother of that redoubtable crusader for temperance, Frances Willard, Oliver Willard had been destined for the ministry by his parents, surely to become bishop, all to make up for the frustrated hopes of his father's own youth. An 1859 graduate of Beloit College, he was ordained just before setting out for Denver. He preached acceptably, but the pastoral life irked him, so he channelled his considerable energies into land speculation—an unfortunate business for the unwary—and into raising money more successfully for the new schools that Evans and others had in mind.

That November 27, the *News* reported that "a board of trustees, composed of the solid men of Denver, has been organized to superintend the erection of a seminary building, in which our youth may find proper facilities for an academic education." In the article, Byers agreed on the need for such a school, arguing that it was the duty of citizens, increasing numbers of whom were becoming permanent residents, to "share the advantages we have had in the states, and no longer deny them to our youth here."

Financing the School

By December 11, Willard had put together the names of individuals and business partners who had pledged a combined total of some $2,475, less than a quarter of the amount needed for a building, all within two and a half days. Evans led off with $500, and Colonel Chivington gave the same amount. Warren Hussey, banker and dealer in gold who lived "way out on California Street," pledged $200, as did Charles A. Cook and Company (general merchandise, mostly wholesale, with banking on the side). Cook was mayor of Denver, so his contribution made good political sense to both himself and Evans. Alfred B. Case, later active in reform movements in the state, gave $150, and W.D. Pease, secretary of the Methodist Sunday School and a dealer in the wagon train business, offered $125. Eight others came up with $100 apiece, including Will Kiskadden, who owned a business near Cherry Creek next to James H. Noteware, another donor, who had been a superintendent of schools in Kansas and was now president of the school board in West Denver and a member of the Territorial Legislature. Lewis N. Tappan, a dealer in miners' supplies and quartz mill fittings, a member of the school board in East Denver, joined the group and put his money on the line. A. and P. Byram, freighters of supplies from Nebraska City to Denver and the mountains beyond, gave their $100, as did Woolworth and Moffat, booksellers and stationers. Others included John G. Vawter, merchant and later president of the school board; John W. Smith, who owned a grocery and feed store and built flour, wool, and quartz mills in a short period of time; and one mysterious "H. Barbour."

That December, the *Tri-Weekly Miner's Register* reported that the Board of Trustees intended to erect a building worth about $10,000, and would later establish an endowment for an institution that would be "under the immediate control of the Methodist church. They are more numerous than any other denomination."

By February 1863, the subscription list had grown to $5,000, and a local contractor, Andrew J. Gill, was showing journalists plans for the building. But, of course, the base of donors was still too narrow to create a durable institution. More help being needed, the number of board members was raised to 25. Evans, probably with the advice and agreement of such men as Byers, Moffat, Willard, and others, canvassed the city for men from business, churches, city council, the educational "establishment," and the territorial legislature for representative members of an informally appointed board. This group of 25 men then met at Evans' office on Larimer, near 16th, to draw up plans for raising more money. That meeting on May 22 is a tribute to the resiliency and optimism of pioneer leaders: Just three days prior, on April 19, Denver experienced the Great Fire of 1863.

The First Disaster: Fire

The spring of that year was unusually dry, and persistent high winds roared over the barren landscape. Sometime after 2 a.m. on the 19th, a fire broke out at the rear of the Cherokee House at the southwest corner of 14th (E Street) and Blake, destroying that building and leaping over streets and around brick buildings, eating up all the wooden structures in its path in less than three hours. Dry timber and resin-permeated wood were consumed in the flames until most of the business district between Cherry Creek and 16th, from Market to Wazee, was covered by heaps of ashes. The dry bed of Cherry Creek was filled with goods, piled up by people who salvaged what they could. Only at daybreak was the fire exhausted. A contemporary witness described the scene:

> In two hours time, the best part of the city was reduced to ashes, and very many who had retired on the previous night, full of the comfort that independence or opulence gives, awoke on the morrow, impoverished or beggard. More than $350,000 worth of buildings had disappeared, few of them adequately insured, the costs of insurance in a community with almost no fire protection being excessive. But the work of rebuilding began immediately: Many of those businesses that looked forlorn one month became prosperous within a remarkably short time.

That first group of 25 that met in Evans' office at 3 p.m. on Friday, May 22, 1863, included men of a dozen different occupations, presumably all chosen by the governor and his closest friends. There were Evans, who considered himself foremost a "capitalist," as he later listed himself in city directories, and Secretary of the Territory Samuel H. Elbert, who later married Evans' daughter Josephine and became governor after her death. They were joined by two lawyers, Lewis Ledyard Weld, who left soon after for the war and perished in one of its battles, and Amos Steck, then mayor of Denver. Four others were Methodist ministers—John M. Chivington, John Cree, B.C. Dennis, and the "agent for the school" Oliver A. Willard. Andrew J. Gill and Richard E. Whitsett were involved in real estate, the former also in the construction business. Most of these men became charter members in 1864.

Byers summarized the accomplishments of the meeting in the *News* of May 28:

> On Friday last there was a meeting of the trustees, who appointed an agent and a working or executive committee. The present intention is to proceed at once toward getting the work under way. A site will be selected and proposals for building

asked. Several plans have already been drawn, and the committee will doubtless have but little difficulty or delay in adopting one. . . . Certainly no citizen of Denver will be backward in contributing to this enterprise. It is the most praiseworthy object ever started here, and viewed in the light of dollars and cents alone it will pay. Nothing can add more to the reputation of our young city than a good institution of learning.

Methodism and the Seminary

While plans for the seminary were progressing, many wondered just how sectarian the new school would be. Methodists were surely at the heart of Evans' thinking, but there were those who thought one more denominational school, in addition to the organizations proposed by the Roman Catholics and the Episcopalians, would be more than the fragile society could bear. Appearing in the *News* on June 3, 1863, a letter, signed "A Sinner," objecting to the "establishment of an academy under the exclusive control of the Methodists or any other religious sect," represented the secular view of a fair share of the populace.

Willard shot back a reply to the effect that the seminary could survive only if it were attached to some established organization, such as a church:

> The members of the M.E. Church in Denver signified their willingness to forego a church edifice for the present and contribute the sum they had intended to give to build themselves a church to the seminary enterprise. This as a fact in the past would be a good guarantee for their devotion to the enterprise in the future. More than three-fifths of the entire amount subscribed up to this date has been given by persons connected with the M.E. Church by membership or sympathy.

By his calculation, however, only 10 of the 26 trustees were Methodists, and only two of the five members of the executive committee were of that persuasion.

The Methodists had been the first to preach in Denver in the winter of 1858. The Rev. George W. Fisher, a "local minister," gave the first sermon under a cottonwood tree in December of that year. In April 1859, the Kansas-Nebraska Conference established the Pike's Peak and Cherry Creek Mission. Subsequently two ministers with long service on the frontier, the Rev. Jacob Adriance and the Rev. William H. Goode, arrived in Denver. Goode presided over the first conference here August 2, 1859. Adriance moved all over the area, now called the Auraria and Denver City Mission. The first Sunday School happened in November. In April 1869 the Rev. John Milton Chivington was sent to what had become the Rocky Mountain District of the Methodist

Episcopal Church. The Rev. A. W. Kenney was appointed pastor of the church, which met in temporary quarters, at one time renting part of St. John's Episcopal Church until Kenney died in 1862, leaving neither pastor nor place of worship. In 1862, the Rev. B. C. Dennis became presiding elder, replacing Chivington, who had received a "fighting commission" as colonel in the armed forces. With the coming of Oliver Willard, the Methodist Society prospered and finally organized the Rocky Mountain Conference on July 10, 1863. A former carpenter shop had been purchased and renovated to serve as a church. Placed in the midst of the dry bed of Cherry Creek, this building was swept away by the great flood early on the morning of May 20, 1864.

Finally, on July 22, 1863, came the incorporation of the First Methodist Episcopal Church of Denver with John Evans, John C. Anderson, John Cree, John M. Chivington, and Hiram Burton as trustees. After the flood, the homeless congregation determined to build a permanent structure. They purchased land on the southeast corner of 15th (F Street) and Lawrence streets and erected the historic First Methodist or Lawrence Street Church in 1864.

The Committee on Education of the first Rocky Mountain Conference presented a report, which was adopted:

> Resolved, that we view with satisfaction the progress already made by the Trustees of Denver Seminary that we heartily approve the officers selected for its management and the steps already taken for the erection of its buildings and the liberality of the people who contributed to its financial stability.

Meanwhile, the selection and acquisition of a site was very much on Evans' mind. He had himself built a box-like, highly utilitarian house for his family on the southwest corner of 14th (F Street) and Arapahoe. Diagonally across 14th was the small brick and wood structure of St. John's Episcopal Church, formerly owned by Southern Methodists before their hurried departure southward. Across Arapahoe from his house, Evans acquired four of the 10 lots, which eventually became the property of the school. All were owned by the Denver Town Company, which had issued certificates of share number 31 (lots one and two at the corner) to one W. T. Parkinson, who sold them to Evans on April 6, 1863. Evans then purchased two more lots, three and four (share number seven of the company) on June 12. These parcels of land were to be given for a building, the very name of which was in dispute. The Methodists talked about the "Denver Seminary" while Byers headlined "Denver University." But given the low estate of primary and secondary training, the latter title seemed to many too pretentious. There was newspaper talk of an academy and a high school, which seemed more accurate designations. An "institution of collegiate rank" could hardly be successful without adequate foundations, particularly in times of Western hardship and given the uncertainties of frontier life.

The national picture was not much better. In the East, the war ground on relentlessly. The assault on Vicksburg was countered by the repulse of Union forces in May at Chancellorsville and by Lee's drive into the North as he crossed the Potomac. The introduction of the telegraph to Denver that year brought news of triumph and disaster ever more quickly. *The Weekly Commonwealth,* however, in an article of June 11, 1863, reported the following:

> It [the seminary] is intended to commence work as soon as a site is procured. A building to cost about $10,000 will be erected. . . . The benefits of the institution are too palpable to require enumeration. We are an isolated community, and though generally supposed to be mostly of the female sex [surely they meant male], have hundreds of children and youth. . . . There is not the slightest reason why we should send our sons to St. Louis or Boston to be educated.

Somehow the sum of $10,000 was raised and Evans called his executive committee to a meeting at his office on July 22. Byers proudly reported on "Denver University" in his paper, announcing that bids had been opened, and a low bid by Andrew J. Gill—some $6,286, with brick work and plastering in addition—was accepted. As the work progressed, one might imagine John Evans fondly surveying the laying of the foundations, taking pride in the building of his own house and crossing the street to see the Seminary walls arise, story by story. Progress was slower than expected, with local masons kept busy constructing brick buildings in every direction.

That October, the exterior being finished, a cupola was placed squarely on the top, looking, some thought, like an awkward bird. Byers, who had earlier commented that "the Denver Seminary, or University, will be the handsomest looking structure in the city," found a final addition:

> The new bell, a large, fine-toned bell, has been placed in the cupola of the seminary. For the present, its ringing will announce the church hour on Sundays, forenoon and evening. It rang for the first time on Sunday last at eleven o'clock. No other little thing contributes so much to the city air of a new town as church bells. Everybody likes to hear them.

The building, stark in its simplicity, fronted 65 feet on 14th Street (E Street) and 36 feet along Arapahoe. The main doors were surmounted by an ornamental balcony. The structure rose two and a half stories with numerous windows with rounded tops, presenting a commanding appearance in a village where there were as yet no three-story structures.

View of Seminary from the river

The Seminary and Evans' house

Lawrence Street church and the Seminary
Denver Public Library Western History Collection

The old Seminary building in 1864
Denver Public Library Western History Collection

The ground floor was divided into three areas by a hall from the front door to the rear and a traverse hall from that to the left, halfway back. On the right were to be a school room and chapel, on the left a parlor and music room. To the rear was the president's room, "a living room by day and a sleeping room by night," as well as the dining room and kitchen.

On the floor above, divided into quarters by two hallways, were the main music room, a separate room each for the primary and secondary grades, and smaller rooms used by teachers and boarding students. It was a tightly organized scheme, in which, as in all the schools on the frontier, every usable space was filled.

The Charter Is Granted

With the building half completed, Evans turned to the territorial legislature to incorporate the school. Having had experience with this process in dealing with the Illinois legislature in the founding of Northwestern, he could, as governor, foresee the problems and opportunities and move the necessary legislation quickly through that peripatetic body, then meeting in Denver. Since its creation in 1861 the legislature met first in Denver, in rooms on Larimer Street, then moved its second session to the primitive quarters of the town hall in Colorado City, then promptly voted to adjourn to its old quarters in West Denver. In its third session, the legislature opened February 1, 1864, in Loveland Hall in Golden City, but adjourned to Denver about a week later to meet in the courtroom on Ferry Street, with the Council in quarters nearby.

On Friday, February 19, Moses Hallett, later a famous federal judge, introduced into the Council, or upper house, Bill Number 22 (also known as House Joint Resolution Number 5), to incorporate the Seminary. The bill was read a second time that Saturday and then referred to the Committee on Incorporations. On Tuesday, February 23, the committee of the whole, having considered the bill, sent it back without amendment and recommended its passage. On Wednesday it was passed unanimously by the 12 members. The House of Representatives took up the bill on Friday, gave it two readings, referred it to the Committee on Incorporations, read it a third time, and passed it to the Committee on Endorsement. Passing that committee, it was laid on the governor's desk.

On Saturday, March 5, John Evans informed the Council that he had approved and signed various acts on March 4, one to incorporate the Beaver Creek Ditch and Fluming Company of Park County, another "to exclude traitors and alien enemies from courts of justice in this Territory in civil cases," one "to enable soldiers to acquire and hold mining and other claims," and "an Act to incorporate the Colorado Seminary."

This charter named 28 men to constitute the board of trustees as a "body politic and incorporate for the purpose of founding, directing, and maintaining an institution of learning, to be styled the Colorado Seminary." As of June 1, they were to be divided into four classes of seven each for a period of one, two, three, and four years. Further, "their successors shall be appointed whenever terms expire, or vacancies for any cause exist, by the Annual Conference of the Methodist Episcopal Church, within whose bounds the City of Denver may be included."

By common agreement, as well as by necessity, it was to be a school for both men and women. As to its religious complexion, the charter specified that "no test of religious faith shall ever be applied as a condition of admission into said seminary." Section 5, which conferred a tax-exemption statement, was crucial for the continuance of the institution, as the experience of both the University of Denver and Northwestern later showed: "Such property as may be necessary for carrying out the design of the seminary in the best manner, while used exclusively for such purposes, shall be free from all taxation." The complete text of the chapter appears in Appendix I.

Twenty-Eight Men Become the Board of Trustees

The board that met on March 14 was composed mostly of men in their thirties and forties. Evans himself was 50, three were in their late twenties, one 55, another 65. Almost all had been born in the Midwest, eight in Ohio, three in New York state, two in Kentucky, and one each in Indiana, Illinois, Massachusetts, Pennsylvania, and Vermont. By occupation, most were businessmen, owners of mills and mines, lumber dealers, bankers, and real estate operators. Three—Chivington, Cree and Willard—were Methodist ministers, and three were lawyers. Evans was governor, Elbert lieutenant governor, and Amos Steck mayor of Denver. At least nine were members of the Masonic lodge,

---

Classes and Officers, Meeting of March 14, 1864

Class I (to 1865)	Class II (to 1866)	Class III (to 1867)	Class IV (to 1868)
Jerome B. Chaffee	Robert Berry (vice president)	Samuel H. Elbert	Alfred B. Case
Charles A. Cook		John Evans, MD (president, Exec. Committee)	John M. Chivington (Exec. Committee)
Joseph B. Doyle (deceased)	Warren Hussey		
	John T. Lynch	Hiram Burton	John Cree
Lewis Jones	David H. Moffat (treasurer)		Andrew J. Gill
Milo Lee		William N. Byers (secretary, Exec. Committee)	W. D. Pease
William A. H. Loveland	Edwin Scudder (Exec. Committee)		John G. Vawter (Exec. Committee)
	John W. Smith	Amos Steck (president)	
Amos Widner			Oliver A. Willard (business agent)
		Richard E. Whitsett	

---

with an equal number of members of the territorial legislature. In all, they represented the business and official part of the Denver community and its vast hinterland.

Life on the frontier assured that men of this sort led interesting lives, filled with alternations of high adventure and the humdrum. They were not, in the popular phrase, "larger than life," but they were able to fill life completely, as seen in the life of John Evans. A brief look at the careers of the president of the board, its vice president, treasurer, and the secretary of the Executive Committee illustrates the point even further.

Amos Steck, president of the board at 42, was an Episcopalian. He had been born in Ohio and was taken as a boy to Pennsylvania, where he attended school near Philadelphia and went on to attend Jefferson College. He studied law in western Pennsylvania at the office of a local judge. By 1846, he was teaching school and practicing law in Wisconsin. Three years later, he joined in the Gold Rush, serving for awhile as assistant postmaster. He married, had a family, and entered the dry goods business only to be ruined in the Panic of 1856. Two years later, in May, he arrived in the mining areas of Colorado. He was admitted to the bar of the Territory in 1861, and served as mayor of Denver from 1863 to 1864. Ten years later, he became a probate judge, then a receiver of monies in the federal land office, a state senator, and for many years secretary of the Denver Public School Board. An elementary school in East Denver was named for him.

Samuel H. Elbert (1833–1899) was born in Logan County, Ohio. The son of a physician, Elbert attended Ohio Wesleyan, graduated in 1854, and went on to study law at Dayton, after which he was admitted to the bar. He moved to Nebraska, for which he served as a delegate to the Republican National Convention in Chicago in 1860. He impressed John Evans mightily, so Evans successfully petitioned President Lincoln to appoint him as Territorial Secretary, a position he held from 1862 to 1866. Elbert married Evans' daughter Josephine, who died of consumption in 1868. The Evans Memorial Chapel of Grace Methodist Church was built in her memory. Elbert served as governor of Colorado from 1873 to 1874, then joined the state supreme court in 1876, serving as chief justice from 1880 to 1888. Mount Elbert, the highest peak in Colorado at 14,433 feet, was named for him.

David H. Moffat Jr. (1839–1911), Seminary treasurer, was born in Orange County, New York. A poor country boy, with few opportunities for schooling, he persevered in self-education, becoming a bank messenger in New York City. He moved up through the hierarchy of the banking system, first as teller in Des Moines, then in Omaha. Forming a partnership with C. C. Woolworth of St. Joseph, Missouri, Moffat arrived by prairie schooner in Denver in March 1860 to open the book and stationery store of Woolworth and Moffat on Larimer Street. Evans appointed this young man, then 25, as adjunct general of Colorado during Indian raids. From his later post, as cashier of the First

National Bank, he became its president. At the height of his activities, he was one of Colorado's wealthiest men, owning three-fourths of the stock of the bank and half of the Denver Tramway's shares and participating in a handful of smaller banks around the state. Turning to railroads, he participated in the Denver, South Park, and Pacific. In the 20th century, at the age of 63, he invested a large part of his fortune in the Denver, Northwestern, and Pacific, the Moffat Road, to build a direct line over Rollins Pass to Salt Lake City. The road terminated at Craig, in northwestern Colorado. In railroad endeavors as elsewhere, the ties between Moffat and the Evans family remained firm and mutually supportive.

The secretary of the first Executive Committee, William N. Byers (1831–1903), was born on his father's farm in Madison County, Ohio. In the absence of formal schooling, he taught himself to read, write, and calculate. By 1852, he worked in Oregon and Washington and later in California as a government surveyor. He next appeared in Omaha, then only a single dwelling-place, as a land company surveyor, marking out the greater part of the town. A member of the board of aldermen, at the age of 23 he became a member of the first territorial legislature of Nebraska. The idea of creating a newspaper in the Pikes Peak region at the height of Gold Rush fever struck him so forcibly that he purchased a press, saw it delivered in Denver, and published the first copy of the *Rocky Mountain News* on April 23, 1859. The *News* was a powerful voice, in which no issue was small and no opportunity to boast of the grandeur of business enterprise or a significant beginning such as the Seminary was to be lost in the telling. At the age of 32, the self-taught Byers was a founding father of a university.

Between Evans and Byers there existed the firmest of bonds. Each appreciated the other's overwhelming desire to build, create, and develop a great city in the wilderness. A boundless optimism accompanied their excitement. Evans provided shelter and sustenance for the Byers family during the Great Flood of 1864. In 1873, Byers built an elegant mansion at the corner of 13th and Bannock, selling it in 1890 to William G. Evans, the governor's son. Substantially enlarged, this Victorian house, with its mulberry-colored brick and widow's walk, was an Evans house until 1982, when it was given to the State Historical Society to be opened as a museum.

Three other members of the executive committee included John G. Vawter, Edwin Scudder, and John M. Chivington. The first of these, Vawter, operated a mercantile establishment, J. G. Vawter and Company. A picture of Cherry Creek after the flood shows the large wooden structure of the American House standing on the bank and next to it the two-story building of Vawter's emporium. Vawter dabbled in politics as an alderman, was president of the school board of district two, appeared as a member of the grand jury, and the like.

Captain Edwin Scudder (1813–1872) was born in Oysterville, Massachusetts, and became pilot of a fishing vessel along the New England coast out of Gloucester and later of a steamboat in Iowa. As a merchant in Cambridge and elsewhere, he made money from the grain trade before pushing west. He arrived in Denver and entered the grocery business with Freeman B. Crocker. The two first operated out of a small tent in which they slept and stored their goods. They plied their trade under the cottonwood trees, with home delivery being made by wheelbarrow. A cheery soul, "a typical New England coast skipper," Scudder entered joyfully into local politics, becoming a county commissioner, a member and the treasurer of the school board, a member of the territorial legislature and the City Council, and president of the Board of Trade.

The Rev. John Milton Chivington (1820–1894), who achieved great glory in 1862—and equal notoriety for a single act in November 1864—was the hero of the Western world that March. His appearance, like that of Evans, was impressive; Chivington was a fine example of the preacher militant. More than six feet in height, of large frame, and otherwise of magnificent physique, with mental powers befitting his physical prowess, he was well designed as a leader of men in warfare.

He was born in Warren County, Ohio, and having pursued various careers as lumberman and carpenter, in the prime of life at 44, he was ordained a Methodist preacher with charges in Ohio, Illinois, Missouri, and Nebraska. Appointed resident elder of the Rocky Mountain District of the Kansas Conference, he arrived in Denver with his family in May 1860. A strong anti-slavery advocate, he longed for action against the Confederacy. Governor Gilpin offered him a chaplaincy, which he rejected in favor of being appointed major in the First Regiment Colorado Volunteers in August 1861. He was promoted to colonel the following April. In the military operations of that unit in New Mexico, he was an inspiring leader, "the bravest of the brave," despite a total lack of previous military experience.

In spite of Chivington's attempts at the end of the campaign to have the troops transferred to the Army of the Potomac, the regiment was re-formed early in 1863 and broken up. Chivington was placed in charge of the Colorado Military District, a position he held until his fateful decision to solve the "Indian Problem" by force, which led to what some termed "the sickening slaughter" at Sand Creek in southeastern Colorado on November 24, 1864. Released from service in January, he spent four months in congressional hearings, then became an agent of the Nebraska Church Extension Society, and freighted and farmed for awhile. He finally returned to Denver, where he wrote and held minor offices until his death in 1894. He was buried at Fairmount Cemetery. Parenthetically, Evans was also blamed in Washington for his part in the Sand Creek Massacre, and, although completely exonerated, was relieved of his position in 1865.

Such were the executive officers of the Seminary in its earliest days. All were hand-picked by Evans and were for the most part businessmen, entrepreneurs, bankers, freighters, and commission agents. Among them, Evans was by far the wealthiest. The reports to R. G. Dun and Co., made by local agents, estimated his assets at $250,000—some 10 times the reserves available to anyone else in Denver. In addition to businessmen, there were of course Methodist ministers. At the heart of the board, the trio of Evans, Byers, and Chivington maintained the drive and continuity that were necessary to launch this fragile ship in a world unaccustomed to giving money, even for good enterprises, or to valuing education, especially education considered suspiciously Methodist.

Natural and man-made disasters of considerable magnitude played a role in dampening enthusiasm for great projects and delaying financial rewards, and always in the background loomed the war, a series of bloody struggles to which there seemed no end.

The Second Disaster: Water

The great fire of April 19, 1863, was followed 13 months later by an equally disastrous flood. It began high in the mountains, when heavy, drenching rain pounded the watershed of the divide and created a tumultuous, irresistible wall of water along Plum and Cherry Creeks and swept into Denver at midnight, Thursday, May 18. Cherry Creek, looked on as a dry bed despite Indian warnings, had numerous wooden buildings perched on stilts and sitting precariously within its banks. These included Byers' *News* plant, city offices, the Methodist Church, and various business houses. Unfortunately, the bridges across the stream were built just above the sands, where piled-up debris contributed to the push of water outside its banks into both East and West Denver. The best eyewitness account is that of O. J. Goldrick in the *Commonwealth*. Filled with purple passages and unreliable statistics, it was nevertheless a vigorous piece of writing:

> Presently the great noise of mighty waters, like the roaring of Niagara, or the rumbling of an enraged Aetna, burst upon us, distinctly and regularly in its sounding steps, as the approach of a tremendous train of locomotives. There was some hurrying to and fro in terror, trying to wake up one's relatives and neighbors, while some favored few, who were already dressed, darted out of doors and clamorously called their friends to climb the adjacent bluffs and see with certainty for themselves. Alas! and wonderful to behold, it was the water engine of death, dragging its destroying train of muddied waves, that defied the eye to number them, which was moving down upon us, now following the former channel, and now tunneling, direct through banks and bottoms, a new channel of its own.

For four hours the flood waters surged along the creek and the Platte River bottoms, carrying buildings and people downstream, burying bits and pieces of equipment miles below the village. The river itself moved an eighth of a mile westward. People were rescued in army skiffs and brought, exhausted, to dry land. The Byers family on its farmstead above Denver was rescued by a group of soldiers led by Colonel Chivington and brought to the Evans home for several days. Later, as the waters failed to go down, the Byers moved into the completed, but not yet occupied, rooms of the Seminary building.

A quarter of a million dollars worth of property was swept away, somewhere between eight and fifteen people in the area drowned, and all the records of probate and property and those of the commissioners were lost, including the minutes of the Seminary's Board of Trustees. It is a measure of the informal nature of those early meetings that later some members found themselves unable to remember the exact class they had been voted into. Evans summarized the problem at the conference of 1867:

> At the first and only meeting of the Board of Trustees, as authorized by the charter, the management was placed in the hands of an Executive Committee and the trustees were determined by lot. But in the flood of May 20, 1864, the records of the meeting were carried away with all the records of the secretary (Mr. William N. Byers) in Cherry Creek. It being impossible to tell whose terms expired, it has been thought best to have the entire board stand, as designated in the charter, until the annual conference of 1868, when their terms will have expired. They continue in office until their successors are appointed. . . . The attention of the conference is, however, directed to the propriety of filling by appointment, at this time, of the places of such trustees as have died or permanently removed from the Territory.

Teachers and Students

Meanwhile, the Seminary building, standing several blocks from the edge of the Cherry Creek, was in no danger from the flood. Indeed, Byers and his family spent several days in the building as they recovered from their ordeal. An advertisement in the *News* of July 28, 1864, announced that the structure was ready for occupancy and that "a competent daily teacher will be secured for the fall." Even more engagingly, the Methodist Conference of October 20 anticipated a "corps of teachers," appointed two of its members as a board of visitors, and recommended to the several churches one sermon each year "On Education," with emphasis on the Seminary.

There was growing competition, however, for students of primary and high school age in the town. Four other private schools were the Rev. A. B. Day's "school for both sexes," Professor James B. Murphy's school for boys, Miss J. R. Glen's "select school for boys," and St. Mary's Academy for young ladies. There were also two public schools, one with eighty pupils in West Denver, the other with seventy students on the east side, housed in rented buildings. By the time the Seminary opened, there were some 11 schools to which parents could send their children, although some of these were small and had but a short life. As for the Seminary, the names of most of its pupils have disappeared.

The names and careers of trustees, ministers, teachers, and administrators appear in some detail in newspapers and written records, so historians can describe them. But what of the students? We know nothing of their daily lives, what share most of them took in the regular routine of classroom and play. In the absence of grade books, attendance lists, and group pictures, it is difficult to put together an accurate picture of the student body in the first four years. The curtain lifts occasionally—at the exercises at the end of a quarter or an academic year or an exhibition of special talent in music or declamation. Two baseball games appear in the daily press, one in the *News* of November 4, 1867 (in which the seminary was beaten by "the Arapahoe Clubs"), the other on November 27, 1867, with the "Occidental Club." Administrators, however, provided more information.

The Presidency of George S. Phillips, 1864–65

The first of the Seminary's four presidents appeared on the scene October 24, 1864. The Rev. George S. Phillips, MA (Ohio Wesleyan University), transferred at the age of 45 to Denver at the special request of Bishop Edward R. Ames. Phillips was born near Danville, Pennsylvania, and was taken by his parents to Ohio at an early age. While still young, he had experienced a deep and moving conversion, which led him to college, then to the ministry. In 1841 he became a circuit rider throughout northern Ohio. Highly motivated to work in the mission field, Phillips and his wife journeyed to California, taking the overland route across Panama, his wife riding horseback on a man's saddle. In December 1851, their ministry began on Market Street in San Francisco. Phillips served in the California Mission Conference for 10 years, first as editor of the *California Christian Advocate,* then for a longer time as president of the "Young Ladies Department" of the University of the Pacific. From 1857 to 1861 he was principal of Santa Clara Female College.

Returning to Ohio in 1861, he was caught up in the desire for military service and became chaplain of the 49th Infantry Ohio Volunteers, serving with General Sherman in his rapid, bloody march toward Atlanta, sharing the hardships and privations of the soldier in the ranks. At Chattanooga, where they were forced to the extremity of subsisting on the flesh of their horses and mules, he contracted dysentery, and, as they neared Atlanta, became so debilitated that he was forced to resign and return to his home in Ohio. After improving somewhat, he took a position with the "Christian Commission" for a few weeks, until he was called to the new presidency in Denver.

Thinking of the invigorating air of the Rockies and what looked like an uncomplicated life there, he came eagerly to the West, his arrival being duly reported in the *News* of October 24, 1864. On Monday, November 14, 1864, the new school opened with 35 or 40 (some said 50) pupils. Following the pattern of many such schools on the frontier, the control lay in the hands of the executive committee of the Board of Trustees, which in turn gave over the management of funds, the hiring of teachers, the control of the curriculum, and, indeed, almost all of the teaching, to the president. Mrs. John Cree was hired as "matron of the boarding department," and a certain Almedia R. Treadway with a certificate from the State Normal School of New York was hired to assist in teaching.

The school year was divided into three quarters, with tuition each term fixed at $15 for primary pupils, $20 for preparatory school students, and $30 for academic department students. As for the curriculum itself, it was obviously designed to attract a wide variety of youngsters: "[It] comprises all the branches of a solid and ornamental education for juveniles and adults of both sexes. It embraces the rudiments of a business, practical, commercial, or scientific course, with music, drawing, scientific experiments, etc." At least, that is how the advertisement in the local papers read.

The winter of 1864–65 was excessively hard. It was unusually cold, forcing Seminary students to busy themselves with feeding fuel to the building's wood- and coal-burning stoves. Food prices were high, even for Colorado, and local crops yielded only meager harvests. The fear of Indian raids was omnipresent, despite the cold and the snow and the "lesson" the Indians were supposedly given at Sand Creek. The hardships of the winter sapped the courage and energy of many a Denver resident, including those of President Phillips, whose constitution was not the best. On January 7, 1865, the newspapers reported his departure on leave. He did indeed make it home to Ohio in safety, but died of tuberculosis at Brookville, Ohio, on March 30, 1865. He served as best he could, but managed to remain in Denver only six weeks. He left one message, a powerful testament.

Just as Evans, Byers, Whitsett, and other Western enthusiasts trumpeted the growth of the community through sober industry and inspired vision, Phillips had carried around in his mind a belief about America's purpose in the world. He worked it out in a series of lectures, which he delivered in Ohio and elsewhere and published in Cincinnati in 1864 as "The American Republic and Human Liberty Foreshadowed in Scripture." The title gives us the whole story, a concept familiar to 19th century Americans as Manifest Destiny. God, so Phillips' thinking went, had in the beginning chosen the Jewish people to be the original federal republic, composed of 12 federated tribes. Unfortunately, with the coming of monarchy, the Jews strayed from the true path, and, until the coming of the American democracy, the way was indeed lost. The "Jewish church" was indeed the prototype of the Christian church, but that latter body, with its pope, was equally far abandoned in the Middle Ages. Only with the arrival of Protestantism was the path regained, and then only in America. The fifth monarchy, which would destroy and replace all other rule, the fruits of the Revelation of St. John, all pointed to a true republic, the offspring of the church and the "restored Israel" spoken of by the Jewish prophets of old. The book points first to one and then another of the mighty acts of God in the Scripture as being parallel to great events in American history. Americans were the new "chosen people," and only in the New World would God's high purposes be fulfilled:

> God seems to have kept the New World, with its vast forests and grand prairies, as the place of his Christian Israel. Here for ages the wilderness remained unbroken; kings and kingdoms rose and fell in other portions of the world, while Jehovah, in His mysterious providence, was preparing the way for the coming nation, which was not to grow up on the ruins of another, but was to receive its birth outside of all other nations, to grow up where monarchy had never cast its dark shadow as an occupant of the country.

The duty of every American was clear, therefore, and most clear to those on the frontier: To be a showcase of democracy in which men and women alike would peacefully bring the advantages of real civilization to the rest of the world.

Phillips' book was significant, not because there was anything new in its message or the reasoning behind it, but rather because it represented the thinking of a multitude of empire builders and their assured and enthusiastic followers.

Similar allusions to the uniqueness of America's destiny and duty permeated sermons and lectures. The Rev. I. D. Clark delivered an address before the Seminary Association at the church and talked about "Our Liberty and Its Destiny." As faithfully reported in the *News* of June 15, 1866,

> He [Clark] showed that our liberty differed from that of any other nation that ever existed, in being founded on the principles of education and pure religion. Neither, alone, was able to sustain a permanent freedom. The pilgrim fathers planted the church and schoolhouse side by side, and if we ever rest the foundations of our government on these two principles, we shall enjoy an enduring freedom. The power in this country rests on the ballot box, and if our liberty is to be immortal, that

ballot must have both intelligence and principle. He believed that in the future this liberty would reach every root of this continent, every nationality and race. That like a great wave of the sea, it would reach the despotisms of the Old World, lifting man everywhere to a higher and holier life.

Meanwhile, on Phillips' departure from the Seminary, Oliver A. Willard added interim president to his other duties as the first term ended February 10, 1865. These were difficult times. Denver of 1865 was a town of some 5,000 people. It was still raw and unfinished in appearance, the frontier uncouthness not yet wholly gone. The tallest buildings were only two stories in height. As Jerome Smiley put it in his inimitable history of Denver, "Outside the area bounded by the two streams and Champa and Twentieth streets, the prairie dogs were little disturbed."

Transportation was difficult. A letter from the bishop who should have presided at the first Colorado Conference of the Methodist Church put the matter succinctly. On October 1, 1864, in San Francisco, Bishop Clark addressed the Rev. Bethuel T. Vincent:

> Dear Brother: I had the question of attempting to return by the Overland route open till today, hoping to hear from you and others to whom I have written and telegraphed. But failing to hear from you, and being assured that the route continues to be impracticable, I have now concluded to take steamer and not attempt the Overland route. I hear that no preachers have come on, and that Brother Willard has not and can not yet return. Still, I would say, hold the conference and make out the appointments, sending me at Cincinnati the result.

The Presidency of George Richardson, 1865–66

That winter of 1865, the Seminary's Executive Committee, casting about for a new president, then picked a comparatively young man, the Rev. George Richardson, at 25 the pastor of the Lawrence Street Church. He had already participated by teaching classes from the opening of the school the previous fall. Richardson was born at Northfield, Vermont, July 21, 1838, of pious Methodist parents who moved to a farm near Marengo, Illinois when he was a small boy. After graduating from Garrett Biblical Institute about 1861, he became preacher in the Illinois Rock River Conference at Rockton (1862–63) and Warren (1863–64).

Although plagued with ill health, he journeyed West with a rifle over his shoulder, prepared to teach the Gospel and regain his health. Leaving his wife and small child behind temporarily, he arrived in Denver November 8, 1864, to assume the pastorate of the church. Here he found his old schoolmate, Oliver Willard, and promptly began boarding with him. On Saturday evening, February 11, 1865, he presented the first sermon in the newly erected church at 14th and Arapahoe, a structure that cost some $21,000.

He was president for just more than a year, from 1865 to 1866. In June 1866 he found himself so overworked that he was forced to resign. As he reminisced in 1903,

> During the first year, I was pastor of the Lawrence Street Methodist Episcopal church, which parish included all of Denver and Arapahoe County. Then the trustees could not afford to divide the honors of professorships very much, because there was not much pay to divide. If I may adopt modern school terms and phraseology to illustrate, I was chancellor of the schools, being at the head of the Departments of Liberal Arts, Fine Arts, Music, Law, i.e., of teaching and especially of administering law, etc. Then I was "dean" of the finances, personally making out and collecting all bills for tuition and board. Again, I was private secretary to the chancellor, attending to all his correspondence and assisting him in his various office duties. I was bookkeeper, treasurer, and hired and paid all teachers and employees, looked after many things in particular, and assisted my worthy wife in running the dormitory and boarding department. When I was professor as well, teaching six hours a day, five days a week, I occupied the chair of mathematics, languages, literature and philosophy, and especially economics. But the Executive Board elected us to do all these responsibilities and work with authority to do all these things, with one condition only, viz: that we should not incur any debts.

Hoping to regain his health with lighter work, he took a pastorate at two busy, growing mission spots in the camps of Empire and Georgetown. By 1867 he felt well enough to return to his old conference in Illinois, but he fell sick again, so he gave up the ministry, becoming at one time a traveling salesman. The Rockies lured him back to Denver in 1880, to a homestead he and his family had acquired in what was then part of the town of Argo, later a part of Denver. His later career included the presidency of the North Side Savings Bank, an organization that became the Central Savings Bank at 15th and Arapahoe, from 1896 to 1903. He died in Denver July 4, 1909.

Despite the difficulties of bad health and overwork, which had forced him to resign the headship of the Seminary, Richardson kept in touch with the University family and performed a valuable service in his reminiscences of those early days. His year in office, though filled with the bright optimism of Western

David H. Moffat Jr., treasurer

George Richardson, president, 1865-66
Denver Public Library
Western History Collection

Bethuel T. Vincent, president, 1866–67
Denver Public Library
Western History Collection

P.D. Barnhart, president, 1867–68

promotion, was one of continual anxiety, played out before the backdrop of post-war depression, the recurrent danger of Indian raids, and the trauma resulting from these and the fire and flood of previous years. On a national scale, victory and despair came close together: The surrender of Lee at Appomattox was followed by the Good Friday assassination of President Lincoln. By August, following the investigation of the Sand Creek Massacre and the forced departure of Chivington from the military, Secretary Seward was demanding Evans' resignation. Although subsequently proven innocent in the whole affair, Evans was removed by President Johnson in October 1865.

These were uncertain and tumultuous times. Even nature attacked, as the first of several infestations of grasshoppers arrived that summer, bringing farmers and consumers to despair by eating everything in sight. They came "in clouds and shoals," as one observer commented. The immediate effect was a rise in prices, added to the steady increase in the cost of transportation and foodstuffs, already higher than in the East. The uncertainty of these years—the fear that the insects would return, as indeed they did in vast hordes in 1865 and in fewer numbers in 1867—added to the general malaise.

Confronted with all these economic and social problems, it was small wonder that so fragile an institution as the Seminary, depending as it did on popular support and calm confidence in the economy, found the going difficult. The short terms of two presidents in two years did not augur well for the stability of the school, since presidents were expected to be all things to all people—in the community, the church, and to students and faculty alike, while their wives were expected to be efficient managers of housing and catering.

Through December 1864, the school having opened November 14, some 35 to 50 students were in attendance, the number varying widely and unpredictably. A "Card to the Patrons" by Phillips had urged strict discipline, regular attendance, proper recitation, and obedience—qualities that were evidently in short supply. A problem lay in the number and size of available spaces for the students. As the *News* commented on December 16, the rooms used for study and recitation were too small for both primary and advanced pupils. As late as the following autumn, there was a promise in the announcement that "a separate room will be opened for the primary scholars and another teacher secured as principal of that department." One solution occurred to the administration and was embodied in the suggestion that "larger day students are recommended to study at home as far as possible, so as to avoid the annoyance of the school room." Another problem lay in the turnover of staff.

Phillips had been aided by Almedia R. Treadway, who had been hired in November but left the following spring to marry, and by Mrs. John Cree, who as "matron of the boarding school" lived in the building with her family until the coming of the second president and his wife.

Encouraging notes were frequently sounded by a friendly press. In February 1865 it was advertised that the seats had been painted and "a superior piano reserved," that a department of painting and drawing was established under "the charge of an excellent artist who has been secured from the East." A "new lady teacher," Sarah F. Morgan, became preceptress, teaching languages, painting, and drawing. Recruited by John Evans from her post as teacher of mathematics and natural science at Northwestern Female College in Evanston, Morgan arrived with him by coach April 24, 1865. She opened the Department of Fine Arts and took charge of the preparatory room. Other staff members were Morgan's sister, Bell, as well as a teacher of German, and Mary Bannister Willard (wife of Oliver Willard) was set up as a "teacher of instrumental and voice music and to teach the rudiments of science."

Curricular Offerings: Hope and Reality in 1865

The fall term started briskly, with some 107 students and new courses of study, so that the announcement read "in this respect the trustees intend the Colorado Seminary shall be equal to the older institutions of the east." As to its religious intent, reflecting the terms of the charter,

> The trustees have established the institution to meet the educational wants of Colorado and have, therefore, planned it upon the broad principles held by all evangelical Christians, and nothing of a merely sectarian nature shall be permitted to disturb the peace or harmony of those gathered within its walls.

The school then consisted of three departments, or levels:

Primary Department	1st Class	primer, speller, first reader, slate exercises
	2nd Class	speller, second/third reader, primary geography, slate exercises
Preparatory Department	1st Year	English grammar, written arithmetic, intellectual arithmetic, geography (included "reading, spelling and penmanship")
	2nd Year	English grammar, written arithmetic, intellectual arithmetic, American history, elementary physiology, philosophy
Academic Department	1st Year	primary and higher arithmetic, primary and higher algebra, physiology, physical geography, English history, natural philosophy (later called physics), botany (included "rhetorical exercises")
	2nd Year	botany, chemistry, bookkeeping, zoology, French history, rhetoric, trigonometry, mineralogy, astronomy

3rd Year	geology, natural theology, mental science, logic, Kames' Elements, moral philosophy, universal history, evidences of Christianity, general review. (A "classical course" could be added, including Latin or Greek. "Young ladies may substitute German or French for Greek.")

Whether all these subjects were ever taught is open to doubt. Obviously some items were projects for teaching in years to come. Further, curricular statements in catalogs were—as they are today—open to diminution from high promises. Nevertheless, some curricular elements provide great insight. For instance, the absence of Hebrew as a language and the availability of Latin and Greek only as options demonstrate that the school was never intended or operated as a "seminary" for the production of a learned clergy. Ministers were trained in the East or in Chicago and made their way on call to the frontier. The development of a theological school came only with the creation of the Iliff School of Theology at the end of the century.

"Philosophy" as a subject occurs several times. First came "natural philosophy," which belonged with the sciences of geology, mineralogy, botany, physiology, astronomy, and zoology. The name given later was simply "physics." "Moral philosophy" was a mixture of subjects that were later separated into such fields as sociology, political science, ethics, and economics. "Mental philosophy" was metaphysics, dealing with the nature and being of reality and the origins and purpose of the universe. The sciences were to be taught by demonstration, without the benefit (with the obvious exceptions of mineralogy, botany, and observational astronomy) of laboratories. Lectures, the most common form of communicating ideas in the modern university, were also absent. Lectures were given by public address, often to raise money, and were open to citizens at large. In the classroom, recitation to a teacher from an approved text or series of assignments was the order of the day. Opportunities for more inventive forms of speech came with public declamation, pageant, and oral examinations at the end of each term.

Art, in the form of drawing and painting, was always available at extra cost, and was considered proper exercise for the leisure time of young ladies and eventual housewives. One course was founded on the textbook version of Kames' *Elements*. Originally in two volumes, *The Elements of Criticism* (1762) was the work of Henry Home, Lord Kames (1696–1782), a Scottish lawyer and philosopher who attempted to equate beauty with what is pleasant to the natural senses of vision and hearing.

It was, for its time and place, a heady curricular program, and not too expensive considering post-war inflation and the continuing difficulties of supply on the frontier.

The Economics of Higher Learning

The 31 pupils of the primary department paid $12 or $15 for each of three terms, the 55 students in the preparatory level paid $20, the 17 scholars in the academic department paid $30. Piano lessons cost an additional $20, vocal music cost $5, and the daily use of the piano $5 per hour or two hours for $8. There was summer school in 1865, consisting of classes in drawing and painting with those skills taught at $15 to $25 a term, and in German and French at $10 each.

The girls who "lived in," four to a room, were charged $120 a term, which included meals, but not the cost of fuel and lights. They had to supply their own furniture. Incidental expenses came to $2 a term. These prices must be considered in light of the high costs of food and transportation and the wages of laborers and mechanics that, although equally high, did no more than pay necessities, providing little for savings. Flour cost $20 for 100 pounds, beef $45 a pound, potatoes $15 a bushel. To pay for this food, laborers received $5 a day, mechanics no more than $8. These were the most available jobs.

Money in support of the school came from sources other than tuition; otherwise the building could not have been kept open. Evans continued his support, while exercising his considerable ability to extract cash and promises from the people of Colorado. There were no national support and wealthy donors to give unstintingly of their resources. Local Methodists, who had been pressed to erect the Lawrence Street Church, gave what they could.

Some income came from such gatherings as the Grand Festival and Fair, held May 18, 1865, offering an art exhibition, supper, and the opportunity to hear the "Colorado Band." At such jollifications, the *News* reported demurely, "For the good, no breath of intemperance or impurity sullied the festal hours." An Ice Cream Festival, a set piece for church socials in those years, followed the next Monday. The profit from these activities was some $1,261.50, almost all of which was used to pay for furniture and other equipment.

It occurred to some that offering a series of public lectures by leading townspeople and charging admission could help further equip the building. The first of these presentations, in December 1865, was by one Professor Maynard, who shared his views on "Mines and Mining," always a popular subject, especially since the fields were down in activity. In January 1866, the audience was properly "entranced" according to the press, by a poem on Columbus, delivered in high elocutionary style by L. N. Greenleaf.

A later lecturer, the Rev. Mr. Marsh of Central City, thought aloud about "The Triumph of Freedom in Italy." He might equally well have talked about Prussian Chancellor Bismarck, who believed "the great questions of the time are solved not by speech-making and the resolutions of majorities, but by blood and iron." At the next session, the Rev. Bethuel T. Vincent, who later became president of the school, talked hopefully about "The Man and the Masses Not

Yet in Church." He was followed in March by the last lecturer, Oliver A. Willard, who spoke "On Women." The attendance being small, the combined efforts of these five men raised little money.

On March 21 of that year, a fire in the cupola was extinguished after some $1,500 in damage. Providentially all damages were covered by an insurance policy which, thanks to Captain Scudder, had gone into effect only the day before. This seemingly insignificant event pointed to two problems. On the one hand, a large number of college buildings in America before and after the Civil War were destroyed by fire, some schools suffering such a loss that they never reopened. As for Denver, a city with no organized fire-fighting equipment, there followed the creation of the Hook and Ladder Company Number One.

Money did come in, though not handsomely, as shown in a report of the receipts on March 15, 1866. From May of the previous year, $3,533.37 had been taken in, balanced against expenses of $2,129.31. The difference, $1,404.06, became the president's salary.

The Presidency of Bethuel Thomas Vincent, 1866–67

To succeed Richardson, the executive committee then chose as part-time president the Rev. Bethuel Thomas Vincent, pastor of the Lawrence Street Church. Vincent, then 32, was born in Tuscaloosa, Alabama, August 9, 1834. His father, John H. Vincent, a Pennsylvanian by birth and Huguenot in ancestry, returned with his family to Lewisburg, Pennsylvania three years later. There he was in turn a farmer and trader, miller, postmaster, and enthusiastic Methodist Sunday School superintendent.

An older son, John H. Vincent, turned to the ministry, having attended local schools, worked in a country store, and served as principal of a small academy. His later career is of importance because of the impact it had on his younger brother. In 1850, John became an exorcist and local preacher. At 23, he became a deacon, and at 25 an elder, before transferring to the Rock River Conference of Illinois. There his progressive ideas about teaching Sunday School classes and the desperate need for better instruction led him to found a Union Sunday School Institute for the Northwest in 1864. Ten years later, his ideas of holding a national training institute for teachers bore fruit in a teachers assembly, which met in August 1874 at Fair Point on Lake Chautauqua in New York state. From this small beginning sprang the highly successful Chautauqua Movement for popular education, which proliferated into a thousand such assemblies across the country. John Vincent began a highly successful career as a Methodist bishop in 1888.

Meanwhile, Bethuel, his younger brother, went through much the same frontier training—some public schooling, then clerking at Erie for two years and in Chicago for another 10. For a short time he studied at Garrett Institute, then entered the ministry in 1860, preaching as a member of the Rock River

The Presidency of Bethuel Thomas Vincent, 1866–67

Illinois Conference for three years. In 1863 he set out for Colorado. At Atchison, Kansas, he rode the stage in grand Western style, paying $75 for a crowded inside seat on a coach that jolted its way for six days and nights, stopping only for meals and a change of horses. Relief came, as he stated: "The last night I slept on the boot, on the mail bags, under the driver's feet, with extreme comfort!"

A short stay at the Planters House on Blake and 16th (G Street) was followed by a more permanent home, on 17th between Lawrence and Arapahoe, with his fellow student and old friend, Oliver Willard. Like his older brother, Bethuel Vincent was especially devoted to Sunday School work, so much so that while he had charge of Central City and other nearby gold camps, he edited and published Colorado's first periodical, *The Rocky Mountain Sunday School Casket,* from January 1864 to October 1868. It was a small quarterly paper, which contained teaching materials and some news items, in an attempt to bring together teachers from isolated places into some common understanding of evangelistic techniques. An "efficient organizer and energetic leader, it has been said of him that no preacher had a greater influence on the evolution of the Colorado Conference."

Those talents, however, were not to be given to the administration of a school. Consequently, Vincent left the principal management of the Seminary to Sarah Morgan and gave only part of his attention to its affairs. He moved on to Colorado Springs in 1867, finally leaving Denver for Philadelphia in 1876. There he remained for 13 years, coming back to Colorado in 1889, where at 55 he was leading the same congregation at St. James', Central City, that he had served in earlier days. Finally retired, he died in Denver July 30, 1920.

School opened September 3, 1866. Two-thirds over, the year looked like a good one for Denver. Some 300 houses were erected during the building season, the prices of real estate climbing in anticipation that Denver would soon be linked by rail to the Midwest and the East. Farming was better, the grasshopper was seen no more, and the mines were producing almost double the amount of ore reached the previous year. The territorial census of the summer enumerated a Denver population of some 3,500, still concentrated in the river area, with only a few houses dotting the area between Stout Street and what was eventually known as Capitol Hill.

Vincent's sense of urgency that if the school were to survive it needed far more pupils resulted in a flurry of newspaper notices requesting parents not to send their children East to school. Meanwhile, in order to stimulate enrollment, the trustees offered the public the chance to support scholarships: $200, the offer said, could support a scholarship for five years, $300 for 10 years, and $500 for a perpetual scholarship. Although these could be attractive memorials with the donor's name attached, there is no further mention of funds acquired or scholarships granted.

The school, like such establishments elsewhere, had a literary society, whose activities, in addition to securing books for a library, included a series of free public lectures. One series, given on weekday evenings at 7:30, attracted a crowd who came through the Arapahoe Street door into the lecture room. On January 4, 1867, for instance, L. N. Greenleaf favored his audience with a lecture on "King Sham," a parody on politics. He was followed by Dr. E. C. Strode, who presented "A View of the Nervous System," then F. Schirmer, who explored "The Surface of the Globe." President Vincent wound up the series with "Finis," the "lesson expressed in General Hooker's military maxim that 'the day is not finished until the duties have been accomplished.'" A reporter found Vincent to be "one of Colorado's best orators," the lecture being a "rare literary treat."

The fourth session of the Colorado Conference of the Methodist Church met at Empire on June 30, 1867, and, among other business, organized a Centenary Fund to celebrate the 100th anniversary of Methodism. Of an unspecified amount, 90 percent of the fund was given to the Seminary, 10 percent to Garrett Biblical Institute in Evanston, Illinois.

That winter, C. F. Bridges of Ogdensburg, New York, was added to the faculty—a man who would have a great impact on the school later.

The end of the school year in June 1867 was marked by "Public Exercises" at the church—declamation, rehearsals, the reading of essays, and a lecture by the Rev. I. D. Clark on "Our Liberty and Its Destiny." These programs were preceded by three days of public examinations, which provided a clue as to what was taught that year. The primary department was put through its paces on June 11. The next day came examinations on American history, geography, grammar, arithmetic, algebra, Latin, and French. Then came practical anatomy, advanced arithmetic, botany, "primary philosophy," and English history.

On June 13, the public was treated to an "exhibition" of students' prowess, for which crowds poured into the old frame building of the People's Theatre at the corner of 15th (F Street) and Larimer for a dollar apiece. "The building was cold, as the temperature outside lowered after sunset, and it was impossible to keep it up inside. The audience was, nevertheless, so entertained that all remained deeply interested until the end." This "literary entertainment" of declamations, reading, scenes in costume, "colloquies, recitations, and songs humorous and pathetic," caused the reviewer in the *News* almost to lose his mind in the delights and to communicate all of them in painfully coy detail. "Taken together, the affair was most novel and interesting, closing a term whose success is perfect." If advertising could make it so, the school was assured of a glorious future.

By the spring of 1867, the Seminary had acquired a debt of $3,000, borrowed at 3 percent compound interest on a property valued at $20,000. Ready payment on such a debt was impossible. Inflation drove expenses up steadily, there was a frequent change of officers and teachers, and there was the news that Vincent would be unable to continue even his part-time presidency. It looked as though fall enrollment would not continue the modest gain of the previous year. Evans later estimated that 103 students had enrolled the first year and an encouraging 186 in the second year, but by the fall of 1867 the school had only 136 students.

The work went on. In the examinations of the previous March, Miss McCoy had dealt with arithmetic, Mr. Bridges with "intellectual arithmetic," Miss Morgan with natural philosophy and chemistry, the latter subjects being publicly explored by some 15 earnest and predictably anxious pupils. There is no full record of those early students: Only occasionally, as in the case of performers in public examinations, exhibitions, musical affairs, or the 15 or so members of athletic teams, did a list appear in public print.

With the need for a new president, Evans called a meeting of the board for August 6, 1867. Twenty-three of the official 28 members were present, including some new faces. That summer, Evans had reported to the Methodist Conference that it was "impossible to tell whose terms expired, it has been thought best to have the entire board stand, as designated in the Charter, until the Annual Conference of 1868, when their terms will all have expired. They continue in office until their successors are appointed." He continued, stating "the attention of the Conference is, however, directed to the propriety of filling, by appointment at this time, the places of such trustees as have died or permanently removed from the Territory." With the Rev. William M. Smith having already been appointed, the conference elected the Rev. Bethuel Vincent, L. M. Vesey, Daniel Witter, a banker, and Fred A. Salomon, J. B. Doyle's old partner in the mercantile business and later mayor of Denver.

The Presidency of P. D. Barnhart, 1867–68

Those present at that board meeting then selected the Rev. P. D. Barnhart, "the late president of Philadelphia Female Seminary," as the fourth president of the school. Born in Alabama, a graduate of Garrett Institute, he seemed to be just the man for the job. The *News* of August 13, 1867, announced his acceptance, and the September 8 issue told of his arrival on that morning's coach. The fall term started September 9, with a smaller enrollment and somewhat reduced tuition and other charges. Coinciding with his arrival, however, was the public announcement that a third religious group, the Episcopalians, headed by Bishop George M. Randall, planned to start a school, or, rather, a series of schools—one for boys, another for girls, a theological college, and a mining school—all of which came into existence in the next several years. St. Mary's Catholic Academy, founded in 1864, was not in competition for students.

Barnhart had come for an initial view early in August. Although not captivated by what he saw, he had some hope for the future of the school and the community. But public opinion during his short tenure was that he was not interested in local affairs; certainly there are few items in the press of the time concerning the Seminary. In the third week of September he was off. As the

News of the 24th reported, "Professor Barnhart of the Colorado Seminary goes east in this morning's coach for the purpose of purchasing some apparatus for the use of the institution. He will be absent about three weeks."

Meanwhile, the work of teaching went on, carried out by Miss Morgan and Mr. Bridges. A month later, Barnhart returned. Even then, however, things never went well. Scheduled to give a lecture appropriately titled "The Conflicts and Vicissitudes of Life" at the Presbyterian church that November, he found the church locked, the sexton apparently having been confused about the time and place. The lecture was not rescheduled.

Shortly thereafter, at the close of fall quarter, the November 23 issue of the *Tribune* noted, "We understand that Professor P. D. Barnhart will go East in a few days, the seminary of which he is principal not being enough patronized to induce him to remain. Barnhart will probably return in the spring." In a lengthy letter to the *Tribune* on the 28th, Barnhart related his disappointments and commented on the failure of the community to secure adequate rail communication with the East:

> My return to Denver will, to a great extent, depend on the final success of the railroad movements. It has been my opinion ever since I first visited this place that the future wealth or woe of Denver rests entirely upon the decision of the railroad question. . . . Whatever I can do in the East during the winter to aid in the work will not be left undone. In nine months from this time, I fully expect to go from Denver to Cheyenne by railroad.

The *News* of December 4 carried a somewhat more astringent message from the president, which began "Departing, but not Without Hope":

> This is the third time I have left Denver for the East since the first of last August. The first time, as the coach rolled away from this hospitable city, the conviction went with me that soon Denver would be a forlorn, deserted town. The second time, my opinion was confirmed that Denver would cease to be a place where strangers seek a home, and some new city would wear the crown of honor, forfeited by the inactivity of the citizens of this place. The third time, I leave beholding a bright day of prosperity dawning upon this beautiful city.

He did indeed come back the following spring, on May 22, 1868. The *News* reported the next day that "he is going on to Montana next week. He will return soon, and expects, in company with three other gentlemen, to go into mining in Gilpin County." But Barnhart was heard of no more.

Decline and Fall

This brief saga of the four presidents of Colorado Seminary points clearly to the problems of administering a small school on the frontier in the post–Civil War period. It is further instructive in showing the elements that both attracted and repelled the Easterner. There were great opportunities for wealth in the mines and along the rivers, but such opportunities were chancy, and more people went home broke and despondent than stayed to become even moderately wealthy. Equally great opportunities came to other entrepreneurs, the grocers, bankers, owners of mining and milling equipment, and real estate brokers, but location and timing were all important. The alternation of boom and bust could leave the people of the once-thriving community derelict and the city desolate. Even Denver was not immune from such painful upward and downward economic thrusts, and the erratic arrival and departure of hordes of people. Some who came, attracted by the booms reported in newspapers and handbills, sought health out of sickness. Rumor had it that mountain air could cure tuberculosis, for instance. It sometimes did, but all too frequently the patient died.

There was, of course, a permanent population, headed by a small group of businessmen, as well as clergy and others—"civic leaders" whose optimism was unbounded, even in the face of crisis and insecurity. The record of their perseverance (the story of Evans and Byers is typical of this group) and the frustration they encountered from both people and nature was evidence of a simple fact: Denver was not automatically and inevitably the capital of a region that increasingly extended beyond Colorado, but rather the product of their leadership, boundless energy, and great faith, expressed in civic enterprise and search for personal advantage.

In this milieu, the institutions of education, religion, business, and government played a decisive role. If impermanence were the order of the day, out of that uncertainty—even failure—the driving force of the people brought eventual success to shape the city. The history of the University of Denver is one such example.

But the leadership of both churches and school in the territory was erratic. Clergy of almost all churches came with enthusiasm and departed with distressing rapidity, discouraged by the lack of piety in small congregations or lured by greater opportunities elsewhere. Of the four presidents of the Seminary, two—Phillips and Richardson—arrived plagued with ill health, the former returning home only to die six weeks later, the latter giving up after little more than 15 months because of overwork. The third, Vincent, found even part-time administration for a single year was harmful to his desire for the pastoral ministry. Barnhart was technically president for nine months, from August 13, 1867, to May 28, 1868, but spent most of that time away from the city before leaving for the greater fulfillment of mining.

The "Denver Directory," which formed a column in the *News* of January 28, 1868, listed Barnhart as principal. The next day's issue reported Sarah Morgan's name in his place. Indeed, in those days, one spoke of "Miss Morgan's School." She remained until June, when, having carried on administration and teaching for a year, she left also. The *Tribune* of February 28 reports that residential pupils had already dispersed: "For Rent. . . . the boarding department of the Colorado Seminary, also a number of rooms pleasantly located in the second story of the building. Apply to J. M. Veasey, secretary."

There was plenty of room at the school when the Territorial Assembly, which had met in Golden, December 2, 1867, adjourned to Denver on the ninth. The *News* of December 11 noted that "Acting Governor Hall has rented the Colorado Seminary for the legislature and executive rooms. All the territorial offices will be located there. The desks and furniture from the old legislative halls at Golden City arrived in this city last night, the entire cost of moving being somewhat less than $500." That session lasted until January 10, 1868, after which the legislature departed from the building, not to return.

Miss Morgan and her pupils somehow worked their way through their studies around the legislature and around meetings such as the Quarterly Conference of the Methodist Church, which met at the school on April 2, 1868. With the end of the spring term, however, the school closed, and no new students were admitted in the fall of 1868. But that October, there were advertisements for a boys' academy, an evening school, and, in November, an "academy for ladies," all the inspiration of C. F. and M. H. Bridges, two brothers, the former of whom had been teaching at the seminary. The *News* of October 10 carried the announcement that Mr. Bridges would open a school in "the Methodists' Seminary October 19." Limited to 30 pupils, it was to be a haven in which "perfect order will be enforced, and every scholar will occupy a separate desk; giving to each unequaled facilities for making thorough and rapid progress in the studies." The cost for "primary branches" ran to $4 a month, "common English" set parents back another $5. Higher English, with Latin, came to $6. Greek, French, and bookkeeping each added another dollar to the bill.

The Bridges brothers probably had a lease on the building. The following March, notices appeared about their school, by now called the "Colorado Academy." At some unspecified time, they moved out of the building and continued their school elsewhere.

The Charter and the Board Continue

The building might have been used for a variety of purposes, including rehearsal rooms for amateur theatricals, but the legal entity that was "Colorado Seminary" continued unaltered. The charter was intact, and the Board of Trustees continued, replacements being elected as terms expired or members dropped out. Meeting in Golden in June and presided over by the redoubtable bishop Matthew Simpson, the Methodist Conference of 1868, at which six ministers were present, elected a board of 28, made up mostly of old hands with a scattering of new appointees.

In each of the four classes there was a Methodist preacher. In the first, for four years, was George Adams, a presiding elder and itinerant minister in mining camps and in Wyoming, who left the following year to supervise missions in Arizona. In the next class was William Smith, who had been on the board for several terms. The two-year class contained W. W. Baldwin, a man who spent two years preaching at Black Hawk and another at Valmont-Boulder-Burlington before being "located," or retired, at his own request. He later left for the East and a successful ministry there. George Murray appeared for a single term and was elected to another one, having preached at Colorado City and Cañon City before being "superannuated," or retired, as the result of a fall from a horse.

Two of Evans' old friends came on the board—Henry M. Teller and George M. Chilcott. Teller (1830–1914), a lawyer from western New York, had been born in the small town of Angelica, attended the local academy where he also taught, learned the law in a local judge's chambers, moved to Illinois, and appeared in the *Gregory Diggings* in April 1861. An old friend of Evans from the days when Evans had been part of the selection of delegates to the Illinois Republican Convention in Chicago, Teller was appointed by the governor as major general of the improvised Territorial Militia from 1863 to 1864, to guard the populace against "Indian depredations."

In 1865, Teller had become an incorporator of the Colorado Central Railroad, along with William Loveland, John Lynch, and Milo Lee. He served as its president for five years. Teller's later career as senator (1876–1882, 1889–1903), as Chester Arthur's secretary of the interior (1882–1889), and as leader of the Teller Silver Republicans of the 1890s placed him on the national stage. Elmer Ellis' *Henry Moore Teller* fittingly called him "Defender of the West." His name is commemorated in a county of Colorado, and the Teller House of Central City, which he and his brother built in 1873.

Chilcott was equally the businessman-builder-statesman, arriving in Kansas Territory in 1859, then settling in Pueblo to ranch, raise sheep, and farm. A member of the House of the first Legislative Assembly of Colorado territory in September 1861 and again in 1862, Chilcott was elected as a Republican delegate in November 1865 and re-elected the following August. Pueblo leaders proposed him as one of their senators from the State of Colorado in 1876, although he failed to be elected. Later, in 1882, Governor Pitkin appointed him to fill the unexpired term of Senator Teller. Chilcott was also an incorporator of the Pueblo and Salt Lake Railroad (1872), and Chilcott's Hall, the Pueblo Opera House, commemorated his name. He died in St. Louis in March 1891, "whither he had gone a few weeks previously, seeking relief from rheumatism and nervous prostration."

Elections to the board in the years between the collapse of the school as an educational venture and its resurrection in 1880 followed a consistent pattern: a Methodist preacher in each class, a majority of hold-overs, and a sprinkling of notable figures from the world of business, legislative bodies, mining, and farming. There was little or nothing for the board to do after being elected by the Annual Conference on the advice and recommendation of John Evans and current board members. Evans held tenaciously to the idea that some day the school would reopen. Year after year, he maintained the fabric, but times were hard.

By 1869, at the end of its first decade, Denver was growing with painful slowness, good years alternating with bad economically, the advent of new people barely balancing the departures. Tents and log cabins had given way, first to frame structures, and then increasingly to substantial brick buildings of two and three stories. Water for irrigation had been brought into town for distribution in streams on every street. Communication with the outside world was quicker, as the telegraph line to Cheyenne was opened the first of the year. In March, Evans returned from Washington with news of the passage of a bill in Congress granting alternate sections of public land to support a railroad to the north. In May, the Union Pacific joined with the Central Pacific at Ogden, Utah, bringing the reality of some link with Denver from both coasts even nearer. Evans' dream of Denver as the hub of a vast interconnected hinterland might very well come alive.

But the Seminary building continued to be used for a variety of non-educational purposes. In 1868, some church leaders even published a brochure that contained a plan for the creation of "Fountain College" at Colorado City, adjacent to Colorado Springs. Ray Bettie, AM, was listed as president, John Mansfield, AM as "professor of languages, etc.," and the Rev. George Murray as agent. Nothing further was heard of this operation, but such planning was a clear indication that the future of the school in Denver was in grave doubt.

Hope, however, kept springing in the collective breast. The Annual Conference of June 1869 in Central City, for instance, having elected seven members to the board, resolved:

> That we respectfully but earnestly urge the trustees of the Colorado Seminary, located in Denver, to activate effort for its relief from pecuniary embarrassment; also to put it, as early as possible, into active operation under their more immediate control.

The census statistics for 1870 tell the story of a static population. Colorado, for instance, which had 34,277 people in 1860, counted 39,867 just 10 years later. Arapahoe County (of which Denver was a part) grew in that decade from 6,566 to 6,829. Gilpin County, to take an important mining region, gained only a few people, increasing in population from 5,429 to

5,490. Denver, which was home to 4,726 souls in 1860, now counted 4,759, by admittedly incomplete returns.

The figures for the number of church buildings and available seats are equally interesting:

Roman Catholics	(14)	8,575
Methodists	(14)	3,815
Episcopalians	(9)	2,000
Presbyterians	(6)	1,200
Baptists	(5)	855
Congregationalists	(2)	
Jewish	(1)	

In all, the 1870 census found some 55 religious organizations, with 45 buildings and "sittings" numbering 1,745. Availability of seats, parenthetically, is not to be confused with church attendance. Methodism, at any rate, was the second most popular faith, and by a narrow margin the largest Protestant body, with 589 members. Local Methodist preachers numbered 18, seven more than the year before, but only one more than in 1861.

The year 1870 was demonstrably the "year of the railroad," for on June 22 the lines of the Denver Pacific reached Denver from Cheyenne, and on August 15 the first Kansas Pacific trains arrived from the Missouri River, some 639 miles away. Shortly thereafter, track laying began on the Colorado Central Railway to tap a mountain of gold and silver. But none of this approach to prosperity benefitted the school. As presiding elder, the Rev. Bethuel T. Vincent reported:

> The Colorado Seminary is practically no more. The building has been sold for debt and is now being rented for the use of the public schools of Denver. All has been done that could be to secure the sympathy of rich men in the East on the subject of the revival of the enterprise by endowment, but without avail. Either it is not considered worthwhile to invest in education, or the field is too frontierish and obscure to pay enough in the shape of benevolent popularity.

Public School District Number One did indeed lease the building on September 6, 1870, at the respectable rate of $150 per month, and established the Kehler School there. The school was so named because the East Side School had been located in the substantial brick building constructed by Father John H. Kehler, the first rector of St. John's Episcopal Church in the Wilderness, on the site of the later Windsor Hotel. The school remained there in two or three rooms until the Arapahoe School was finally finished in 1872.

At the time the Seminary shut down in 1868, the debt totaled $3,000. In October 1868, a mortgage in the amount of $4,000 was held by John Evans and

Edwin Scudder, two of the trustees. That mortgage was foreclosed in 1870, after which Evans, Elbert, and others began buying up the 10 lots along Arapahoe, from what is now 13th to 14th streets. On September 22, 1874, Elbert gave Evans a quit claim deed to the 10 lots, all of which were in Evans' personal possession when the school reopened in 1880.

The early and middle years of the 1870s were filled with high expectations for Denver, little of which aided the cause of the Seminary. The Methodist Conference of 1870 had heard the report of the educational committee: "We learn with regret of the financial embarrassment of the Colorado Seminary, located at Denver, and whatever may be the action of the trustees thereof, we most respectfully urge them to guard well our educational interests." The following year, a more hopeful note was sounded by the conference:

> Resolved, that we learn with pleasure that the financial embarrassments, which have so long retarded the prosperity of the Colorado Seminary, are, under the providence of God and the kindness of friends, likely soon to be removed.

There was more evident prosperity in the Denver of 1872, with five railroad lines entering the city. The characteristic report of city promoters was that "large and substantial stores and elegant dwellings have been built in great number. The Holly Works furnish an abundant supply of pure water, the streets are well lighted with gas, and everything, as one wanders about the city, betokens a vigorous and most gratifying prosperity." By the end of the year, Denver became the hub of an increasing hinterland. Baskin's *History* noted that in 1880 "the Rio Grande road had been opened to Pueblo and the new town of Colorado Springs had become a place of considerable importance. The Greeley Colony was flourishing. Mining industry was making rapid strides, and Denver was on the high road to prosperity as she had never been before at any time in her history." The Annual Conference of 1872 was less ecstatic, but at least impressed to hear from the educational committee:

> We are glad to note that the building known as the Colorado Seminary is still in possession of the excellent brethren who have saved it from falling into unmethodistic hands, and these brethren are rapidly reducing the debt, with a view to the restoration of the property to the use and the possession of the conference.

A year later, however, the committee could report no further progress:

> The condition of the seminary building in Denver remains unchanged, the rents of the past year not having more than paid

the interest and the insurance. In consideration of this fact, and the further fact that the collections of the charges [that is, through churches and missions] are small, and some have been taken in connection with the children's day celebration, the creditors waive their claim to them, and we, with their approval, recommend the rescinding of the first resolution of last year and the use of our small collections in holding our connection with the general educational interests of the church.

Evans Conceives the Union Evangelical University

Faced with the possibility that the school would never reopen, Evans then turned his thinking to the creation of a school that could be supported by all the Protestant churches of the area. He was himself no narrow sectarian, holding for his time advanced ecumenical views, contributing nearly $100 to each new church edifice, regardless of denomination. Why not, then, approach the various church bodies with such a proposal?

He first talked to members of the Denver Board of Trade, an organization he had helped found several years before to further his Denver and Pacific Railroad. He came to that meeting fresh from the Annual Conference in Colorado Springs, on August 1, 1874. His vision was spelled out:

> If we will cooperate in this enterprise, I believe that we can concentrate the influence of those different denominations I have mentioned in an effort to build a great and glorious enterprise for the Rocky Mountains, a university that shall be a university in fact, and that here, in the growth and prosperity of the city of Denver, we can secure the means of effecting an ample endowment for the institution that will necessarily come from the growth of the city, if it owns enough of the soil in and around the place to enjoy the benefits of the enhancement of the property.

As he saw the role of such a true university, he waxed ecstatic:

> A well-founded university lives as long as the country in which it is founded lives. It lives for ages. Its influence runs through all time, and therefore . . . [it] is more important than all the other propositions we have had before us put together. . . . There is nothing in all a man's lifetime that he can do that will be so permanent in its beneficial results as in founding an institution of learning that will live on and work, year after year, age after age, after he is laid in the grave.

After such ad hominem remarks, the board thought of all the objections anyone might make to such a proposal. A union of denominations would disperse funds, not consolidate them, there was no first-class high school in the region to furnish a pool of suitable entrants, and so on. They did finally choose a committee to consider the plan, consisting of Evans, Charles B. Kountze, Frank M. Case, Mayor W. J. Barker, and one Alderman Wilson. There the matter rested. Evans might approach the churches on his own.

He later recollected the events that led to his proposal and its subsequent failure. The occasion was the dedication of the Colorado Woman's College, at which he gave the principal address on March 26, 1890:

> In the year 1874, I solicited the general convention of the Baptist Societies in Colorado to join in a union college movement at Denver, and they appointed three of the members to be trustees. The synod of the Presbyterian Church did the same. The standing committee of the Protestant Episcopal Church in like manner joined the movement, and the Colorado Annual Conference of the Methodist Episcopal Church also gave its endorsement and appointed three trustees.

The Congregationalists were approached, but as they were fully occupied in organizing and opening Colorado College in Colorado Springs, they merely "received" the proposal. The rest did indeed appoint men to consider the proposal. To continue with Evans' recollections,

> The twelve trustees among the eminent men of these churches met, devised an admirable agreement and modes of operation and plan of endowment, and asked for a charter from the Territorial Legislature to enable them to hold without taxation lots and lands for the endowment of their great educational enterprise, which was not to be sectarian, but strictly moral and religious in its teaching.

Despite all these arrangements, the plan failed. According to Evans, the failure was solely and simply the result of legislative oversight. He detailed those steps:

> General Bela M. Hughes in the council and Judge William B. Mills in the house carried the bill through their respective branches of the legislature by almost unanimous votes in each. But when adjournment made it too late to correct it, it was found that precisely similar bills had passed both branches, and yet failed to become a law for the want of either having passed the bill originated in the other house.

But why didn't the trustees come back to the legislature with their proposal another time? Surely the answer lies in the predictable reluctance of the various religious establishments to cooperate with one another, especially in an enterprise that would shower glory on only one of their number. Even the Methodists, who could be presumed to benefit most by the use of the building, although they duly appointed a committee of three, declared the plan "not likely soon to be put in operation." The Episcopalians had been busy with the creation of the "University Schools" at Golden, an ambitious scheme that included a seminary, a boys' school, and a school of mines. Burdened by an increasing debt, two of these became defunct in 1874, leaving only the mining school, later acquired by the state. The seminary and the boys' school, in addition to a school for girls, Wolfe Hall, were all located in Denver. With the death of the saintly Bishop Randall, most of that church's hopes for a university came to an end.

John Evans Persists in His Vision of a School

Evans persevered. As he later put it in an exchange in the local papers,

> There is no other cause to which you can more profitably lend your influence, your labor and your means, than that of Christian education by aiding in founding a university. We may do good by improving the country, by defending it in a righteous cause, by serving in the councils of legislation on the bench or in the forum, but these labors are more or less transient, and the impress we make is temporary, but when we found an institution to mold minds and characters for good that will continue its operations and accumulate influences from generation to generation through all coming time, we have done the very highest and noblest service to our country and our race, of which we are capable.

With all these aspirations in mind, Evans then heard with pleasure at the Annual Methodist Conference in Central City in July 1875 that the bishop strongly urged the establishment of an "institution of learning" in Colorado, and that the delegates pledged themselves to redeem the outstanding debt on the seminary property, amounting to more than $5,000. The ministers present asked the bishop to appoint a committee of three of their members to meet with three laymen to make an appeal to "the church at large" for "a Methodist institution of learning" within the bounds of the conference. Even with the selection by that group of Evans "to serve as a committee on education," however, their meetings produced no results, except for greater determination that a Methodist school should be undertaken.

The centennial year of 1876, coming after months of considerable business depression, grasshoppers that "came down and devastated the land," and huge early snow storms, brought some psychological relief, though that surcease was punctuated by a flooding of Cherry Creek in May and the slow revival of business. The Great Centennial Exposition, opened in May in Philadelphia by President Grant, did show forth an array of new communication inventions, including the telephone, which reduced the West's feelings of isolation. Colorado was more firmly independent when Grant's proclamation of August 1 made it the "Centennial State" of the Union. The legislature then elected Jerome B. Chaffee and Henry M. Teller as state senators.

Evans, appearing again before the conference with his plans in 1876, offered to liquidate the debt of $5,000 against the property and deed it to the continuing board, on the condition that the conference raise $10,000 to add a wing for dormitories and other appurtenances, remodeling the original structure to "fit it for a first class school." But the money would never come from the offerings of the various Methodist congregations: In 1877, they amounted to a total of only $27.20.

In extenuation, the secretary of the conference undoubtedly had a point when he wrote that "this deficiency, doubtless, arises from the absence of some central and definite object for which to plead." Dead horses were obviously not in this category. The old seminary building was still there, occupied by a variety of tenants. For instance, one H. B. Gillespie rented the whole structure for $100 a month, to be increased to $150 the following October. His use of the building was not specified. By that time, however, Evans had sole possession of the property, having paid all its debts. In 1878, the conference put the whole matter of education in the hands of the Preachers Aid Society with power to act.

Evans was not present at the anniversary session of the Preachers Aid Society held in Golden in August 1878, but he delegated a preacher to present his views that the school, whenever it should be back in business, "must be under the control of Christian philanthropy and Christian churches." He was still of a mind to propose some sort of interdenominational college. Not all of his hearers were of like mind as to the need for an edifice. The former president of Hamline University, in St. Paul, Minnesota, the Rev. Dr. B. F. Crary of Golden, spoke against a building with a substantial mortgage:

> We once had a college in Denver, a fine building with a complete mortgage on it. It stood on the east bank of Cherry Creek. It ought to have been in the Cherry Creek itself, for it would have been swept away in the midst of its glory. Now it is the deadest thing you ever saw.

Meanwhile, other forces had been at work, among them the presence of publicly financed higher education. Up to now, such schools had existed only on paper. But the University of Colorado, authorized by the Territorial Legislature in 1861, opened at Boulder in 1877. The Colorado School of Mines had started offering courses in 1874 in Golden. The State Agricultural College of Colorado, established as a land grant school at Fort Collins in 1870, began operation in 1879. In private education, the Congregationalists were doing quite well with the Colorado College, opened in 1874 in Colorado Springs. But what of Denver and the seminary? Would Methodists fail where others had succeeded? Would Denver fail where lesser towns had their educational centers? As for the Methodists, Bishop Matthew Simpson, Evans' old friend and supporter, was doggedly pursuing his vision. In a visit to Colorado in August 1878, he addressed the anniversary session of the Freedman's Aid Society in Golden, speaking glowingly of the need for the leadership of the church to renew their efforts for Christian education in Colorado.

That year, the conference, tackling the subject of the school and its lamentable state, passed the initiative to the Preachers' Aid Society and its president, the Rev. F. C. Millington, giving it the power to act for the conference. Franklin Ceylon Millington (1841–1887) was inspired. A man of action, a church-builder by deepest conviction, he knew in his heart that the Seminary could be operative once more, in a new and changed environment. Consequently, in the spring of 1879, he called a meeting of the members of the society and a few friends, predictably in Evans' office. He had great plans, as well thought out as those he later developed for University Park. But he was not destined to bring them before the meeting. As Millington was preparing to advance his proposals, worked out with prayer and much meditation, Evans arose, addressed the meeting on the absolute necessity of reopening the Seminary, and concluded, "If you gentlemen will now undertake to reorganize this institution, all there is of the old Colorado Seminary is placed at your disposal."

The next step was to call a public meeting, to be named "the Educational Convention of the Annual Conference." It was partly inspirational, largely informative to press and public, and designed to transact enough business to get the school going again. Consequently, the faithful were gathered at the Lawrence Street Church on Tuesday, June 10, 1879. Composed of 20 ministers and 16 laymen, presided over by Supreme Court Justice Samuel H. Elbert of Pueblo, the body joyously received the proposals for the reopening of the building and the promise of substantial gifts.

Even Dr. Crary, who had a justifiably sour attitude toward mortgaged schools, was enthusiastic, as reported by the *Tribune* in June:

> Among other things, he said the church does not antagonize the state in its efforts to educate its children, but supplements that work. . . . We believe an institution can be formed here that not only would be the glory of the state, but the pride of Denver.

We Methodists, he said, want to raise up preachers from among us who have learned the ways of the people and have 'tried the climate.' From the young men of Colorado, if properly educated, we may raise up a class of ministers even better than we now have.

Given a chance to speak again later, Crary waxed ecstatic about the possibilities for the school and spoke his mind about its shape:

This is a growing state, beyond all the predictions of the most enthusiastic prophets of the past. The wildest predictions of the most reckless have fallen far short of the reality. Let me give a very safe calculation of the growth of our church. In 1900, 21 years hence, there will be 35,000 Methodists in Colorado and 400 ministers. We must raise now a school of liberal arts, backed by one hundred thousand dollars. In twenty years we will need five million dollars backing for a theological school, a medical school, a school of art, a conservatory of music, and last, a school of oratory.

By a deed dated April 13, 1880, Evans donated the seminary property to the new Board of Trustees. That deed provided that the property must remain "forever free from any and all liabilities" and could not be mortgaged or sold except with the unanimous consent of both the Board of Trustees and the annual Methodist conference. He offered an additional cash donation of $3,000, while John W. Bailey, Methodist layman and mining and milling investor, gave $10,000 more, all this toward the $35,000 necessary to pay for the planned remodeling. As money continued to come in from large and small subscriptions, the school—Evans thought the name ought to be "the Denver Seminary" or "the Colorado Conference Seminary"—seemed to be off and running.

Some Causes of Educational Collapse

Why were the earliest years, from 1864 to 1868, so unproductive, involving four presidents within that brief time and ending with the collapse of the institution? With this short and dismal record, how was it possible within another 12 years for the same school to sail a much more direct and successful course? The answer to each question is a complicated one, involving the whole history of higher education on the frontier, the religious support of education in general, and the special conditions affecting Denver and the West.

Anyone searching for reasons for the collapse of the school after only a few years of operation would do well to reflect that it was a miracle the Seminary was started at all and, once under way, that it lasted in its first phase as long as it did. With this condition in mind, it is possible to set down a variety of causes:

(1) The Seminary shared in a common frontier experience of failure. The history of "colleges" on the frontier, from the earliest colonial days down to the Civil War, shows continuous struggle against disaster. Fires often burned down the single building in which the "president" taught the classes and his wife ran the housekeeping department. Itinerant teachers struggled with unruly students through the mazes of mathematics and the rest of the classical curriculum. The indifference of many citizens to anything more than the rudiments of training and the constant toil and loneliness of daily life diminished the zeal even of dedicated teachers. To all this, there were heroic exceptions among the greater school, but they were few indeed. Intermittent leadership, as in Denver, was a common problem.

Even in the states usually thought of as settled and stable, a high percentage of the schools expired, often within a few years. An analysis of colleges founded before the Civil War shows that of a total of 516, some 104 were still alive while 412 had closed, an average mortality rate of 81 percent. Pennsylvania experienced a toll of 48 percent, New York 58 percent, Ohio 60 percent, Virginia 69 percent, and Maryland 78 percent. Florida and Arkansas had by this time lost 100 percent of their colleges. Essentially a frontier church, which came late to the field of higher education, the Methodists had launched 34 permanent colleges in 19 states, beginning with Randolph-Macon in Ashland, Virginia, in 1830, and including the College of the Pacific (1851) in Stockton, California, Willamette (1853) in Salem, Oregon, and Baker University, (1858) in Baldwin, Kansas. These successes were balanced against more common failures and against the imminent possibility of their own demise.

(2) The Colorado frontier presented its own problems. Mining booms from 1858 onward brought hordes of people westward, resolved to become rich, to educate their children in the East, and to return home as soon as possible. But in the mid 1860s, the placer deposits of gold in the mountain streams were exhausted, and with inexpensive methods of extracting gold from the mines being unavailable, a steady decline in Colorado's prosperity set in.

(3) Even in good years, the nature of the population and their expectations were calculated to weigh against expensive educational experimentation. At the beginning of the gold rushes, as Frank Fossett pointed out in his *Colorado* (1880),

> There was a smattering of good, bad, and indifferent characters, all desirous of bettering their fortunes, which in many cases could not have been worse. Probably more than fifty thousand men aided in this eventful year of 1859 to enlarge that western trail of immigration, which bursts into states and empires as it moves. The wide awake speculator, the broken down merchant, the farmer, mechanic, gambler, or the wanderer from foreign lands, the cultivated and the illiterate—all combined to swell

the human tide that was setting in so strongly for the new land of gold out toward the setting sun.

The point is reinforced by Hale, in his *Education in Colorado:*

> It must be borne in mind that the early settlement of Colorado was somewhat anomalous. The pioneers and immigrants of the new regions, Michigan, Illinois, Kansas, etc., were families seeking permanent homes, while those of Colorado were fortune-hunting men only, whose wives and children were left behind, whose highest ambition and only intentions were to remain here long enough to gather wealth with which to return and enjoy. Schools were not, to them, of much importance, even if there had been the material to make them.

All this is not to say that the great modifying influences of church, family, fraternal organizations, and the like were slow to penetrate the wilderness. They did take time to settle in and civilize their world. Consequently, it is understandable that a school could be created in 1864, go broke in 1868, and be totally revived in 1880.

(4) Isolation was a factor in every personal and social calculation. Without rapid communication with the outside world, in which the telegraph and railroad were being extended across America, a community would perish. The joy with which the coming of those two media was welcomed is almost unimaginable. In their absence, gloom descended on the business community and the adventurous alike. The mid 1860s were the darkest years in Denver's history. In 1866, the city had 1,000 fewer people than it had had in 1860, and it seemed well on its way to becoming a ghost town. When the Union Pacific decided to bypass Denver and strike its route across Wyoming, many people closed their shops and moved to such places as Cheyenne. As new lodes were reported farther west, others left town for the rewards of newer camps. Greater numbers simply returned eastward, broke. Consequently, the census of 1870 counted a Colorado population of 39,867, only 5,000 higher than 1860.

(5) Nature itself seemed hostile. It was a wild, rough, lonely world, in which the amenities of housewifely care and the consolation and steadying influence of the great institutions of civilization, churches, schools, family, and business, were the only exceptions. The difficulties and dangers of travel were on the lips of all. Indian depredations were a constant menace, and the forces of nature were hostile. After all, Denver lay at the edge of the Great American Desert and could survive only with water for irrigation and the beautification of the town. Grasshoppers plagued the area in vast hordes in 1864 and 1867; fire destroyed many of the wooden buildings in 1863; the Great Flood of 1864 was followed at intervals by others. Washington and the federal government seemed remote, if

not inimical, and the collapse of a movement for statehood produced dismay among leaders of the territory.

(6) A continuing scarcity of ready funds made support difficult. In the midst of all these dangers and difficulties, it proved almost impossible for those people who were the greatest friends of church and school to aid in the survival of such institutions as the Seminary when more vital problems had to be solved. All waited for a more propitious time. Meanwhile, the charter continued in existence, and John Evans and his allies remained consistently hopeful. New members of the Board of Trustees continued to be elected by the annual conference of the Methodist church.

Thus ended the first stage of the history of the university. It began as a glimmer in the eye of the territorial governor, aided by a small number of businessmen who saw, as he did, the necessary mixture of economic, political, social, and even spiritual advantages of such a school—all failed against the vicissitudes of the institutions of frontier man and nature's inexorable demands. As John Evans remarked, a debt of $5,000 at compound interest of 2 percent was enough alone to bring the seminary to a close.

Nevertheless, a new era dawned with the 1880s. The year that had begun the decade saw the reopening of the school, with confidence in Denver and throughout the State of Colorado powerfully on the rise.

David Hastings Moore, chancellor, 1880–1889

II. Years of Building, Years of Recession: The University, 1880–1900

One might well ask why, if the school was so unsuccessful as a seminary after 1867, was it able to push forward so successfully as a university in 1880, some 13 years after its closure? The answer lies, in large part, in the spectacular development of Denver from 1878 on, in events that created a momentum against which no subsequent adverse economic forces were expected to prevail. The intimate connection between population growth, transportation availability, and business expansion on the one hand, and the greater expectancy and dogged persistence of Denver's promoters on the other, brought about, through days of depression and bust, a viable center of Western culture. The harbinger of good days was the discovery of gold in Leadville in 1879. Of all this renaissance, the University was beneficiary and, in turn, a creative force.

Denver Is Born Anew

Denver was both an "instant city" (as a perceptive comparison of the explosive growth of San Francisco and Denver calls it) and a speeded-up adaptation of Eastern culture laid down on the frontier. It moved rapidly from tent and shack to town and then to city. A French traveler, Rezin Constant, saw this same phenomenon:

> Denver was founded as though by the wave of a fairy wand. It is said that the pioneers of the Far West went into the prairies with a roll of twine and a dozen stakes in their hands; as soon as they arrived on a favorable spot, they planted their stakes, marked off the streets with twine, and said 'Here will be Babylon, Thebes, Memphis.'

The pulse of the city, he thought, could be felt:

> The movement of life is everywhere. One would hardly believe himself at the end of the prairies, 2,000 miles from New York. Rapid carriages pass everywhere, or heavy wagons laden with

commodities from the East ready to leave for the mining towns. Ingots of gold and silver come from the mining towns, precious merchandise, though not as bulky. From the mountains and prairies come skins and furs, of which Denver makes a considerable commerce.

A Denver journalist of later years, looking back fondly on the early 1880s, thought that the change "from the big village to what we proudly called the Queen City of the Plains, started in 1878" and was going full tilt by 1880, in which year "our town leaped forward with seven-league boots." Building was everywhere, symbolized by the opening of the Tabor Opera House in September 1881, which initiated the building boom up 16th and 17th, away from the principal business thoroughfare, Larimer Street. At 18th and Lawrence, the Windsor Hotel opened in June 1880. The Eighties saw remarkable gains: a new city hall, a county court house, the union depot, three hotels, imposing churches and schools, banks, business blocks (including Evans' skyscraper, Denver's first), and the railroad block, an eight-story building between 15th and 16th on Larimer. In 1880, a free postal service was established in Denver, the last step to join Denver with the East.

Visitors' laudations were frequent. Rezin Constant, arriving from Pueblo in July 1880, averred:

> I have been around Denver some time since I came, and am surprised at its magnificence. . . . Denver is the most substantially built city and costliest I ever saw of its size, contains 36,000 inhabitants. . . . No person can conceive of the vast amount of building going on up here unless seeing it. . . . Such quantities of brick as I saw! If I could accurately describe it, it would seem fabulous, as also the quantity of stone on every street. The clicks of the stone cutter's chisel are heard in every direction. Two-story buildings of stone and brick are begun and reared up in a few days. Nothing that I ever saw begins to compare with it.

Others, a bit more astute, saw the old still present in the new. A physician, arriving on the train from the East in the fall of 1881, noted that there was a surprisingly large number of brick buildings, a few of stone. There were enough frame buildings with icky second-story fronts to mark the town as a Western one, just shedding some of its youthful pretense and awkwardness. He found many structures built with brick that had a small clay and high sand content, already beginning to crumble from dampness around their foundations.

But despite the dangers and false promises of the past, Denverites knew in their bones that the future was with them. They were fond of using figures to prove it. Dean Martyn Hart of St. John's Episcopal Cathedral remembered a visit he paid when he first came to Denver in 1879:

> One afternoon I had the honor of consulting Governor Evans and Bishop. The governor was whittling a piece of stick; the bishop, a large and apostolic-looking man, was rocking in a cumbrous chair, smoking a cigar, with his leg over one arm. I asked them what they considered the population of the city might possibly attain within a reasonable limit. The bishop deferred to the governor, who, mechanically whittling his stick, looked up to the ceiling for inspiration. 'Well, Bishop,' said he, 'we'll give her a million.' 'Within what time,' I inquired, 'do you think the city will attain the population of a million?'

The governor deferred to the bishop and the bishop deferred to the governor, and they then both agreed that within 25 years Denver would be a city of a million souls.

The figures turned out to be quite different, although still encouraging to any city booster. In 1860, the federal census takers had reported some 4,749 people in Denver, of whom 4,140 were men, only 609 women. Ten years later, local citizens, who were bemused by all the noise and confusion of their fellows, estimated a population of at least 6,000 (probably more like 9,000) and were surprised when the census reported a gain of only 10 people, for a total of 4,759 citizens. But by 1880, a leap had indeed been made, to a total of 35,629, more than a sevenfold increase, with a more even balance between the sexes: 21,539 men and 14,090 women, the latter constituting some 40 percent of the population. In 1890, 10 years after the reopening of the school as the University of Denver, the city had become the third-largest Western urban center after San Francisco, which had almost 300,000 people, and Omaha, with just more than 140,000. Denver then had 106,713, a 10 year increase of 71,000, or almost 200 percent.

A continuing problem faced by the University was the public image of its religious commitment, and here population statistics are important. Granted, the public was aware in the 1860s and 1870s that the name "seminary" referred to any educational (usually pre-collegiate) institution and not to a clergy training operation. But how exclusively a Methodist institution was it? Certainly the quarterly and annual conferences of the ministers and laity of the church considered the University their property, and the more conservative among them thought it a bastion-in-readiness against secularism, immorality, and the excesses of Romanism in particular. Simonin, writing in 1867, commented:

> In the United States there are properly no little cities, and Denver has also a college, schools, and several newspapers, not

to mention the churches, of which the number is already large. M. Talleyrand was right when he said that in North America he had found only one dish and thirty-two religions. There are no cooks in this country, but everyone is a little religious.

The frontier had, indeed, outstripped the churches in its move westward, and had placed a peculiar imprint of civic religion on its people. There were several factors at work. First, the terms of the charter in 1864 specifically stipulated that there would be no test of religion for admittance. Further, any such attempt to limit applications would have flown in the face of the fact that there was no substantial pool of high school candidates, and these students were divided among the various religious communities. In 1890 some 2,858 Methodists were second in size among the denominations, out-distanced by the Roman Catholics (18,039). There were Baptists (2,498) and Presbyterians (1,896), closely accompanied in numbers by the Episcopalians (1,820). The first and last of these groups had their own schools.

As for specific religious instruction—the sure test of denominational emphasis—there was apparently none of the exclusive nature, nor was there in later years, though to be sure the presence of a sturdy Christian faith and active church membership on the part of administration, faculty, and students alike was pretty much taken for granted.

Reorganization of the School

With high hopes for the continued growth of Denver and the whole Rocky Mountain hinterland, 16 members of a new board of trustees, elected by the Annual Methodist Conference at Pueblo, August 9, 1879, met at the Lawrence Street Church on September 16. In a meeting chaired by Governor-elect Frank W. Pitkin, they chose officers and an executive committee, which they empowered with all financial and operational affairs. These men then set out to locate an appropriate building or site and to raise the necessary funds for its erection or remodeling, furnishing, and equipment.

The full board of 1879 consisted of eight ministers, seven businessmen and nine lawyers (including government officials and two generals), three physicians, and one educator. Of course, a man could, and did, practice a number of activities—a physician becoming a pharmacist, a lawyer a businessman. In this list, the Rev. Earl Cranston is of importance in the resurrection of the school and the choice of its first chancellor.

Cranston had come to Denver in 1878 to be pastor of the First Methodist Church (on old Lawrence Street). Born in Athens, Ohio, in 1840, he graduated from its local school, Ohio University. The school, founded in 1804 as an outgrowth of American University, had graduated its first class as the first collegiate institution in the Old Northwest Territory. Cranston graduated just as the Civil War broke out. Joining the military in a company recruited on campus, he was later elected first lieutenant, then became adjutant of a union battalion in Virginia, and suffered through the campaigns of the Wilderness as captain. He was finally mustered out for sickness.

Unable to do much work, he traveled for a wholesale grocery concern until he completely recovered his health. He became an ordained Methodist minister in Ohio, feeling a strong call to evangelical duty and church service there and in various neighboring states. From Cincinnati he began receiving letters from his friends in the West, urging him to come to Denver. After moving to Denver to preach and administer a growing parish, he became vitally interested in the redevelopment of the Seminary and stayed on its board until he left in 1884 to become manager of the Methodist Book Concern in Cincinnati and a bishop in 1896.

During the discussions between Evans and others on the pressing subject of a leader for the school, Cranston brought forward the name of a man who, he was sure, had all the qualifications of health, personality, drive, and adequate means to become a splendid president of the University. That man was David H. Moore, DD, the president of the Wesleyan College for Women in Cincinnati. The careers of Cranston and Moore had been continuously intertwined through most of their lives, and continued to be so for the rest of their careers.

The Chancellorship of D. H. Moore, 1880–89

David Hastings Moore was born in Athens, Ohio, September 4, 1838, of New England ancestry, the son of Eliakin Hastings Moore—congressman, patriot, and stirring orator. Young Moore received his bachelor's degree at Ohio University in 1860, his master's in 1863. At the outbreak of the war, he became a private in an Ohio regiment, was elected captain, and served in Sherman's campaign until the fall of Atlanta. An ordained minister, he served as a pastor in Columbus, later in Cincinnati. In a fond reminiscence, Moore later noted the similarities between his career and Cranston's: natives of the same town, graduated from the same university, both members of Beta Theta Pi fraternity, converted on the same day, decided to become ministers in the same meeting, Civil War soldiers, later editors and publishers of the same Book Concern. Their wives had been roommates at college, and their sons were both lawyers in Denver—Earl Montgomery Cranston and William A. Moore. During part of Moore's five-year presidency of the Wesleyan college, Cranston had been the local pastor. Small wonder, then, that Cranston could give enthusiastic testimonial to this man's qualification for a most difficult job. The board echoed his feelings, and brought Moore on two visits to Denver to begin setting up the school.

The meeting of the executive committee of the board on September 16, 1879, laid out the requirements, financial and otherwise, for the relation of the chancellor (still called the president) of Colorado Seminary:

The University's first three chancellors. Dr. McDowell and Dr. Moore are seated, and Dr. Buchtel is standing.

> We agree to furnish the necessary buildings and school apparatus, including laboratory and all heating and lighting fixtures for the buildings, and to grant free use of the same for the term of 5 years to said president, on condition that he shall open and maintain during that period, without risk to this body or the Annual Conference represented by it, a school or schools, in harmony with the spirit of the charter incorporating this institution.

Moore agreed to supply the "moveable household and dormitory furniture." In return he was to have a suitable physical milieu in which to work. Receipts of tuition and any rentals were to be his. His income was not to exceed $2,500, and his teachers "as a body" not more than $7,500. Faculty were to be housed, if they chose, in the building.

A month later, Moore appeared in person—a stocky, well-set individual, self-possessed, jovial, and convincing in speech. He set about the difficult task of reconstituting the school, which he hoped would in time become a true university, with departments, faculty with special expertise in the most important academic subjects and advanced work in some of them, and, of course, a substantial and qualified student body.

It was by no means certain that the school would continue operating at 14th and Arapahoe. Evans and others had seen possibilities at 24th and Blake, but the offers they made were not accepted, so the decision was made to enlarge the Seminary building to accommodate a much larger student body. Evans and the board were exuberant over the substantial improvement of the economy in all areas. The events of the Eighties seemed to justify such optimism. Even though the line of frontier settlement in the Midwest had showed no advance in 1870 over that of 1860, the next two decades witnessed rapid increases. The mid Seventies were marked by depression and falling prices for agricultural products, but the movement westward was unabated. There was a marked expansion of the settled area in the mining regions of Colorado and along the foothills, all the way from Wyoming southward through New Mexico.

The decade of the Eighties brought an equally rapid movement to the West as times became more prosperous, railroads opened up new areas, and the realization spread that the supply of free and desirable land was fast disappearing. Indeed, the end of this decade is usually noted as marking the disappearance of the unsettled frontier.

Evans was prepared to take immediate advantage of new times. The old building had to be greatly changed by adding a story to the original two stories, adding a "Boys' Hall" of four stories some 40 by 50 feet along Arapahoe, and preparing for a "Girls' Department" of some 50 by 100, four stories tall along

The new University building, 1880

14th. This handsome brick building, trimmed with brown and red sandstone, cost some $35,000. Time was of the essence, the architect being informed that the building must begin "upon the first of May and be finished on or before the first day of September 1880." Evans offered to match dollar for dollar the subscriptions of the board members to pay off the debt, up to $12,500, for a total of $25,000. As a result, John W. Bailey, who had originally offered $10,000, increased his donation by $3,000; the rest came from Elbert, Dr. J. Durbin, and Nathaniel P. Hill. Smaller sums came from a host of others, so the building could commence. (But on opening day, the inside of the edifice was far from being completed.) It was high time, for two forces were at work—one contributive, the other highly competitive. Evans welcomed the first permanent public school building in an address for the occasion, April 3, 1873:

> Today . . . is the proudest day Denver has ever seen. She is doing the noblest work for her country, in the great system of public schools that is possible for her today. Wealth amounts to but little compared with it. He who glories in a great but an ignorant and in a vicious population, glories in a disgrace. He who glories in a population high on the plain of moral rectitude, high upon the summits of intelligence, glories in that which is true and an everlasting glory.
>
> And as this public school is established for the education of all, it is but preparing for the perpetuity of the institutions of our country. They cannot subsist permanently except they are based upon the firm foundation of the intelligence, the morality, the rectitude, and the justice of people. On no other foundation can a republic stand.

In 1876 the first class graduated from the high school in Boulder; in 1877 the first class came out from the Denver High School. There were more students for a university to attract. And by 1880 there were other centers of higher learning. The Colorado College opened under Congregationalist auspices in 1874, suspended operations, and reopened January 5, 1880, with a class of 122 students. The Colorado School of Mines, succeeding a school established by the Episcopalians in Golden, opened in 1874. The University of Colorado, which had been authorized by the Territorial Legislature in 1861 and created by law in 1870, finally opened September 5, 1877. One professor was in charge of 44 students, 10 in the university and 34 in preparatory or high school studies.

Into this situation came the Rev. Dr. David Hastings Moore, a robust figure with a well-trimmed beard, a man who was "surcharged with mental and physical vigor, a splendid mixer, a swinging orator, and a born leader." If he was sanguine about the future, he had no illusions about the past of the institution.

In a speech on "My Decennium," delivered in 1914 on the occasion of the 50th anniversary of the University, he commented on the origins:

> It was heir and descendant of the Colorado Seminary, an unsuccessful but worthy enterprise, which was born in 1864 and lived three struggling years, after which it survived only in the immortality of its charter, until it was resurrected and incorporated into the University in 1880—the privileges and powers of the old charter being exceedingly valuable.

Speaking of the third president, Bethuel T. Vincent, Moore commented that the death of the school "was no fault of his; the mother was too weak to give it nourishment. The Conference had only six preachers; less than 300 members; one church and one parsonage, together valued at $700!"

The New Curriculum

All could now be changed. "I began preparations immediately, drafted the curricula, advertised widely in the leading magazines and in our church papers; engaged a faculty."

First, the curriculum. The student of 1881 faced a choice of two degrees—a bachelor of arts and a bachelor of science. The arts degree was heavily classical, salted with some science (astronomy, physiology, chemistry), a year of German, and two terms of French. The senior year included Moral Philosophy, Christian Evidences, Political Economy, and Logic. It was a highly prescribed regimen, deviation from which was possible only with the consent of the president. Thus, in the fall term, the students were exposed to physiology and zoology (a single course), Livy, and Greek selections. In the winter came Trigonometry and Surveying, Odyssey and Greek Composition, and Chemistry. Spring term brought more Trigonometry and Surveying, Horace's Odes, and another term of Chemistry. The bachelor of science course work emphasized Physics, as well as other sciences, and included Anglo-Saxon Grammar and Reader, three quarters of German, two of French, and a senior year much like that of the arts degree. For a short time, one could major in mining engineering, but the development of the school at Golden put an end to that. Also for a short time, a bachelor of painting degree was available, as well as a bachelor of music.

By the end of Chancellor Moore's service, the curriculum had been modified somewhat by the disappearance of some of the classical authors, the appearance of a choice between classical and literary majors, a term each of International Law, History, and one French Historian, Guizot. Laboratory work was given, although it was more of a demonstration than student participation.

A Faculty Hired

The Prospectus of 1880 showed a full-time faculty of five. Moore assumed the title of professor of philosophy and belles lettres with the honorary degree of doctor of divinity. Sidney H. Short, BS, would teach physics and chemistry, acting as vice president. O. B. Super, AM, soon left to teach Greek at Ohio State; Frances A. Fish, AM, appeared as the lady principal and teacher of languages. D. Sauren Blanpied, MusB, occupied himself with instrumental and vocal music; Ida DeStiguer with Italian, drawing, crayoning, and painting. Other part-time faculty contributions included the Rev. Earl Cranston's "Lectures on Christian Evidences," General Bela Hughes' "Lectures on Political Science," and Chief Justice Elbert's "Lectures on Political Science."

It is not remarkable that none of the faculty had a degree beyond an MA, for the first earned PhDs were awarded (by Yale) only in 1861. In 1876, when Johns Hopkins entered the field, a total of only 44 degrees were being awarded by some 25 institutions. Some of these were of manifestly poor quality, given to faculty to improve the appearance of the catalogue.

On the other hand, the dedication of many professors to teaching and learning (if not to publication) and their loyalty to their schools was of a remarkably high order. A case in point is that of Sidney Howe Short, "Colorado's Edison," the first of a long line of inventive geniuses at the University. Born in Columbus, Ohio, in 1858, Short demonstrated at an early age remarkable mechanical ingenuity, becoming a telegrapher at 14, then equipping his home with a burglar alarm and other devices. He graduated from Ohio State in 1880 with a BS in physics. Moore immediately invited him to come to Denver as vice president and professor of chemistry and physics.

Short's earliest interests were the telegraph and telephone. He invented and patented a loud-speaking transmitter, which he sold to Bell Telephone. An electric light secured the backing of Ohio businessmen for a total of $100,000. In Denver, he addressed enthusiastic audiences on the telephone; the address, the papers assured people, would "thoroughly explain the philosophy and working of that wonderful machine. . . . The occult workings will be made visible by means of projections upon a large screen. The lecture combines most happily the elements of popularity with sound science."

One of his most interesting inventions was a mid-slot track for cable cars, a 400-foot track on which he experimented on the University grounds at 14th and Arapahoe in 1885. That year, a small car, the "Joseph Henry," the first of eight, went into use on 15th Street and branch lines. Unfortunately, the project was abandoned in favor of overhead trolleys by the time Short left for school. He remained a fine example of the commitment to exploration and development that has characterized the University's contribution to Denver and the wider world for more than a century.

Moving back to Cleveland, Ohio, Short continued his career in street-

Chancellor Moore and first faculty
(S.H. Short, Dean Howe, Moore, O.B. Super, Frances Fish)

Ammi Bradford Hyde

John Hipp, first graduate, 1884

railroad construction. At the time of his death in 1902, he had received patents on more than 500 substantial projects.

Another commanding figure on the campus was that of Herbert Alonzo Howe (1858–1926). Born in Brockport, New York in 1858, he received his bachelor's degree at Chicago in 1875 at the age of 18 and taught at American University, Cincinnati, struggling with two coronary hemorrhages before he was 21. Offered a position as professor of mathematics and astronomy at Denver, he gratefully took it and regained his health to become one of the most creative and respected astronomers of the 20th century. One wonders what he might have achieved had he not been immersed in administrative duties for much of his life. Although, by necessity, he taught for long hours, he found time to earn a doctorate in science at Boston University in 1884. Years later he played a role in the development of Chamberlin Observatory.

Ammi Bradford Hyde (1825–1921) offers a third example of the dedicated scholar-teacher. Coming out of Oxford, New York, he graduated from Wesleyan University, Middletown, Connecticut, having been advanced to the junior class soon after his arrival. After ordination as a Methodist minister, marriage, and teaching in Cazenovia, New York, he moved on to Allegheny College in Pennsylvania, where he demonstrated his skill in languages—seven of them by this time, Latin, Greek, Sanskrit, and Hebrew among them. Chancellor Moore found Hyde and set him to teaching his great loves, Greek and Latin, in addition to the usual round of administrative chores.

Faculties in Arts and Medicine

The liberal arts faculty grew slowly, from six in 1880 to nine in 1883 and 20 at the end of Moore's term. He had adequate housing for them, but if the school was to become a true university, buildings, faculty, and curriculum were needed. In this area, Moore was highly successful in arousing the interest of men of the caliber of John Evans, among them members of the medical and legal professions. Moore's thoughts turned to the operation of a medical school; he thought it would not be a great expense. Indeed, as Dr. Charles S. Elder looked back on the time, he reflected:

> A medical school, such as several that appeared a few years later, required much less than a block of ground. A room for lectures, another for dissections, and strong influence with the county undertaker who was to furnish bodies for dissection, were the primary requirements. As potential

Sidney H. Short, Colorado's Edison

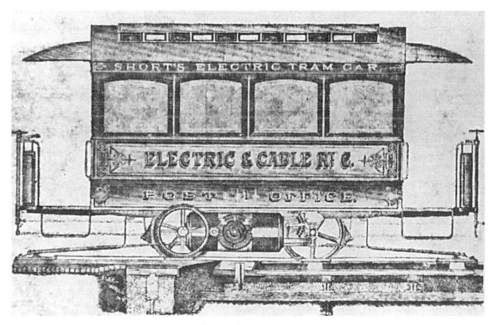

Short's electric tram car

professors were exactly as numerous as physicians in the state, it was not necessary to resort to military conscription in forming a faculty. Even chemistry was taught by lectures.

In the fall of 1881, the Medical Department of the University opened its doors, and for several years lectures were given in various spaces in the old building, moving for a time to the Chamber of Commerce building at 14th and Lawrence. Finally, when the Haish building was completed in 1889, the school moved into quarters there, where it remained until it became defunct. The standard curriculum of the day was followed, embracing two years of six months each until a third year became the national norm.

> Although the faculty was made up of men of high character and considerable learning, they rarely weighed the responsibilities of the professorships. If it happened to be inconvenient to give a lecture at the appointed time, the professor was absent. The students felt no resentment at this neglect. They had their text books and would have relied on them in any event for accurate information. . . . The students were not disappointed at having been spared a tedious hour. These opposing ways of viewing a teacher's delinquency maintained amicable relations and gave longevity to a school that might otherwise have perished before it matured.

The school opened in the fall of 1880 with a fine display of local talent serving as professors covering all the important fields of medicine. Fifteen students showed up, to be taught by a faculty of 17, an enviable ratio at any time. By 1889, the school had given degrees, one of them an honorary degree, to 42 embryonic physicians. Meanwhile, the University of Colorado, whose officers also felt that a school calling itself a university ought to offer more than undergraduate collegiate degrees, began a medical department at Boulder in 1883. That school opened bravely, with two students beginning a four-year course, each year nine months long. Soon that was reduced to a three-year curriculum, with students there as elsewhere anxious to get on with the practice of medicine on their own.

Bishop Warren Raises Funds

Meanwhile, other leaders arrived to share in the burden of raising money and erecting buildings for the University, among them Henry White Warren, who came as the first resident bishop of the Methodist Episcopal Church in 1884. Of Massachusetts birth, a graduate of Wesleyan University in Connecticut, he had served pastorates in Philadelphia and elsewhere. In addition, he served briefly as chaplain during the Civil War and as a representative in the Massachusetts Legislature. He became a prodigious writer of sermons, articles, and books, among them a volume on mountain climbing and (in 1879) *Recreations in Astronomy*. Physically robust, he had climbed the Matterhorn and essayed the Colorado mountains. Elected bishop in 1880, he chose to serve in Atlanta, where he threw himself with his customary energy into helping found Morristown Normal College and Gammon Seminary to aid African-American students. As bishop he traveled in South America, Europe, and Asia to places where Methodist missionaries were at work. In 1883, he married Elizabeth Fraser Iliff in Evans Chapel in Denver.

Elizabeth Fraser, who had been born in Fitzroy, Ontario Province, Canada, was a woman of equal energy and devotion to the church. After coming to Denver in 1868, she married John Wesley Iliff, the undisputed "cattle king" of the West, in 1870. Iliff was the widower father of one son, William Seward Iliff. J. W. Iliff died in 1878 at the age of 46, leaving the Iliff real estate investments and cattle business, including ranches along the South Platte and in Wyoming, in the hands of his widow and son.

In their happy relationship, the Warrens continued their service to the community, the bishop always at work on several projects at a time, traveling to collect money and moving at a fast pace, year after year. At one point in his travels, he reported that he had secured a significant promise from one Jacob Haish, a barbed-wire dealer in DeKalb, Illinois. Haish agreed to give the University one half of the receipts from the sale of his barbed-wire made in Colorado, Wyoming, Utah, and New Mexico, up to a total of $50,000. In return, the University agreed to erect a building for manual training classes and other purposes, and name it for the donor.

The Manual Training Department opened in 1885 as a high school with 11 students. It was designed to train boys of 16 and older a skilled trade and teach them respect for the dignity of manual labor. The school had a difficult beginning, so Warren offered to pay the tuition for needy boys, repeating his offer for several years. In 1887, some $40,000 had accrued from the sale of barbed-wire, and the building was opened across 14th Street from the University. The imposing stone structure, 85 by 65 feet and four stories in height, housed the medical department as well. The manual training department ceased operation by 1892, as East High School entered the field with a substantial program of its own.

Other ideas had been on the mind of the board, including a law department, so on June 30, 1881, the executive committee adopted a resolution to begin such a department, to be headed by Judge Elbert and the Hon. W. B. Mills. The law school, however, remained dormant for a decade, the idea later revived under Chancellor McDowell in 1891. At the same time, the committee voted in favor of Moore's suggestion for a School of Commerce and appointed Robert B. Wallace, who had been Moore's bookkeeper, to head it. That fall, the school was offering courses in bookkeeping and penmanship. With such practical areas attended to, it was time to turn to a matter close to Evans' heart and that of others—the question of theological training.

In June 1884, the Board of Trustees was informed by Bishop Warren that his wife had offered the University $100,000 toward "the establishment, under the auspices of the Methodist Episcopal Church, of a school of theology for the better preparation and education of persons called to the high and holy office of the Christian ministry." The offer was made verbally and did not appear in the minutes of the board meeting. The joy of anticipating such a gift, the largest so far in the history of Colorado higher education, may have kept the trustees from mere recording. A further stipulation for the gift was that an additional $50,000 would have to be raised to further the endowment. Two years later, the executive committee was jubilant that more than $56,000 had been assured, almost $11,000 in cash, $13,000 in real estate deeds, and $33,000 in notes and pledges. Mrs. Warren, rightly interpreting that last figure as representing scholarship sales, concluded that the action did not comply with her original requirement that the sum should be in cash, something the board had by no means anticipated. Even her tender of a mere $1,000, having caused "embarrassment" to the board, was withdrawn. Only during the incumbency of the next chancellor was the original gift completed.

The Clark Gift and the Move to the Park

Another of her requirements, however, had immediate impact—that the University seek a permanent location away from the distractions, noise, and smoke of downtown Denver. The school no longer sat at the edge of a town, but at the crossroads of commerce and industry. A committee headed by John Evans explored three alternative sites. The first, of 260 acres, was east of Montclair; a second was in the Barnum subdivision, an area larger than the first. The third offer came from a group of farmers, headed by one of Colorado's most picturesque characters, Rufus Clark (1822–1910). Clark had left the Connecticut farm of his family at the age of 16. He sailed on whalers operating in the South Atlantic and around the Horn into the Antarctic. At one point, he was even shipwrecked off the coast of Australia. In 1859, Clark was in Colorado, growing potatoes along the Platte. After one crop sold for $30,000, he acquired his nickname, Potato. By his own words, he became a "confirmed drunkard, a slave to drink, so deep in the mire of sin and drink I never cherished a hope of getting out." But he was suddenly converted by the "Gambler's Sermon" of the Rev. E. P. Hammond. He denounced alcohol and acts that had made him Denver's biggest spendthrift and artist of blood-curdling profanity and began a life of prayer and service to his church and community. He was a genius at money-raising, paying taxes on 4,500 pieces of property at one time. He later built a college for missionaries near Freetown, on the West coast of Africa.

Bishop Henry White Warren

Elizabeth Iliff Warren
Archives, Iliff School of Theology

Jacob Haish

Rufus (Potato) Clark

The group headed by Clark had, meanwhile, offered 150 acres, with water rights on 115 of them, located some three miles southeast of Denver city limits, then at Alameda Avenue. There were stipulations. Within six months of November 30, 1885, 200 acres had to be identified as a town site with lots, blocks, and streets platted, next to the site of the school. Further, within a year the school was committed to planting 1,000 forest trees along the streets and in the parks. Last, the school had to begin its principal building as soon as the board could get its money and planning together. Favorable responses from people on the edge of town, in the amount of $6,500 cash and pledges of work, whetted the appetites of board members, as they saw that water was available from artesian wells and the Highline Canal, and transportation was available from the Denver, Texas, and Gulf Railroad and the Circle Railroad of Denver.

Thus the "University Park Colony" was born, and into its development John Evans threw himself with characteristic energy and vision. "The dominant controlling idea," he said, "shall be conscience and culture, the two essential elements to a great civilization." Here was a "superbly healthful location," where people could relax and children grow up unhampered by the troubles of a growing industrial world. There were the Circle Railway, which would make four daily trips each way, and the Pan Handle Railway, which would have a depot for lumber, stone, lime, and coal. Streets were laid out: Evans Avenue eventually extended far west of Broadway. It was intersected at the corner of the campus by University Boulevard. Streets were named for Methodist Bishops Asbury and Warren and for John Wesley Iliff. University Park as then platted extended from South Race Street on the west to Colorado Boulevard on the east, from Jewell on the north to just beyond Iliff on the south, the Circle Railway running across the northern perimeter.

One other connection with the city was made secure in February 1889 by the incorporation of the University Park Railway and Electric Company, formed by men interested in real estate in the Park. That March, under a South Denver town ordinance, a line was constructed westward from South Milwaukee Street and Evans, eventually joining the Broadway cable line, some four and a half miles to the junction.

A prospectus offered lots for $300 and $400 a pair, depending on desirability. Evans himself brought prospective buyers out on the railway at five cents a trip. He placed his carriage at Hilltop (where University Hall and the Iliff School of Theology eventually came to stand) and addressed the onlookers with his best oratory, reminiscent of his earlier days at Northwestern. His advocacy of Denver as the natural hub of a great civilization was apparent to his audience. But sales were slow, it being difficult to imagine a fine suburb growing up on wild and empty prairie land. The first house was built by one of the trustees, J. A. Clough, at 2525 East Evans Avenue, between Columbine and Clayton, in 1886. That house still stands today. The second house was built by Bishop Warren and his wife, Elizabeth,

Humphrey B. Chamberlin

Herbert Alonzo Howe, astronomer

Chamberlin Observatory

at 2184 South Milwaukee Street, called Grey Gables. Much gentrified in recent years, it is well worth a viewing. At the corner of South Milwaukee and Evans Avenue, the original store still stands (although with different tenants). It was built by former governor Evans, who in 1888 established a market, a post office, and the first Sunday School in the Park. It has been handsomely refurbished, a testimony to park residents who have maintained zoning laws as best they could. Through years of depression and hardship, William Evans (no relation) offered store credit to hard-pressed faculty and staff families, who, as they took up residence near the University, would keep a cow and farm animals in their yards.

A promising addition to the Park was the location there of Chamberlin Observatory. Humphrey Barker Chamberlin (1847–1897), who had come from England at the age of six, served in 1863 as a field telegrapher in the Civil War. Mustered out, he worked as a drugstore owner. A physical breakdown brought him to the Colorado mountains for recuperation. He spent part of 1880 hunting and fishing, then formed a company known as Chamberlin and Packard to sell insurance in Denver. On that dissolution, he began land purchases and sales, exercising a canny instinct for investment at the right time and place. As head of the Chamberlin Investment Company, he extended his operations to Pueblo, Trinidad, Texas, and elsewhere, bringing important manufacturing interests to Denver.

An amateur astronomer, he wrote Chancellor Moore, asking if a good telescope could be purchased for $5,000 and if the school were interested in such a donation. An enthusiastic affirmative from the University astronomer, Herbert A. Howe, led not only to the purchase of the instrument at $11,000, but to the construction of the Chamberlin Observatory at 2900 East Warren Avenue. This splendid stone building is in the Richardsonian style, the work of Denver's premier architect, Robert Roeschlaub. The cornerstone was laid in 1890, ground having been broken two years earlier. To the south was a small building, also with a telescope, known as the Students' Observatory. That complex has played a key role in the scientific history of the West, both in broadening popular understanding of astronomy and as a teaching and research facility. Unfortunately, Chamberlin fell victim to the great Silver Panic of 1893 and lost all his money. Thereafter, he frequently visited the campus and commented that "all I have left is what I gave away."

Chancellor Moore as Developer

In 1914, looking back over his "decennium," Moore could proudly point to the development of the school—in bricks, students, program, and faculty. He had begun in 1880 with a bare and unfinished, though imposing, structure. "We hung up canvas for doors, covered window-spaces with muslin, and while carpenters, gas-fitters, and painters were working on every floor, opening day came October 4, 1880."

Chancellor Moore as Developer

He could say that at the end of his chancellorship in 1889, he left three excellent buildings at 14th and Arapahoe, the site of the University Park campus, the pledge of the observatory, a total enrollment of 665, and certain important colleges—liberal arts, music, fine arts, medicine, pharmacy, dentistry—as well as the schools of manual training, business, and oratory. The pharmacy and dental schools are an example of Moore's way of operating, the development of professional schools being close to his heart and those of the trustees. For a pharmacy school, or any others for that matter, a top manager was essential. And one was available in the form of Joseph Addison Sewall.

In March 1877, the newly opened University of Colorado had chosen Sewall as its first full-time faculty member and first president. Sewall was born in Maine, received MD and PhD degrees from Harvard University, and served as professor of chemistry at Illinois Normal University. His idea of education linked the concept of a strong core of liberal disciplines to an emphasis on scientific and practical studies. He was sure the school would, in due time, become a major American institution in the developing West. But the school at Boulder, like that at Denver, was beset by a multitude of problems.

The University of Colorado, with practically free tuition, was dependent on a legislature indisposed to grant large sums of money to a school that had to accept students from quite primitive high schools, that found only nine men and one woman to enter the freshman class in 1878, and graduated only six men in 1882. Two graduates in 1883 and only one in 1884 augured for very slow growth, hardly enough from which to build professional schools. Nevertheless, the medical department opened bravely with two students, over whom Sewall served as head in addition to his duties as professor of chemistry. The mill levy being hardly enough to keep the school open, unfounded charges of mismanagement brought Sewall's resignation after what he called the most frustrating years of his life.

His experience at Denver was a more serene one, as he served on the medical, dental, and pharmacy faculties. By the end of Moore's administration, the medical department had graduated 42 physicians. Over the years, 191 had been in attendance. Pharmacy had taught 11 students, dentistry another 10.

The dental school came into being in 1887 as the Denver Dental School, with a faculty of eight assisted by another nine demonstrators, special lecturers, and clinical instructors—all volunteers and practicing dentists from the Denver area. They graduated four students in 1889 from the first class to complete its studies.

The costs of founding new professional schools and maintaining equipment were compounded by the difficulties of fund-raising. Much of the burden of maintaining the school was placed on the shoulders of the chancellor, the board having heeded the advice of Bishop Matthew Simpson, John Evans' old friend, that the school should never again go into debt by advancing funds without immediate return. Moore was able to control the finances through June 1885, at which time his personal indebtedness amounted to over $10,000, while the

University's was only $2,500. The board proceeded to purchase Moore's share of the debt, at the same time directing him to work for only five months each in 1885 and 1886, after which time he was again on the payroll for a full salary. Meanwhile, he kept busy with cattle raising in Wyoming, preaching there and in Colorado and engaging in a considerable amount of partisan political activity. From all these affairs, Moore garnered some opposition, which came to a head in due time. Meanwhile, in addition to the debt, which, according to the board had reached a "frightening amount" by 1889, there was the ever-present problem of the possible taxation of University property.

John Evans had been highly successful in keeping Northwestern University off the tax rolls, despite arguments in the courts that the operation of the school should be taxed by state and local bodies. He brought the same thinking to Colorado. The Charter, or articles of incorporation of 1864, stated in Section 5 that "Such property as may be necessary for carrying out the design of the Seminary in the best possible manner, while used exclusively for such purposes, shall be free from all taxation." For Evans and the board, these words meant a blanket coverage for all property acquired by the Seminary in perpetuity. But local authority thought otherwise.

In April 1881, not quite a year after the University reopened, James B. Avery donated some 200 acres of prairie land in Jefferson County. The county treasurer promptly assessed a tax for the year at $25.65 and put the property up for sale the next year without informing the University of the action. Jefferson County then "sold" the land to itself. When the board attempted to sell the land, it found to its consternation not only that the land had been alienated, but that any of its property might be subject to taxation. It appealed to the courts.

On April 6, 1885, the case was opened in the District Court in Golden. The University's lawyers asked the court to declare that the taxes were void, and would continue to be so in the future, and that the University, therefore, had the right to sell the property. Jefferson County then appealed to the Colorado Supreme Court, arguing that such an exemption from taxation violated the state Constitution, which had come into existence in 1876 and took precedence over the Charter of 1864. Further, Jefferson County lawyers argued that the charter itself limited the tax-free exemption to actual use, not ownership, of the property. In 1889 the court ruled in favor of the validity of the charter itself, but declared against the University, deciding that the exemption applied only to the campuses, the buildings on them, and the like. The trustees later sold the land, relieved that the charter was inviolate and hoping that no further claims would be possible against property actually in use. But the struggle had only begun.

Student Life

The faculty had an impact on Colorado, traveling as often and as far as their heavy teaching schedule permitted—advertising the school, soliciting funds, and visiting prospective students. One such young man, John Hipp, later became famous as the first graduate of the University. Moore encountered him in a restaurant, when Hipp approached him asking for help to enter college. Born in 1856 on a farm near Hamilton, Ohio, Hipp moved with his father first to Indiana, then to Kansas, and finally in 1873 to an unirrigated farm at the head of Cherry Creek, five miles east of Palmer Lake. There, bent over from years of laborious farm work, he was determined to get an education. He attended East High School in Denver, where he studied, eating graham mush without sugar or milk for weeks, until he could graduate and apply for higher education.

Delighted at the prospect of a young man with such persistence, Moore hired Hipp to serve as janitor in lieu of tuition, ensconced him as a steward in the boarding department, and in his last three years saw him teaching Greek and Latin in the preparatory department. Finally, at commencement in 1884, Hipp appeared as the student with the highest—as well as the lowest—grades in the class, and he performed the office of all the leaders and gave the Commencement oration. The ceremony, held in the newly completed Baptist Church located at the corner of 18th and Stout streets, inspired the minister to lead the assembly in a rousing cheer, "Hipp, Hipp, Hoorah," which the papers noted as "a sincere tribute to the first graduate's perseverance."

Hipp then became a stenographer for S. H. Elbert, read law, and passed the bar examination in 1886. He enrolled in the University Law School, which was organized in 1892, and graduated in 1894. A successful attorney, Hipp was one of the men who incorporated the town of South Denver, and he spent many years as head of the Prohibition Party of Colorado, serving, at one time, as its candidate for governor. He died in Denver in 1928.

Other students shared in the highly regulated undergraduate life in the 1880s and '90s. Campus life was bounded by biblical precept, the careful inculcation of the virtues in and out of class. Students did find outlets in literary societies, art shows, declamations, "readings," musical recitals, orations, and games. Typically, each day in 1884 opened with the chapel exercises at 8:45, "at which all are required to be present, unless specially excused." Each Monday, the "church roll" for the previous day was called. The school day itself was divided into two sessions, one from 9 a.m. to noon, the other from 1 p.m. to 2:30 p.m., filled with "recitations and study halls." The German infusion of the learned profession, research, and publication, with the lecture at the heart of the course, had not yet penetrated to the Colorado frontier; however, much of it had been "settled."

There were, of course, literary and oratorical societies, which were often the source of change in American higher education in the 19th century. Students at Denver and Boulder set out to create a state oratorical society, an organization that did much to foster the art, staging their first production in 1888. Denver enjoyed two literary societies, both a beginning group and Phi Alpha, for advanced courses. The first, named for Alcyone, the first star in Howe's constellation, collected books for a library, debated such subjects as "Was the Execution of Charles I Justified?" and "Should Landlordism in Ireland Be Abolished?" The "cultivation of the minds of its members" and the program "to make them more accustomed to public speaking" allowed students to represent their school to the public.

Other representation came through collegiate sports: baseball, which had been played on neighboring sandlots since 1867, and football, which was introduced in 1885. Frank O. Haraway commented on this beginning:

> William Seward Iliff might be called the godfather of Rocky Mountain football, for it was he who returned to Denver after his collegiate days at Pennsylvania to organize and captain the first DU football team in 1885. The squad was made up of just 11 men, and they played without the benefit of padding or shoulder pads. There was no forward passing and there was little or no resemblance to the game that evolved in the next century. Denver played only one "formal" game that year, losing 12-0 to Colorado College.

Sporadic games with high school and club teams, and a few with other colleges, were the order of the day through the rest of the century.

William Fraser McDowell Becomes Chancellor, 1890

Meanwhile, despite encouraging increases in enrollment and great hopes for the future of the newly organized University Park campus, relations between the board, various friends of the University who had given substantial sums of money, and Chancellor Moore became so strained that the chancellor resigned June 11, 1889, "from the task under which I had struggled for ten of the best and most self-satisfying years of my life." He and the board had tried every device for securing funds. "I caught," he said later, "at every straw—even a promising gold mine proving disappointing." In 1888, in order to attract more and better students, free tuition was offered to the top graduate of any high school in Colorado, New Mexico, and Wyoming. Finally, the board turned over to each individual department the management of its own finances, requiring that 25 percent of all profits be turned over to the central administration. All efforts, however, failed to reduce the budget, so the separation of chief and board took place. Such action could probably have been avoided, since Moore was in the prime of life and still full of enthusiasm for his church and its work. But the Warrens and John Evans were willing to let him go, and the public, still suspicious of a school that leaned toward sectarian control, was surprised and delighted by the rumors and insinuations that filled the pages of the daily press and kept equally to one side.

William Fraser McDowell, chancellor, 1890-1899

But Moore himself moved rapidly. For a short time, he taught political economy at the University of Colorado and was pastor of the Methodist Church in Boulder. He was then elected by the General Book Committee of the national church to be editor of the *Western Christian Advocate* in Cincinnati, Ohio, a post to which he was re-elected in 1892 and 1894. The General Conference of 1900 then elected Moore a bishop, with jurisdiction in Shanghai, China, and special supervision over Methodist work in China, Korea, and Japan. In 1904 he transferred to Portland, Oregon, and in 1908 to Cincinnati, where he continued his work as president of the Freedman's Aid Society. He died November 23, 1915, at the age of 77.

After the resignation of Chancellor Moore, the board persuaded Herbert Howe to take the helm on an interim basis, in addition to his already burdened schedule. He performed with his usual quiet determination. Bishop Warren then journeyed to Lodi, Ohio, where he knew a young minister, William McDowell, whom he had appointed to his first post after graduation from seminary. Here was a good organizer, a confirmed optimist, and a Midwesterner who would fit well in the burgeoning Colorado of the 1890s.

McDowell was born February 4, 1848, in Millersburg, Ohio. He received a BA from Ohio Wesleyan, an MA from Delaware, and finally a doctorate in sacred theology. A man of handsome and commanding presence, he was deep-chested, with a carefully combed head of hair and well-trimmed mustache, large eyes, and aquiline nose. On his arrival, he became pastor of Trinity Church and then served for another year as interim pastor of the Congregational body. The *Colorado School Journal* of 1892 commented that his oratorical style was "brimfull of juicy sweetness and genial light." His later reports to the board and students showed the impact of the ministry and its sermon-delivering force—somewhat overblown, but forceful, always tending to the improvement of the character and lives of his hearers.

McDowell saw it as his opportunity, indeed as his duty, to restore complete confidence in the school, to drive forward on all fronts—curricular, financial, and intellectual—and to carry the board with him in a multitude of endeavors. Their response was generous, earning for them his heartiest thanks and respect. Meanwhile, opportunity, countered by danger, was at hand. The first challenge came with the prospects of a new campus.

University Park Takes Shape

The campus today extends from the western boundary at High Street eastward to South Colorado Boulevard, and from Buchtel Boulevard on the north to Iliff on the south. Four areas were to be set aside as parkland, each with elaborate walkways and considerable expanses of lawns, trees, and flowers. The first of these, bounded by Jackson and Madison, Evans and Warren, was matched by another full block to the west. In the midst of this second part, the

Warrens built their second house. The third, Observatory Park, lay between Evans and Iliff, from Milwaukee to Fillmore. Once a single green area, it is now bisected by Warren Avenue. A fourth, Asbury Park, was located on both sides of Asbury, between Josephine and Columbine. Here the Warrens gave lots for the Wycliffe College for Women.

Despite the continual efforts of John Evans, the board, and active church leaders to attract people to the park, sales of lots were few in number. Boosterism was the order of the day in spite of people's misgivings about living so far from town, without adequate water, in an area where the jackrabbits outnumbered humans. The *Denver Republican*, a paper favorable to the University, reported in 1888:

> Sequestered from intrusive mundane concerns, both students and teachers will be able to devote themselves to the study of the most all-embracing range of knowledge. It sounds like a revival of the Middle Age idea of a university, a sort of philosophical monasticism, tempered (for the teachers) by marriage.

Today, almost 30 houses of those built during McDowell's tenure and before remain. A trip around the park, with a knowledgeable guide or Don Etter's *Four Walking Tours* in hand, is a rewarding and illuminating experience. Two of the most interesting of these early houses are the ones built by Bishop and Mrs. Warren, Grey Gables, at South Milwaukee and East Warren, and Fitzroy Place at East Warren and East Cook. Two professors' houses, A. B. Hyde's at East Evans and South Milwaukee, and H. E. Howe's at South Fillmore and East Warren, are both substantial and properly restored. It is difficult to imagine a time when faculty kept cows and chickens in their yards and worried daily about their next paycheck.

The Silver Panic of 1893 caused great hardship for the school. Only the generous credit of both W. W. Evans, who owned the Milwaukee store, and the owner of the nearby coal yard saved faculty in their distress. But buildings were being built. In February 1890, the board signed the contract for University Hall, 200 feet west of University Boulevard and 60 feet north of Warren Avenue (had it been extended westward). The cornerstone, with the motto Pro Scientia et Religione, was laid April 3, 1890, in a ceremony attended by more than 200 spectators. The *Republican* commented:

> The laying on of the cornerstone of the University provided a cheap advertisement for realty dealers holding land in that locality. Some of the crowd present at that ceremony were greatly struck with the locality, and yesterday they invaded the real estate offices with the result that many sales were consummated.

The cornerstone of Old Main is laid, 1890

The Iliff School of Theology

The board was fortunate in engaging Robert S. Roeschlaub as their architect. He fashioned a splendid edifice of Castle Rock rhyolite, the same stone he had used for Trinity Church in downtown Denver. Modeling, with improvements, the design of Sever Hall at Harvard, he fashioned an imposing structure to house the chancellor's and other offices, with a chapel on the ground floor and lecture halls and laboratories on the second and third floors. For several years, this was the University's only structure, commodious enough to present parlors for entertainment and meeting rooms for the two Greek letter groups, one of which, Beta Theta Pi, had been founded in 1888. For $80,000, it was a real bargain, although the school had to go heavily in debt to complete and furnish it.

Across the circle to the south, a matching building, the Iliff School of Theology, a department within the University, rose grandly in 1892, created with a modified library plan, and offering spacious halls, lecture rooms, offices, and, on the second floor, a chapel. A gift of William Seward Iliff, a University graduate and Mrs. Elizabeth Iliff Warren's stepson, the sum of $50,000 was enough to complete the structure. It enrolled its first class of six full-time and five part-time students in September 1892. Two faculty members were enough to keep them busy. But the endowment was adequate to pay only half the running costs of the department, and, as the total debt of the University mounted, Iliff was separated from the former in 1897 to protect its investments. Finally, in 1900, after McDowell's resignation as chancellor, Mrs. Warren announced the closure of the school "for the time being." It did not reopen until 1910, and then under private ownership, having been formally separated in 1903.

Meanwhile, McDowell was happy to announce that the University "possesses all the departments necessary to make a complete University," which was true in large part, at least on paper. The chancellor had still other problems. As the organization of the new campus took shape, the relationship between town and gown, between an avowedly religious University posture and the secular society of Denver as a whole, continued to be strained. Was the University a sectarian school? McDowell was at pains to show it was not. In 1898, for instance, he invited a number of ministers from various denominations to serve as "pastor in residence," an act he hoped would "overcome denominational stigma." The catalogue of two years earlier firmly stated that "the University is under the auspices of the Colorado Conference of the Methodist Episcopal Church. Its management is thoroughly Christian, but in no wise sectarian. Several denominations are represented on the Board of Trustees and in the faculties." Somewhat earlier, the conference minutes of the church, apparently representing an agreed-on position, averred that "our University does not produce students who so misrepresent nineteenth century thought or who are so inspired by anti-Christian ideas as to produce actions pregnant with the defunct teachings of eighteenth century skepticism."

The University Curriculum of the Nineties

How reflective, then, was the curriculum of such values? McDowell was an avid proponent of curricular reform, hoping thereby to enlarge the offerings and attract more students. And, of course, more specialized courses—balanced with carefully selected fields of general study—provided, as he put it, "Something of everything and everything of something." The undergraduate students found what they wanted—a bevy of required courses and a good number of electives, divided into three options of classical, literary, and scientific studies. In the 1897–98 catalogue, for instance, 16 available courses appeared in the three terms of the school year. There were the sciences—chemistry, physics, some biology, astronomy—and languages—led by Latin and Greek with French and German. Courses in "The English Bible," taught by Bishop Warren, were prominent. Mathematics and oratorical courses were also available. As usual the chancellor had a hand in teaching, having been appointed as professor of political economy and Christian evidence, later as professor of mental and moral philosophy and evidence of Christianity. Research into the nature of the textbooks shows an emphasis on Calvinistic writers, and the courses were generally of an apologetic nature. In the senior year, students could choose from a series of courses. How difficult was it during these years for a graduating high school senior to enter the University? The catalogue presented an imposing list of requirements.

Reading further, students found that the chancellor would personally review each transcript and that good high school averages would assure them of entrance. There was always, of course, the Preparatory School, later called the Warren Academy.

Departments were moved around, some added, others dropped. In 1892 the law school came into being, with Albert E. Pattison as its head. With a two-year course of study, the school was housed in the old Haish Building at 14th and Arapahoe, along with medical and dental schools. The College of Music was greatly expanded in the old seminary building across the street. A School of Oratory was added to the College of Liberal Arts in 1884, but the following year the School of Pharmacy and the School of Business were dropped.

By the turn of the century, a new type of faculty member was being added, a person who not only sought the warm personal relationships with students with which the college in America had always been associated, but who also possessed a positive attitude toward specialization and publication, an attitude that had been introduced into America from Germany after the Civil War. An example of this group was James Edward LeRossignol, who remained at the University from 1894 to 1911. Born in Quebec in 1866, he was educated at McGill University, Toronto, where he earned honors in mathematics, science, and the classics. After a year of public school teaching, he studied at the University of Leipzig, earning a PhD in 1892. He then became professor of ethics and

Medical and pharmacy buildings, Arapahoe Street

The Haish Manual Training Building

psychology at Ohio State. In 1894 he was appointed professor of history and economics at Denver. He was a gifted teacher, counselor, and author, producing five books in 10 years on subjects including economics, monopolies, socialism, and taxation. Later he wrote a critique of Marxism and Stalinism. His *History of Education in Colorado* became a classic.

Howe contributed much to the measurement of celestial bodies and their movement and to two books, *A Study of the Sky* and *Elements of Descriptive Astronomy.* Hyde created a book of poems, another of essays, and *The Story of Methodism.* Even Bishop Warren took time from a busy career to issue three books on the Bible. Early on, McDowell became interested in the extension movement, both as a public relations effort and as an opportunity to bring University courses nearer to the public. In this he was a pioneer in Colorado, beginning with his lecture in Greeley on "The French Revolution." He then brought in Daniel E. Phillips to organize the Department of Pedagogy, the first of its kind in Colorado, to offer extension work for teachers leading to a University degree.

Other members of the faculty included Joseph C. Shattuck, who came from New Hampshire with a doctorate from Dickinson University in 1886 to become superintendent of public instruction in the state system. As professor of pedagogics and dean of the academic faculty, he found students interesting and exciting. He became a full-time business manager, and, as the students put it, "our genial registrar." When he died in 1921 at the age of 86, he had spent 50 active years in Colorado education.

By 1896 Herbert Howe had come to some conclusions about the nature of the student body:

> In some respects, Western student life is different from that in the East. In old institutions, cane-rushes, hazing, and various acts of vandalism keep alive a misnamed college spirit, which lends a lurid hue to college life. Very little of this false college spirit is to be found at Denver. The students realize that the aim of a residence at college is not to paint red, nor to while away the small hours of the morning in riotous carousal. Two literary and four Greek-letter societies take care that no student need lack social affinities. The collegiate YMCA and YWCA are exceptionally strong. Each occupies a well-furnished hall and does substantial work.

But great forces were at work, well beyond the power of University officials to resist, and they proved almost cataclysmic in their impact. It seemed the University would be free from market fluctuations and the recurrent recessions the West in particular had been prone to. But the decade of the Eighties found great speculation, excessive borrowing, and other instances of breach of credit to be increasingly the norm. The board told the *Rocky Mountain News* in June 1890 that it was "determined not to follow the general tendency of all such enterprises, which is to go faster and faster in its operations, while its credit will enable it to raise the means to do so, until it results in embarrassment if not in bankruptcy." These were brave words indeed, but not always put into action. The University property was valued at more than $1 million, but most of it was in unproductive real estate, so the institution needed—more than anything—a large increase in its endowment.

The Silver Panic of 1893 and the University

The boom days of the Eighties were particularly hard on Colorado farmers, who found their increased crops receiving lower prices in the market. Miners as well were seriously affected. In 1873 the federal government discontinued the coinage of silver dollars. Soon, however, the supply of silver materially increased. A compromise in 1878 increased the purchase of silver, but the amount produced in the mining states of the West continued to increase substantially, thus forcing the price down. In 1890 the Sherman Act required the government to purchase 4.5 million ounces of silver each month, a sum calculated to be the aggregate of silver produced in the country. But the supply continued its upward climb, exceeding the amount the government and business could or would absorb. By 1893, the price of silver was still declining. As over-extended businessmen saw a bleak economic future, commercial houses began to add up huge losses, and banks contracted their loan programs.

By mid-July, 45,000 Colorado workers were out of jobs, multitudes of businessmen declared themselves penniless, mines closed, and Denver banks were stormed by worried depositors—10 closed their doors. The Sherman Silver Purchase Act was repealed on November 1, 1893, adding to the confusion. What happened to business and farming life immediately affected the University. McDowell reflected on that period in his "Recollections," given in 1914 at the 50th anniversary of the University founding:

> It was not a swift and sudden storm that came and went, leaving devastation in its wake. It was sudden enough in its coming, but showed no haste in its departing. The University shared the experience of individuals and institutions. Every individual, institution, or corporation that had fixed charges was doomed to like experience. The University of Denver had both debts and fixed charges. I presume that we made more than one blunder in our management of affairs. I know perfectly well that the long strain stretched our nerves and irritated them before we were

through. But as I look back at it, I marvel that the institution was kept going, and I marvel through it all we held fast to our ideas and kept the faith, waiting that better day we confidently expected, but could not see.

LeRossignol, looking back in 1903 in his *History of Higher Education,* noted a school that had 10 departments, several graduate programs, and assets of $1 million, largely in pledges backed by real estate in University Park:

> It would have been well had the University possessed less land and more money. It would also have been well had there been more concentration of effort and less expansion. It is easy to see that now; it was not easy to see it then. As has been well said by a friend of the University, 'The trustees gave the same attention to the University affairs as they did to their own.' Nobody was to blame. It was a mistake. The 'boom' did not last. Land values fell. The prospective million dollars could not be realized. Many friends of the University became poor. The University, with Colorado and the country as a whole, entered into a period of depression.

For the state, that depression lasted at least through 1897. But the University continued to suffer financial distress, as evidenced by the mounting debt. That indebtedness amounted to almost $80,000 in 1891, increased to more than $145,000 in 1892 as a result of the building of University Hall, and by 1900 amounted to $170,000.

Another even greater challenge had come to the fore. In 1892, the Arapahoe County Commissioners, taking the ruling of the Supreme Court that non-taxable land had to be property in actual use, began to tax land in the University Park area that was demonstrably idle. The University responded by hiring lawyers to bring action against the commissioners. The case was argued in District Court beginning October 12, 1893. The presiding judge granted a temporary injunction against payment. Renewed each year from 1893 to 1899, the pattern consisted of an assessment by the county, the levy of a tax, and another temporary injunction. A final decision in 1899 declared that the school was liable only for some $2,500 on a portion of the lots, but not all. The University, however, then appealed to the State Supreme Court and there it rested until the problem was tackled in the administration of the next chancellor.

McDowell as All-Around Administrator

The second chancellor brought to his office considerable dedication and a willingness to be all things to all people: administrator, money raiser, public relations man, teacher, pastor. And the board saw his functions the same way. The minutes of June 9, 1898, state:

> The chancellor must meet with all the faculties or lose his relation to the educational work of all the departments. He must confer constantly with students or have only nominal relations to the student body. He must be ready to represent the University in all public educational ways, in education councils and elsewhere, and this he must do not as a man of affairs, but as a scholar.

In many of these duties he was successful. He was twice appointed by the governor of the state as president of the State Board of Corrections. He traveled widely in search of endowments for chairs. He experimented with novel ways of attracting students, including the abolition of tuition in favor of a fee of only $10. In 1894, he introduced the wearing of caps and gown by faculty and students. But the heartbreaks following the Panic were everywhere, as he saw in 1895:

> The year just closed has been a harder year for institutions like ours than the year 1893–94. The excitement of the panic has subsided, but students have found it more difficult to get places to earn their living, which is a very important item with our students, a large number of whom each year earn their way by caring for furnaces, carrying newspapers, etc. This year, positions like these named were taken by men who could give their whole time to them, so that the number of such situations for our students has been considerably reduced.

Independent vs. Public Education: The Rivalry

Sharing the deep feeling of John Evans, McDowell was convinced that the University of Colorado was encroaching on the territory of his school when it recruited students from Denver High School and tentatively put out extension courses. The greatest contention arose over the location of CU's medical department. Since President Baker found Boulder less than an ideal place for such a school—isolated from many practicing physicians, good quarters, and a sufficiency of patients—he was able to move the last two years of teaching to downtown Denver in 1893. The course was extended from three years to four, and enrollment climbed. McDowell rightly feared the program at the new location would tempt University faculty, as well as students. Consequently, the case was taken to court. The DU board argued that the state constitution specifically located the university at Boulder, and by implication denied it the right to offer any courses elsewhere. In 1897, the State Supreme Court upheld McDowell's contention, forcing the school back

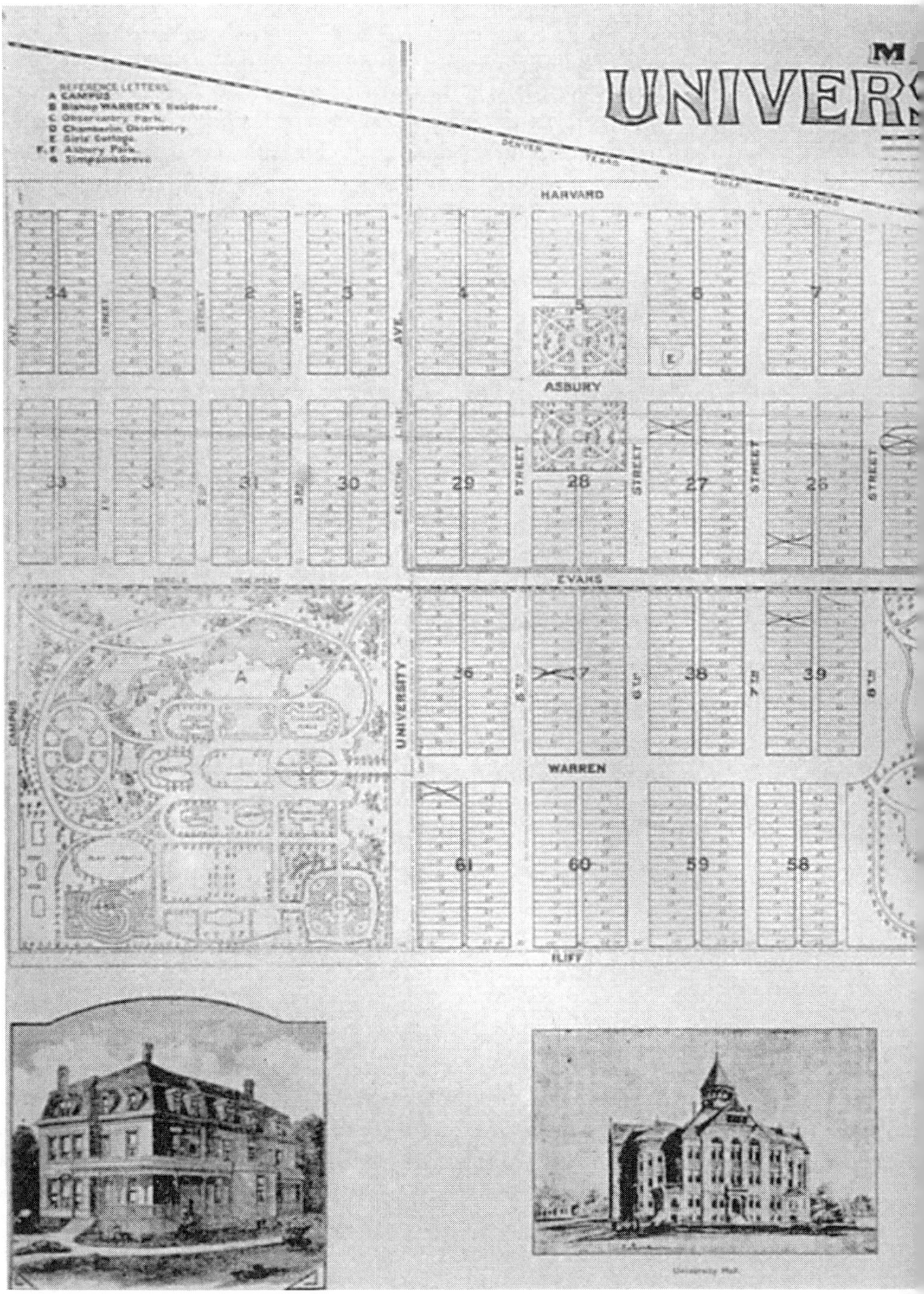

UNIVERS

REFERENCE LETTERS.
A CAMPUS.
B Bishop WARREN'S Residence.
C Observatory Park.
D Chamberlin Observatory.
E Girls' Cottage.
F, F Asbury Park.
G Simpson Grove.

DENVER TEXAS & GULF RAILWAY

HARVARD

| 34 | 3 | 2 | 3 | 4 | 5 | 6 | 7 |

ASBURY

| 33 | 32 | 31 | 30 | 29 | 28 | 27 | 26 |

EVANS

| 36 | 37 | 38 | 39 |

WARREN

| 61 | 60 | 59 | 58 |

ILIFF

University Hall.

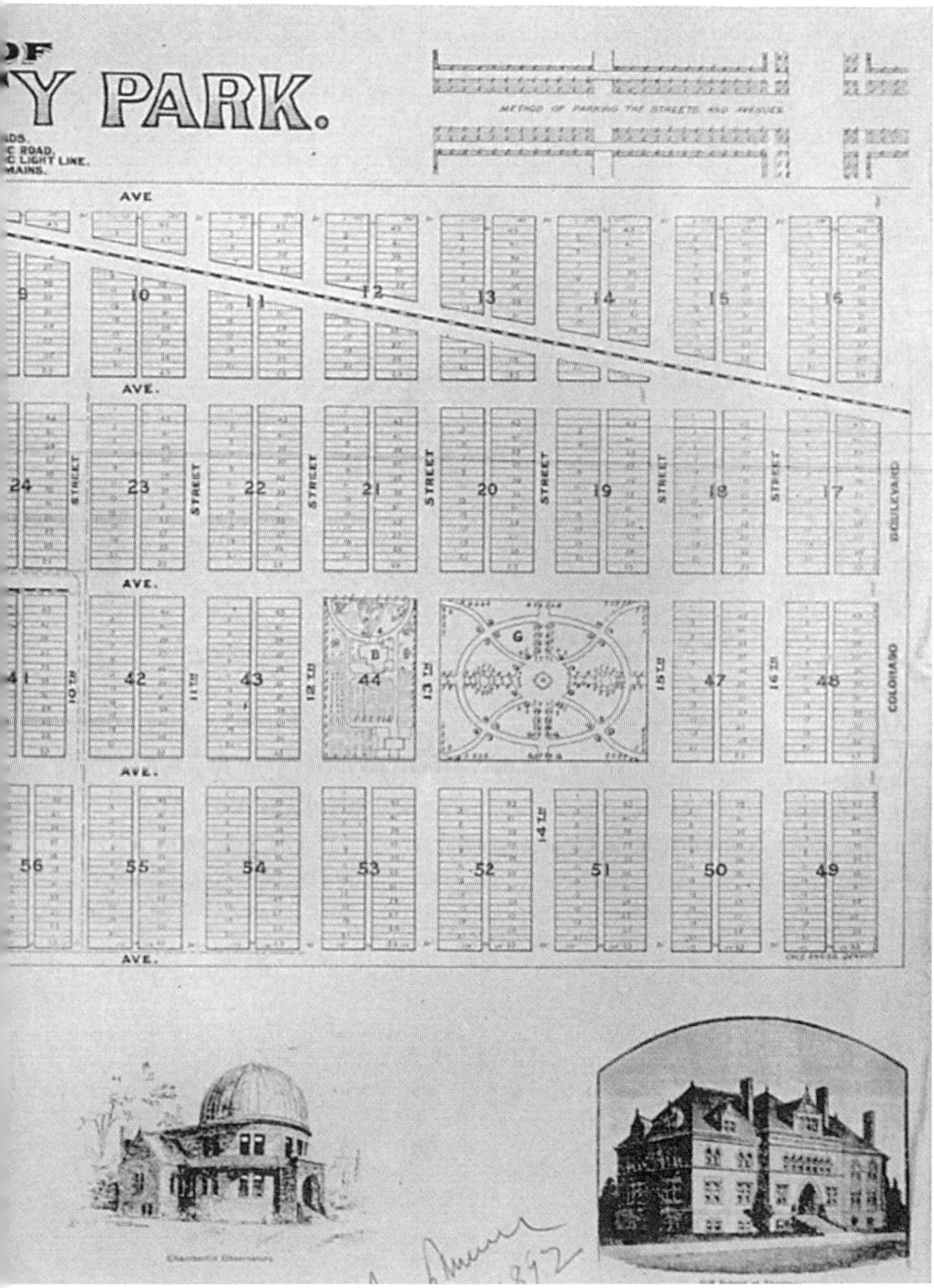

METHOD OF PARKING THE STREETS AND AVENUES

AVE

9 10 11 12 13 14 15 16

AVE.

24 23 22 21 20 19 18 17

AVE.

41 42 43 44 G 47 48

56 55 54 53 52 51 50 49

AVE.

STREET

BOULEVARD

COLORADO

Chamberlin Observatory

1892

93

to Boulder, where a dwindling student body and less enthusiastic faculty forced the reduction of the curriculum back to three years. That, of course, was not the end of the affair.

Meanwhile, DU's medical department, which had been the largest department in the University from its inception in 1881 until 1892, enlarged its own curriculum from three years to four in 1895 and then merged in 1898 with the Gross Medical College. That school had been established as a proprietary institution in 1887 under the charter of The Rocky Mountain University. Named for a world-famous Philadelphia surgeon, the writer of several fundamental textbooks, and an acclaimed lecturer, Samuel David Gross (1804–1884), the Denver and Gross College of Medicine was a significant addition to the University.

McDowell Resigns the Chancellorship: An Assessment

Chancellor McDowell tried every expedient to keep the school not only afloat, but headed upward in every dimension. The campus was moved, enrollment increased, there were new departments and a renewed curriculum, court decisions seemed to go in its favor, the University of Colorado was held at bay. Fraternities and sororities were developed, new student publications came into existence (including *The Kynewisbok*, "The Royal Book of Knowledge," so named by Professor Hyde).

But the debt, the unpaid salaries of professors, and the suits threatening to foreclose on mortgages all added up to crisis. With wry humor, McDowell reflected in his 1914 address:

> I marvel that we did not go all to pieces. . . . I never see a sheriff now without dodging, from force of habit. I lived in mortal dread of having the institution closed to satisfy the claims against it, until it almost became an obsession.

By the spring of 1899, he knew that someone else would have to carry the burden and resigned, effective at the end of that summer.

He was appointed secretary of the Board of Education of the National Church, and in 1904 he became resident bishop in Chicago. He was transferred to Washington, D.C., in 1916. From that position he retired in 1932, having been president of the Board of Temperance, Prohibition, and Public Morals. He died in Washington on April 26, 1937, at the age of 79, having just returned from one of his highly successful speaking tours.

The campus extends in lonely splendor

In retrospect, Denver had experienced 20 years of fervent hope, disciplined austerity, and a greater-than-average expansion of physical facilities. In a remarkably short time a small provincial school had been transformed into a liberal arts college with outlying semi-independent professional schools. The campus had been moved out of downtown Denver and onto a hilltop with a commanding view, water rights, and a well planned suburban village that was attracting permanent faculty and well-disposed neighbors.

The University had survived (if only barely) the Silver Panic and had warded off all attempts to put it on the tax rolls, something that would have certainly closed its doors. It gave the chancellor some small satisfaction to see in Governor Thomas' biennial message of 1901 that his old rival, the University of Colorado, was staggering under a large debt that rendered it "the shadowy and emasculated semblance" of a university. Colorado College was doing very well, in part because it had not attempted to become a university, even in name. There were those who thought Denver might well follow that example. But the school was rich in land and in debts, the chancellor and board seeing a vision of what a great university in a great city might become. Oxford, Cambridge, Harvard, and now Chicago, had all, in turn, started from nothing. The arrival of a new chancellor with fresh energy and renewed vision would set Denver on its way.

Henry Augustus Buchtel, chancellor, 1900–1920

III. From Tragedy to Triumph: The Buchtel Years, 1900–20

A second stalwart chancellor having confessed his defeat before the force of debt and the threat of extinction, the minds of Bishop Warren, John Evans, and Joseph Shattuck were cast back to another minister, one who had had the remarkable ability not only to preach, but to charm money out of his parishioners' pockets right into imposing edifices. So Warren set out once again on his travels, this time to East Orange, New Jersey.

The Early Career of Henry Augustus Buchtel

The man he had come to see was then 51 at the height of his powers, a stocky—even bulky—large-boned man, just above medium height, clean shaven, with still a mane of greying black hair. He was born November 30, 1874, at East Liberty, near Akron, Ohio, of a family that had come from Würtemburg, Germany, in the 18th century. They pronounced their name "book tel," with the emphasis on the first syllable. Moving west to Indiana, his father became a trustee of the Methodist College of Northern Indiana, where Buchtel studied for a short time before his restlessness took him to Chicago and the druggist trade, then back home to a grocery business. Then, at the age of 22 he entered Asbury College (now De Pauw) at Greencastle, Indiana. It was a Methodist school, founded in 1837, that by 1871 had decided to admit women as well as men.

He was a pale, thin youth, slender and delicate-appearing but enormously popular, an orator of sorts, a member of Delta chapter of Beta Theta Pi social fraternity. He was on his way to full-time ministry, having been "licensed to exhort" by the father of Kate Thrush, who later became the wife of Denver Mayor Robert W. Speer. From that relationship came a life-long friendship between the politician and the minister. Appointed to a circuit in Ohio, he stayed four months before accepting a call to do missionary work with his wife, Mary, in the small Danubian village of Rustchuk, then part of the Bulgarian section of the Ottoman Empire. Their stay there was less than a year, as Mary fell ill to typhoid-pneumonia and lay near death. In the summer of 1873 they were back in Greencastle. Here Buchtel demonstrated his ability to raise money by inspiring congregations to build significant structures, in this case two churches, the first of which was all but wrecked by a tornado. A stirring preacher, he developed the practice of conducting every service as a revival meeting, then counseling with the youth of the parish, boys in particular. Moving on to Knightstown and Richmond, he was successful in eliminating the debt on the latter church. He repeated his success at Trinity Church in LaFayette, Indiana, the seat of Purdue University.

The Buchtels might have stayed in the Midwest, where Henry certainly would have become a bishop, had his physician brother, William, not become desperately sick in Denver. In June 1884 Buchtel was at his brother's bedside, taking time out only to preach at the chapel next to Grace Church at 13th and Bannock. Known as the Evans Chapel, it had been erected by John Evans in memory of his daughter Josephine, wife of Samuel H. Elbert. Buchtel's preaching brought crowds. In style, it was vivid, intense, commanding, framed in lyric words, filled with hyperbole, and directed to the conversion of his hearers. Offered a chance to stay, he elected to return to his congregation until the end of his agreement.

At 37, a seasoned preacher, he won the hearts of such men as John Evans, himself 70, and the leaders of Colorado Methodism. Finally, he was persuaded by Bishop Warren to return to Colorado as pastor of the old Lawrence Street Church. After 13 months, that congregation was ready to build a new edifice—Trinity Church at 18th and Broadway. It was a magnificent structure, costing $145,000 exclusive of land, pipe organ, and parsonage. On Easter Sunday 1887, the congregation moved into the basement; they held their first full service in the sanctuary the following Christmas. Buchtel remained at Trinity the full pastoral term of five years before moving on to the Central Avenue Church in Indianapolis, where he stayed five and a half years, again building an impressive edifice, modeled this time on the Pantheon in Rome.

From there he went on to pastorates in Mount Vernon, New York, and East Orange, New Jersey. Everywhere he went he brought ferment, exhortation, and emphasis on the individual, character, and commitment. It was at East Orange that Bishop Warren found him and asked him to "have the spirit of sacrifice in sufficient measure to come and get under our load." The offer was accepted, despite the fact that Buchtel took a decrease in salary and missed opportunities for his four children in school and elsewhere. He found the University in a sad state, every square foot of land and buildings mortgaged, faculty salaries in arrears. The debt, as far as anyone could estimate it, was approximately $200,000.

Buchtel Sets to Work

There were those who thought Buchtel had come to "bury the school," but he had done monumental work in building his churches, especially Trinity in Denver, and he was confident that with great sacrifice and determination his vision of a significantly improved campus and the further development of a solid liberal arts curriculum would prevail. From the beginning, he looked toward a library building, a science hall, and a chapel of commanding proportions. He was convinced that money could be secured for them. The professional schools on the downtown campus were almost independent; the focus of development would be at University Park. Here should be the "Harvard of the West."

Consequently, the new chancellor set out on a pattern that became a highly productive fund-raising standard. It was also one that required much energy. In that first year, Buchtel visited 45 Colorado communities, securing money or pledges from five church members for a total of $220 in one community, $136 from nine members in another. Others could be more generous—$3,000 from one donor, $10,000 from another. By April, some $50,000 appeared to be in hand. For football appearances, he wore his red vest for the first time, a token of double victory, in money and in men. Buchtel's approach was simple. He was available to speak at the dedication of a church, to preach at any time, to meet prospective donors and students individually, and to give formal lectures to all kinds of audiences. His topics ranged from "How We Got Our Bible" and "Practical Values of the Christian Faith" to "Success" and "The Pleasantness of American Life." He read from the poems of James Whitcomb Riley. He was particularly successful in his lectures on Theodore Roosevelt and Lincoln, especially on the Chautauqua lecture circuit through the Midwest. A born orator, he immensely enjoyed large audiences and reaped a considerable financial benefit. Chautauqua alone produced some $27,000 between 1909 and 1917. Most of his money went directly into the University treasury; he died in 1924, poor and in debt. For the University, however, he was so successful that by September 1903 the last mortgage could be burned. He had brought the University a long way from that time when it seemed University Hall would have to be sold, the only prospective buyer being a man who wanted to turn it into a glue factory.

Buchtel's great success in restoring fiscal responsibility and economic life to the University should be seen within the context of a multitude of people who gave the funds, nurtured the students, and developed the school's reputation through difficult years. The most generous supporters, both in terms of money and of moral support, included William Gray Evans, son of the founder. Buchtel had known John Evans well, but by the time he arrived in Denver for the second time, Evans had died, on July 3, 1897, at the age of 83. Evans' contribution to the health of the school had been enormous, as it was also at Northwestern. It is estimated that his total contribution to Denver amounted to nearly $150,000, a demonstrably large sum in those days. He left two sons, William Gray and Evan Elbert, and two daughters, Margaret and Anne.

Young Will attended Colorado Seminary, then various local "academies," before graduating with a bachelor of science from Northwestern in 1877.

Returning home, he plunged into various business enterprises, helping his father with his railroads and Denver's street railway operation. Finally adopting his father's motto, "Develop the Country," on January 2, 1902, he brought his business genius and economic intelligence to bear on the financial problems of the University. The team of Buchtel and William Evans, as chancellor and president of the Board of Trustees, exemplified not only a firm friendship but an ability to conjure up money from unlikely and unexpected places.

The University's curriculum in the Buchtel years was similar to those prevailing across the nation. Most courses in classics were replaced by offerings in psychology, sociology, history, English, and modern languages. A change from the quarter to the semester system had little effect on the curriculum, though it was accompanied by a modest increase in required courses. In general, freshmen were required to take a prescribed series, seniors being allowed much elective freedom. The number of courses offered doubled between 1900 and 1920.

In 1900 the faculty consisted of nine members, only two of whom (Hyde and Howe) had been there since the beginning. Five lecturers were added to this group. Of the regular faculty, well-remembered names included Herbert E. Russell (mathematics), James E. LeRossignol (history and political economy), Ira E. Cutler (biology and geology), Daniel E. Phillips (philosophy and pedagogy), and Wilbur D. Engle (chemistry).

The student body increased from 640 in 1900 to 1,020 in 1910. Graduate school enrollment went up from 20 to 86, liberal arts from 114 to 502, law from 44 to 87, dentistry from 47 to 91, and Warren Academy (the preparatory school) from 94 to 140. The schools of medicine and music had by now been dropped, and the School of Commerce, with 39 students, University College, with 129 students, and a summer school with 107 students added. The student population then increased to 1,695 in 1916, and to 2,780 in 1920. The curriculum had moved from a highly classical liberal arts format to one that included majors and minors in numerous fields, with greater choice of electives. Students had greater access to social activities, with five times as many Greek groups on campus, the YMCA and the YWCA, a students' association formed in 1910, and an athletic committee created the next year. Extracurricular activities were in strong competition with the structure of class lecture, homework, and the like.

It was a highly moral faculty and student society, in which the rules of polite decorum and public behavior were carefully spelled out. Chapel was compulsory (even through the 1930s), although already diluted with some secular presentations. A set of regulations, which appeared in the 1920 bulletin, prohibits the visiting of places of "immoral or questionable resort," swearing, the use of intoxicants or tobacco, and dancing and card playing at parties given "in the name of the University." The school considered itself in full measure in loco parentis, capable of offering all the advantages of a small, closely knit college in which "the collegiate way" prevailed, but (as Professor Hyde and others were quick to note) without the hurly-burly, the hazing, and the rough life associated with Eastern colleges and universities.

The school and the city had not yet embraced each other, but the war and the willingness of the faculty to share their expertise with business and the professional schools was making a significant impact. By 1920, the University had launched more than a thousand teachers into the local system, and there were 600 physicians, 200 missionaries and ministers, 600 dentists, and 350 lawyers with the stamp of the school on them.

The University and the Question of Religion

The University Charter of 1864 had specifically opened the school to all religious groups, but it was obvious that the tenor of discourse, the appointment of the chancellor, and the emphasis of instruction was supported most actively by the Methodist Church. One example is the creation of the Iliff School of Theology in 1892 and its support by Bishop and Mrs. Warren, who had asked that it be set up as a special unit within the University. By 1900, Mrs. Warren saw the debts of the University exceed endowment income, at which point she suggested that Iliff secure even greater autonomy, even independence. For this, she would see that an additional $100,000 would be made available. But in the absence of definite commitments, Iliff closed at the end of the term in 1900. In 1903 the school was deeded over to Bishop Warren, to open in September 1910 with an endowment of some $200,000. A member of the first graduating class, David Shaw Duncan became the sixth chancellor of the University, serving from 1935–41.

Buchtel was asked to defend the school against the charges of the Denver Presbytery in 1919 that the University and Iliff were "hotbeds of infidelity." Although two professors—Wilbur F. Steele (English Bible and religion) and Frank Dickinson (philosophy)—were singled out, the schools together were charged with religious liberalism, in particular for failing to emphasize the divinity of Christ, and with denying the divine inspiration of Scripture.

The controversy arose when the Presbytery sent a letter of inquiry to professors at DU and Iliff asking about their religious views. Some of the faculty replied, defending the right of teacher and student to explore issues in all fields of knowledge. On receipt of these replies, the Presbytery then charged (in the local press): "1) The theory of evolution is the basic explanation at these institutions of all phenomena of life, from the physical down to and including the psychical; 2) the text books and reference books used at the Denver University and the Iliff School of Theology are inimical to the integrity of the Scriptures as evangelically held; 3) the deity of Christ is questioned by the higher criticism taught in these institutions."

Buchtel's reply, given at equal length in the press, was a stout defense of the Christian loyalty of these professors and others and pointed out that the

University had produced more than 200 ministers of a variety of denominations, and further commented that 40 percent of the students in liberal arts and 30 percent of the students in the whole University were from Methodist families. The charges were dropped that same year, to surface from time to time later.

Financial Stability and Two New Buildings

Good news came along. In January 1903, the tax suit pending in the Supreme Court was settled when the court sustained the University's contention of exemption in all particulars. And money came in. An entry in Buchtel's diary for 1904 reads: "Mr. William G. Evans promised by phone to loan me $3,000 tomorrow until he and I can find it."

Now that some of his worries about money had been alleviated, Buchtel could turn his attention to planning a campus beyond the two monumental buildings facing each other at Hilltop. For such an undertaking, he was able to engage the attention of Denver's foremost architect, Robert S. Roeschlaub, who had been designing structures ever since his arrival in Denver from Munich in 1873. Eleven public schools, Trinity and Central Presbyterian Churches, the Central City Opera House, and Chamberlin Observatory were all the work of his genius. In his last years, he turned to a pavilion-type style, somewhat similar to the French classical garden pavilions at Versailles. A library in that style would be just the sort of building to attract, in its simplicity, the eye of Andrew Carnegie, who had been funding libraries across the country and abroad. An appeal to Carnegie was met with a reply in 1906 that $30,000 would be available, provided Buchtel could come up with an equal amount. The money was found, so this building, one of 108 academic libraries funded by Carnegie—and almost the last to be personally approved—was dedicated in 1909 and available the next year for student and faculty use until 1932, when the books were moved into the Mary Reed Building (the author, himself, participating). Carnegie, located between Mary Reed and Penrose, was eventually demolished.

In January 1909, Buchtel made a second visit to Carnegie, asking for a grant to construct a science building. For this he obtained a promise of $50,000, the money again to be matched. The matching funds were quickly acquired from five individuals and the building constructed, just northwest of the library. Built four-square of light brick, it housed the departments of chemistry (hence it was called "the gas house") and physics, with laboratories, lecture halls, and offices.

William Gray Evans

A typical note from Buchtel

Andrew Carnegie

103

A Solution to the Endowment Problem

Although the University was free of debt in 1906 for the first time since 1885, the annual deficiency amounted to some $10,000, a sum that had to be made up with hurried appeals to Methodist churches and to friends at the end of every budget year. It was comforting, though of no help, to learn that all the other Colorado schools were in a similar plight. And there was no endowment fund to provide interest money to cover current expenses and provide for any enlargement of programs.

So, in 1906, Buchtel appealed to the General Education Board, founded by John D. Rockefeller, for $100,000—to be matched by a three-fold sum to be raised by the school. Buchtel was able to argue successfully that the University was at a turning point. It had balanced its books, but in the absence of an endowment, no funds were available for enlargement of faculty or student body. His plans included more buildings, additional funds for faculty improvement, and the like. The board's pledge was not secured until 1912: Then began the long and arduous task of raising money to wipe out the accumulated deficits, for the board stipulated that its quarterly payments were contingent on a positive balance in the school's account. It was almost a full-time job for the chancellor, so in 1917 Wilbur D. Engle was appointed vice chancellor. Buchtel had already taken on, at his own expense, the Rev. Charles F. Senter to travel and raise money across the state and to participate in running the school. But Buchtel himself was indefatigable in his efforts. He was as accomplished an orator as preacher, and skilled on the lecture platform, to which he brought real drama and a concern for patriotic and religious symbolism. He could weep, and his tears were, as his audiences averred, genuine. Between 1907 and 1919, he toured the Midwest in the Chautauqua circuit, with lectures on Roosevelt, Lincoln, and, after 1915, on the topic "Are There Moral Gains in the War?" He turned over most of his earnings to the University. Finally, in 1921, the last of the matching funds had been received and the account closed.

Buchtel as Governor, 1907–09

In 1906 Buchtel made a one-term foray into Colorado politics, running for governor on the Republican ticket against Alva Adams of Pueblo and Ben Lindsey of Denver. It was a Republican year, for three candidates were returned by them to national office and an overwhelmingly Republican legislature sent Simon Guggenheim to Washington as senator. Buchtel's inauguration took place at Trinity Church on January 8, 1907, with a parade to the State House escorted by DU students in caps and gowns. As governor, Buchtel brought a keen desire to correct abuses; to move forward against trusts, lobbying, and saloons in residential districts; and to support an active, elected railroad

The Carnegie Library

The press sees Buchtel as governor/chancellor

commission, pure-food legislation, and insurance laws—all worthy aims for a reform-minded governor. But he had his opponents.

Chief among them was Benjamin B. Lindsey, later famous as Denver's juvenile judge. Lindsey charged Buchtel as a simple-minded person who had given in to Evans, Guggenheim, and others—the "Traction and Smelter Interests"—and even of having tried to bribe him with an honorary MA in 1904. Lindsey's attacks, which were successfully rebutted, appeared in book form as *The Beast* in 1911. Ten years later, Upton Sinclair produced *The Goose Step: A Study of American Education,* in which he included a chapter along the same lines, "The Mining Camp University." But such attacks, in word and cartoon, being a part of the common language of politics, failed to agitate Buchtel and Evans. The house Buchtel had constructed at 2100 South Columbine Street served as the governor's mansion for what was, overall, a successful term of office.

More Buildings Appear on Campus

There were other opportunities on campus, among them buildings. In 1907, the cornerstone was laid for Templin Hall at the northeast corner of Josephine and Evans. This structure, the gift of Elbert M. Templin of southern Colorado, served first as a dormitory for men, later for women, and finally as the home of the School of Social Work before it was demolished. In 1910, came the gymnasium, which stretched along South University, the gift of University alumni. Last came the opportunity to erect a substantial chapel to replace the original meeting hall in Old Main. Methodists of the Colorado Conference began collecting funds in 1907 and were able to lay the cornerstone in 1910, but the building was not dedicated as the Memorial Chapel until December 1917, to honor those who had given their lives in World War I. The service flag on the north wall eventually held 566 stars, of which 11 were gold and 18 silver, representing the dead and wounded.

The building itself was described as "Moorish Baroque," and was distinguished by four corner towers, those at the front more massive, all capped with copper domes. The red brick interior and furnishings were the gift of Denver philanthropist J. K. Mullen, a Roman Catholic. A plaque on the west wall testified to the ecumenical nature of the University. The gift was made "in hope that religious prejudices may vanish from the life of all Christian bodies."

By 1930, the chapel was used mainly for "freshman assemblies," at which attendance was required. These were of a purely secular nature, with occasional talks by visiting clergy or the governor of Colorado, many orientation lectures, and some musical presentations. Other gatherings such as the annual alumni meeting were also held there.

The Alumni Gymnasium

Alumni Gymnasium Annex

The Memorial Chapel and Old Main

Interior of Memorial Chapel

The Medical School Is Merged

The loss of the medical school offset such creations. Organized as an affiliated department in 1881, it had been rejuvenated in 1898 by a merger of DU with the Gross College of Medicine, but neither this school nor its rival at the University of Colorado was able to meet the increasingly rigorous standards of the American Medical Association. Finally, in April 1909, Abraham Flexner, a distinguished scholar, visited the school and reported that the two schools should immediately merge. Citing low standards and a serious lack of funds, the association established two requirements: a full-time faculty and the availability of 200 cots in a university hospital if there were fewer than 100 students enrolled in the school. In the face of such needs, the board reluctantly agreed to the merger with CU, which left the state university in 1911 with one strong school replacing two comparatively weak ones.

A Pioneer Business School Is Launched

In 1908 an independent School of Commerce, Accounts, and Finance opened in the Haish Building at 14th and Arapahoe after incorporation by the state of Colorado. The faculty of 12, ten being local business people—specialists in their fields—and two liberal arts professors, was headed by its founding father, John B. Geijsbeek. Patterned after schools at New York University, Pennsylvania, Illinois, Wisconsin, and Dartmouth, it was one of the first such in the country and the first in the Rockies. Indeed, one of the problems was the absence of textbooks in the various areas. Courses were offered in "banking, practical accountancy, the philosophy of accountancy, transportation problems, and kindred subjects." Students studying three nights a week could earn a degree in commercial science in three years, a master's in four. Morning courses were available later, and in 1922, a full day's menu.

It soon became obvious that the school would be better off if it were attached to an academic body, so an informal agreement was made with DU that the school would manage all operational costs and the University would grant the degrees. The school remained an autonomous operation within the scope of DU until complete amalgamation in 1931. In 1923 it became a member of the American Association of Collegiate Schools of Business.

Frequent moves took the school from the Haish Building to 1330 Arapahoe, then to Champa between 16th and 17th, then to 211 15th, then to Grace Community Church at 13th and Bannock. A last temporary home was found in September 1922 at 2011 Glenarm. Here, among many creative activities, the Bureau of Business and Social Research was founded. In 1946 it became the College of Business Administration. The next move was to a grand new classroom building next to the Civic Center, the cornerstone of which was laid March 5, 1949. Here the college remained for the next 22 years.

Troop training in World War I

The First World War and the University's Response

With the U.S. declaration of war against Germany on April 6, 1917, the University moved with dispatch to acquire a retired colonel as professor of military science and tactics to command a unit of the Student Army Training Corps. It detailed Professors Ira E. Cutler and David S. Duncan as instructors and Professor Etienne B. Renaud as battalion commander. Two hundred and fifty men from liberal arts and a number of dental students were enlisted. Military training was required for all men under 30 who were fit for duty, as was Red Cross training for all women, the latter by vote of the students. Courses in military history, drawing and engineering, camp sanitation, and hygiene were all coordinated with the curriculum. The gymnasium became a barracks for 285 men, and a small building to the north was constructed as a hospital and latrine. This building later became the history department office, then offices and classrooms for the Department of Theatre. The basement of the chapel became the mess hall. The summer of 1918 was filled with drilling, hand-grenade throwing, bayonet practice, charging, and elements of trench warfare—all across the campus. An influenza epidemic restricted men to quarters, but across South University Boulevard relatives waved to their loved ones, tearful and hopeful in their distress.

Public acceptance of the University became more pronounced during this period. The faculty were active and patriotic, giving lectures on food conservation, war savings opportunities, and the causes of war itself. (One member of the faculty, however, was dismissed for failure to cooperate.) Finally, on December 20, 1918, demobilization took place, and with it there developed a distaste for military services. When the Reserve Officers Training Corps was reinstated in March 1919, few signed up.

Buchtel's Last Years

The beginning of 1920 marked 21 years of service for Buchtel, and it looked as though the chancellor had many years to go. However, that September Buchtel suffered a collapse that disabled him for more than four years. On October 22, 1924, he died, worn out from those many years of fund-raising and caring for the school he loved. As Thomas Garth rightly said in his life of Buchtel, "The University is the embodiment of Henry A. Buchtel." The chancellor and his associates had brought the school out of heavy debt, and library, science hall, gymnasium, and chapel were in full operation.

Summarizing Buchtel's character in 1937, Garth had this to say of a man who was cast in a heroic mold:

> He was a man of terrific physical power. . . . His energy never failed him. . . . He built three churches and resuscitated many dying ones. He directed all his pastorates with contagious enthusiasm. At fifty-one he took hold of a dying independent university and in time performed the Herculean task of making it a vigorously active institution. So great was his energy that in later life he extended his sphere of influence beyond the University to the state and later on to the whole West, so that his name was known far and wide. . . . Here we have the trilogy energy, sociability, and love of beauty. To these add as an instrument of their use a keen intellect and you have Henry Augustus Buchtel in concentrated form.

Ralph Waldo Emerson's remark that "an institution is the lengthened shadow of one man" is in large part applicable to the University in the Buchtel years, if one adds the ingredient of an enthusiastic and dedicated teaching faculty. Buchtel saw the ends of a DU education clearly: graduates with firm religious and civic convictions, men and women with a sense of public duty and private probity. The curriculum should mold character while providing students with the tools necessary for financial success in a chosen life work. Buchtel's hopes were admirably fulfilled. The war years produced more solid relations with Denverites, enrollment was up, and new buildings were in place to care for almost all foreseeable needs. The collegiate spirit of a friendly intellectual and social life among faculty and students was the capstone to a successful chancellorship.

*Anne Evans cuts 1931 Founders Day Cake, with Gladys Cheesman Evans,
Chancellor Frederick M. Hunter and Daniel K. Wolfe*

IV. The Twenties and Thirties: The University Between the Wars

Between 1920 and 1940, popular images of life in America, especially life on the college campus, are usually of two vastly different periods, separated by the Great Crash of 1929. The Twenties are pictured as universally happy, filled with the pseudo-sophisticated, hard-drinking, carefree collegiates seen in the cartoons of John Held Jr. and the novels of F. Scott Fitzgerald. Hedonism, living for the moment, obliterated time, it was—The Jazz Age. Such a stereotype hardly fit the majority of campuses, least of all Denver. Here the spirit of the YMCA and the YWCA prevailed. Life was earnest, a job all important, and innocence more dominant than worldly experience.

Hence, the Depression came as less of a shock to students and faculty used to austerity. The mood on campus during the Thirties was powered by the fact that although they were poor by worldly standards, few realized it. It was increasingly difficult to get a job, but there were jobs out there, if one were properly trained and sufficiently motivated. For these people, the environment was admirable. It was a school still searching for its true mission, but remaining loyal to its collegiate roots as a small college, yoked together in a single enterprise, with a teaching faculty facing students on the whole eager but unsophisticated.

Wilbur D. Engle as Vice Chancellor and Acting Chancellor

With Chancellor Buchtel incapacitated, the board appointed Wilbur Dwight Engle, then 50, to carry on the leadership. Engle was born in Portland, Michigan, and received his bachelor's and master's degrees from Albion College and a PhD in chemistry from Columbia University. He arrived in Denver in 1895 to serve as professor of chemistry. In 1914 the University presented him with an honorary doctorate in science. He went on to become vice chancellor and director of the summer school, leaving the field in which he had made a name for himself—toxicology and the chemistry of uranium and vanadium. He returned to the acting chancellorship in 1927 and 1928, became dean of the newly created School of Science and Engineering, and later became dean of the Graduate School. As the long and difficult search began for a new chancellor who would be as good as Buchtel, Engle saw his job as one of maintaining the credit of the school, so dependent on tuition, and paying the bills, knowing that with due care the school could continue to exist.

In May 1922, Engle designed a campaign to raise $2.5 million for increased endowment and merit pay for qualified faculty, as well as for the erection of nine new buildings in the downtown area. Meanwhile, the search for a new chancellor went on. The task was a formidable one, as the committee could offer a salary of no more than $5,000, half of what Buchtel had estimated it would take to find a successor. Further, the successful candidate would have to be an active Christian with advanced degrees, a person who could relate to students and faculty, and, of course, be a diligent and successful fund-raiser. The president of the University of Arizona was asked, but declined; he later became president of the University of Southern California. The president of the University of the Philippines was offered $7,500, but found himself unable to get away. Finally, after 18 months of searching and the consideration of some 200 candidates, the ideal man was secured for the post.

Heber Reece Harper, Chancellor, 1922–27

Born in Manchester, England, in 1885, Harper had come to Avalon, a suburb of Pittsburgh, with his parents at the age of five. He graduated from Allegheny College in Meadville and was ordained for the Methodist Episcopal ministry after receiving a degree in theology from Boston University. He served in various pastorates until 1915. He studied at Halle and Leipzig Universities in Germany in 1913–14. During the war he served overseas, first with the American and then the British YMCA, going with the Army Education Corps of the Army Expeditionary Force to France and Germany in 1919. He then spent a year as educational specialist with the Navy to assist in creating a new educational system.

When the Denver University committee found Harper, he was executive secretary at Boston University. He accepted the chancellorship with the proviso that he delay his arrival in Denver to mid-November so he could finish a $4 million campaign. On his arrival, he launched a campaign to secure the allegiance of Denverites, indeed to increase their appreciation of the University as a top institution in the West. As an Easterner, he brought authority and wide experience to appreciative audiences, to people who had been generally disinterested in their local school.

In speeches to civic leaders, Harper expressed his surprise and delight at the freshness and openness of the land of opportunity in the West, as well as his pleasure in the natural and man-made beauty of Denver and its surroundings.

He then pointed out the city's role in the development of civilization and the necessity of urban leadership in a region, especially in the West. In the development of Denver, he saw the University's part as crucial:

> My hope will be to keep the University apace with the city and state. Whatever programs the University adopts will be designed to bring the student to self-realization, thereby enabling him to serve, in a large degree, the city or community into which he eventually will go.

He set his words to action, reworking the administrative structure to make Denver University more than the sum of its parts by integrating all the semi-independent professional schools into one body, commanded by the chancellor and the board.

Speaking on "Some Opportunities of the Urban University" in his inaugural address, February 17, 1923, Harper told the people that there should and could be the same relationship between town and gown here as in Boston, New York, and Chicago. At the same time, Walter Dill Scott, president of Northwestern University, expounded on the monetary value of the school to the community. Harper pointed out that more than 2,000 students spent at least $50 apiece each month, saving the city more than $500,000 each year in numerous ways. Indeed, 77 percent of the student body came from the Denver area. The Chamber of Commerce was informed that the University "must occupy a place in the front rank of the institutions of the city as the intellectual and spiritual fountain head" and as its greatest cultural asset, one that would help make Denver to the United States what Florence was to Italy at the height of the Renaissance. In 1926, the *News* commented :

> Every year the University is entwining itself in the work of the community. Denver could not be without the fine influence of the law school and the school of commerce of the University. In a subtler way something of the intellectual life of University Park is creeping in on the city.

These were kind words to a chancellor's ear, but the school's great financial and operational problems were constant concerns. Here Harper brought his experience to bear in restructuring the internal organization, making the vice chancellor the dean of the college and making him, and all the other formerly autonomous deans, directly responsible to the chancellor, thus creating "a family of schools" and insuring tighter administrative and fiscal responsibility. Funding was next on his list.

*Heber Reece Harper, chancellor
1922-1927*

Wilbur D. Engle, acting chancellor

James H. Causey

University Building, 16th & Champa

Fund Drive and a Stadium "of Grand Proportions"

In the fall of 1924, the board authorized a major campaign for $2.5 million and found to its delight that $1 million was subscribed locally within a short time. The faculty and staff led off with a donation of $165,000. In February 1925, John Evans, newly elected chairman of the board, pledged a further $100,000. He was continuing the tradition of loyal service and the donation of significant sums of money that his grandfather began and to which his father, William Gray Evans, had contributed time, talent, and treasure during the Buchtel years. The campaign was brilliantly conceived and faultlessly executed. In speech after speech, Harper had pointed to the significant contributions the University was making through the schools of commerce, law, extension, and the college of liberal arts to the development of the city. And then came the great opportunity to cement this relationship, an opportunity Harper seized with enthusiasm.

Denver had long needed a major stadium, but city officials had delayed a decision about its location. Citizens, especially the press, were pleased with the announcement that a stadium of major proportions would be erected at the north end of the University property. A bond issue was floated to cover an estimated cost of $475,000; the final figure was $570,942. Chief among the proponents of the stadium was William Seward Iliff, son of John Wesley Iliff and a member of the first football team in 1884. A trustee and chairman of the athletic council and the stadium committee, Iliff represented the unflagging interest of many University alumni. He died of a heart attack at a Homecoming game, October 19, 1946.

The stadium opened to a game with Colorado School of Mines, October 2, 1926. The massive structure held 26,000 people on the west stands, later another 5,300 on the east. Unfortunately, although games proved popular, the facility failed to generate money. In addition to the initial cost overrun, ticket sales were fewer than anticipated, leading to a loss of more than $20,000 each year. But there were other, hopeful signs.

James H. Causey and the Social Science Foundation

Harper and James H. Causey, men of widely dissimilar backgrounds, came together at this time to open the University to a wider world—that of international affairs. Causey was born in Baltimore in 1873, worked in New York business establishments, and moved to Colorado in 1901, when he began a partnership with William E. Sweet and Alexander Foster to sell municipal bonds. The firm later became Sweet, Causey, Foster, and Co., Investment Brokers. During the First World War, he left business to work for the YMCA in France, returning to Denver to form James H. Causey and Co. A tribute written at his death said,

Fraternity houses and Stadium

The Stadium

> In 1923, inbred with an idealism which characterized him to the day of his death, Mr. Causey decided that he wanted to make some lasting contribution to the widening spirit of liberalism and to the cooperation between people which he deemed essential to human happiness. He selected as the instrument for his contribution to this cause the Social Science Foundation of the University of Denver, his creation.

The Foundation was a joint venture, close to Harper's vision of the need in Denver for a greater understanding of the world to combat the obvious parochial-mindedness of Midwestern and Western America. To this end he purchased the Foster Building, an office structure at the corner of 16th and Champa. It was appraised at $1,544,000 against which there was a mortgage of $705,800. He obtained by purchase all the outstanding stock of the building company and presented it to the University. He secured an annuity, but gave up those rights when he saw the pressing need to begin the great work. He contributed an additional $55,000 for the first three years' exploration of the needs of what was to be called the "Foundation for the Advancement of the Social Sciences." It was designed to "promote the cause of liberalism and focus on vital social and industrial problems of the day." The search for an executive director finally brought Ben Mark Cherrington to Denver, during a leave of absence from his post as executive secretary of the national YMCA.

An autonomous board of trustees was created, and given discretion over spending the endowment income. It was an arrangement fraught with difficulty, but one in which harmony prevailed on the whole. Offices were opened in the basement of the Carnegie Library, with lectures given among the books on the first floor. A seminar attracted honors students from the various departments, and regular dinners and luncheons (at such places as the Blue Parrot on Broadway downtown) balanced large scale lectures with speakers from around the world. Throughout its existence, the foundation was in no small way encouraging a regional populace to become interested in world events and their meaning.

The Reed Family and Their Donations

Verner Zevola Reed was one of those who came from the Midwest (he was born in 1863 in Ohio) to Colorado Springs to make their fortune. There he married Mary Dean Johnson, also from Ohio. She found him dabbling in newspaper work, in mining, and in "promotion." In 1901 he took a commission of $1 million in the sale of the Independence Mine in the San Juan Territory of southwestern Colorado, allowing the couple and their three children to spend the next 11 years in European travel. The Reeds' commitment to the University was firm enough for Buchtel to wire them in Europe in 1915 to ask for a pledge

Mrs. Mary Dean Reed

Margery Reed Hall Alma Mater statue

School of Commerce building, 20th and Glenarm

to help wipe out the current debt. He received a favorable reply. Their daughter Margery graduated from the school and later married Professor Paul Mayo. Meanwhile, on their return from Europe, Verner Reed, relying heavily on this wife's advice and counsel, staked a large part of his fortune on Wyoming oil fields and won another fortune.

Continuing her interest in the school, Mrs. Reed announced in June 1927 that she had increased her campaign contribution to $100,000 for the construction of a liberal arts building to alleviate the almost unbearable crowding on the University Park campus. The Margery Reed Mayo Hall, named for their daughter, was finished in 1928 at a cost of $255,611. The designing architect, Charles Klauder of Philadelphia, developed an imposing edifice in Collegiate Gothic style, containing 17 classrooms, 10 offices, five large experimental rooms in the basement, and the Little Theatre, seating 300 on the first floor. It was hoped that this style, with its lavish use of decoration, would be the model for all other edifices to be built on the campus, but only the Mary Reed Building continued the pattern. Other gifts followed, including a substantial sum given by James H. Causey to furnish lighting and sound for the theatre, by now called the University Civic Theatre to underline the interest of the University in serving the public as well.

Success was balanced by failure in other endeavors. In 1924 the Association of American Universities denied admission to its roster, citing high professor-student ratios, unwieldy class sizes, and other problems. In 1925 Harper approached the Colorado Methodist Conference, asking for a $1 million campaign to assist all Colorado Methodist institutions, including the Iliff School and a student program. That campaign netted only $65,000, however, barely enough to cover expenses. The General Education Board turned down a request for $300,000 in matching funds for support of the liberal arts, and the Carnegie Foundation failed to support a new dentistry building, for which $500,000 had been requested.

But on the whole, the picture was encouraging. Student enrollment had held up reasonably well, reaching a total of 3,467 in 1926–27. Of this number, 1,062 were in liberal arts, 811 in the Summer Session, 711 in commerce, 88 in law, 139 in dentistry, 156 in engineering, 40 in pharmacy, and 807 in City College (formerly the Extension Department).

The student population was still predominantly local, 75 percent or more from Colorado and 90 percent of those from the Denver area. An increasing number was coming from adjacent states, however.

By now Harper's mind was turning to other fields, so late in 1926 he informed the board that he would resign the following year, despite the board's offer to let him name his own salary. The following June, he did resign the chancellorship but maintained, as he did throughout his life, an active and contributive interest in both the school and the foundation. His most active and varied years were before him. Receiving a Laura Spellman Rockefeller

Fellowship in comparative education, Harper earned his PhD at Columbia University where he taught from 1931 to 1936. He then moved into government service, as regional director of the Social Security Board, consultant with the United Nations Relief and Rehabilitation Administration, and chief of the European Section of the Division of Science, Education, and Art of the Department of State. He died October 6, 1969, while swimming in the Sakonnet River near his summer home at Little Compton, R.I.

At that time, Chancellor Emeritus Chester Alter said that, "Although Dr. Harper did not serve long as chancellor, he did remain for nearly 50 years very much a part of the University of Denver." Remarking on Harper's love of beauty and his "faith in the international brotherhood of man," Alter continued:

> In all these ways, and indeed by his very style of thought and living, he contributed more than we can ever know to the well-being of his friends, who are legion, and to mankind at large. Heber Harper has left us, but the impact of his long stay with us will remain forever.

The Hunter Chancellorship, 1928–35

After an 11-month search, while Wilbur D. Engle again took over the acting chancellorship, the board selected Frederick Maurice Hunter as the fifth chancellor. He had impressive qualifications. Born in 1874 in Savannah, Missouri, he attended the University of Nebraska, where he was a football letterman and a member of Phi Beta Kappa. Over six feet tall and weighing some 240 pounds, he showed promise in academic administration. From 1905 to 1911 he was superintendent of schools at Fairmount, Ashland, and Norfolk, Nebraska, then of the Lincoln City Schools in 1911–1917, finally becoming superintendent of public instruction in Oakland, California. In 1920 he was president of the National Education Association, and in 1923 he became chairman of a committee of 100 to investigate the problems of teacher tenure. His book, *Teacher Tenure Legislation,* was an exemplary manual. His master's degree was from Columbia University, his doctorate in education from the University of California.

Sensing a fitting successor to Harper, a man of strong physique and vigor, the board selected the first layman and the first non-Methodist in the 63-year history of the school; Hunter was a Congregationalist. On being approached about the Denver position, he wrote his old friend Jesse Newlon of Teachers College, Columbia, asking, "Is the main problem educational or financial? . . . Just what is the job of the chief executive of DU? Is the position one which offers a real opening for a progressive program in higher education? Would one be swamped with financial difficulties and the problem of finance?" James Causey and Heber Harper were on hand to assure him that there were

Frederick Maurice Hunter, chancellor,
1928-1935

David Shaw Duncan, chancellor,
1935-1941

Mary Reed Library Building

boundless opportunities for constructive change and that finances were of decreasing concern. The record, they said, spoke for itself. Hunter was convinced, and from his arrival in 1928 he made clear his intention to make the school a true urban university, with the control of finances, athletics, salaries, and all business operations centered in his office. For the first time, relations among chancellor, board of trustees, and faculty and staff were defined and subject to more rigid fiscal control. As a result, the chancellor could move more rapidly as he saw the need for development. Early on, there was a stiffening in both entrance and graduation requirements. But without long-range planning and careful scientific study of its resources and opportunities, the University could never, in Hunter's mind, achieve the goal he had in mind.

The Suzzallo Report and Its Impact

Consequently, the board appointed a three-man committee of distinguished educators to suggest and, in a way, direct policy. It consisted of Henry Suzzallo, president of the Carnegie Foundation for the Advancement of Teaching; Ray Lyman Wilbur, president of Stanford University; and Samuel P. Capen, president of the University of Buffalo. They issued two confidential reports, one in May 1929 (five months before Black Thursday), the other in 1930. Their recommendations were wide-sweeping. They pointed to the need to discontinue the schools of dentistry and pharmacy. They pointed to the yearly deficit of the dental school, to the fact that it was being downgraded to Class B by the Carnegie Foundation, that it needed a third of a million dollars to build and equip a new school, and that there was no medical school at the University. Subsequently, both schools were eliminated. A recommendation that the programs in chemical and electrical engineering be dropped, however, was not accepted. Two other recommendations were acceptable—the addition of a school of fine arts, a school of social work (at least an embryo), and a library school. The committee recommended that the first two years of liberal arts be divided into a junior college to survey and concentrate on the students' cultural heritage, and a senior college permitting specialization, with a major and minor emphasis. A quarter system would replace the semester pattern, a five-interval letter system would replace the current percentile system of grading, and there would be honors courses. All these suggestions were adopted by the faculty as Hunter proposed them. Two other proposals involved increases in faculty and staff salaries and the hiring of faculty with more adequate graduate degrees. These last two were more difficult to achieve in the midst of the Great Depression, which by now affected every aspect of faculty and student life. By 1932 the Depression caused unemployment for 13 million people, and college placement offices around the country were reporting that 80 percent of their graduates were entering a world that did not want them. But there were encouraging developments on the Denver campuses.

Buildings and Programs, 1929–35

The Greek System had always been strong on both campuses, but members moved irregularly from one rented space to another. The Lambda Chis, for instance, started in rented rooms in the Metropole Hotel in downtown Denver; later they found themselves in rooms above the drugstore at Evans and University, across the hall from their advisor, Professor E.B. Renaud. They then inhabited a bungalow where the General Classroom Building now stands. In 1929 the University contracted with four fraternities—Beta Theta Pi, Sigma Alpha Epsilon, Lambda Chi Alpha, and Kappa Sigma—for the construction of four large houses in Collegiate Gothic style along East Evans and South Gaylord. The houses were occupied in late 1929 and 1931. At this time, there were 11 social fraternities and an equal number of sororities. The first of these were the Betas, who came to the University in 1888.

An Art School and a Library Appear

In 1929 Hunter and Suzzallo, interviewing a prospective professor of art in Chicago, one Vance Kirkland, explained that they had a fine setting for at least a department at 1300 Logan Street. A palatial old mansion built in the 1880s, it had first been the property of David May, then of engineer and industrialist Delos Chappell. The Denver Allied Arts Association acquired this 22-room stone mansion in 1922. The University was able to purchase the building in 1928, sharing it for a time with the Denver Art Museum. For a time, the University even oversaw the operations of the Santa Fe School of Art.

Another project in Hunter's mind was an adequate library, as the old Carnegie building was by then totally inadequate. So when Mrs. Reed approached him asking what project she might put her money into, he was ready. The result was the Mary Reed Library Building, formally dedicated October 28, 1932. Constructed of reinforced concrete faced with specially burned, deep rose brick of variegated hues and trimmed with Indiana limestone, it was designed in modified American Collegiate Gothic style and completed the Warren Circle quadrangle with University Hall and Iliff School. The view from the west terrace was a span of some 125 miles, from Pikes Peak on the south to Longs Peak on the north. It contained 64,000 square feet, with an American Renaissance reading room on the front of the second floor, stack space for 400,000 volumes, room for 400 readers in the reference rooms, a treasure room, and 34 private study rooms for faculty research. The tower, 126 feet high, contained the Paul Mayo Room for faculty and other floors for book collections. Carnegie became the Student Union after being completely refurbished and furnished.

The University Enters the Field of Opera

In Central City, a mountain town some 50 miles northwest of Denver, along Eureka Street is the famous Opera House, built by Cornish masons in 1878. Nearby are the Teller House and Bar, built in 1872 at a cost of $107,000. By the 1920s the Opera House had declined from its former glory and was showing films on occasion. Owned by Frederick McFarlane and his family, heirs of Peter McFarlane, the original builder, it attracted the attention of Ida Kruse McFarlane (also a member of a pioneer family there) who was professor of English at the University. She and her good friend Anne Evans, sure that the building could be returned to its former usefulness, enlisted the help of Allen True, Denver muralist, Burnham Hoyt, Denver architect, and the famous New York stage designer Robert Edmond Jones to propose restoration. The building was as sound as ever, and even the old hand-made hickory chairs were as good as new. The Opera House was given to the University by the McFarlane family, along with the Teller House and other properties in 1931. The next year saw the reopening of the theatre with Lillian Gish playing the title role of "Camille." In order to administer the properties and their financial affairs, the University formed the Central City Opera Association as a non-profit corporation. In 1953 the association took title to some of these properties, including the Teller House, the Bank Block, and the Chain of Mines Hotel, and in turn gave the University title to some properties it then held.

Encouraging Signs and Financial Difficulties

By the end of his administration, Chancellor Hunter could point to further success in response to challenges. The decline in student enrollment was in large part halted by an aggressive recruiting campaign combined with an increase in the number of scholarships. The federal government, through the Civil Works Administration and later the Federal Emergency Administration, gave work grants to more than 300 students. A professor of music position was made possible through affiliation with the Juilliard School of Music, and departments of international relations and journalism were on the books. The University was then accredited by the Association of American Education and the College of Law by the Association of American Law Schools. A doctor of education and a doctor of philosophy degree could now be obtained again, both degree programs added without additional faculty or staff.

The most important good news came on December 30, 1934, when the Colorado Supreme Court, with only one dissenting vote, reaffirmed the University's tax-exempt status, thus ending a process that had dragged on over two years and had threatened the University with the loss of more than $200,000 in taxes and penalties and conceivably the very existence of the school itself.

As the Depression worsened, however, any university that depended on tuition receipts for 75 percent of its income anxiously watched any drop in enrollment. The numbers for the School of Commerce showed a high of 1,059 in 1929–30, dropping to a low of 574 in 1932–33 before rising to 931 in 1934–35. And new programs, however attractive, brought new costs.

The School of Librarianship Is Established, 1932

Malcolm Glen Wyer, the founding father of the Library School, came out of Kansas to the University of Minnesota, where he received his bachelor's degree, then went on to master of letters and bachelor of library science degrees at the New York State Library School. He served successively as librarian at Colorado College and the Universities of Nebraska and Iowa before he came to Denver as city librarian in 1924. Concerned with establishing a school for training librarians in Denver rather than Boulder, he approached Evans and Hunter in 1928. He envisioned a school that would require three years of undergraduate study and a further year for the degree. Suzallo's committee agreed that such a school would meet real needs and could be afforded. The Carnegie Foundation, through the American Library Association, offered a grant of $5,000 and then $10,000 for each of the following three years, contingent, as usual, on matching funds being found. The board was willing to increase funds up to $18,000 and secured a temporary location at 13th and Broadway.

In addition to fulfilling his city duties, Wyer became dean and found Harriet Howe, who had been with the Graduate Library School of the University of Chicago, to be the ideal director. The school then moved to quarters over Mapelli's Grocery and Meat Market at the corner of 15th Street and Cleveland Place, where half of the second floor was already occupied by the College of Law. Miss Howe, who believed that one could never read too much and that librarians were largely responsible for readers' tastes in literature, later remarked that "there are some reference books which still bring to my mind the flavor of smoked sausage." Some 33 librarians graduated in 1933, 46 the next year, and 63 in the following year. But they entered a depressed economy in which there was little need for their services.

Costs for this program, the development of the law school, and the hiring of a full-time alumni director and a professor of religion with duties in religious activities were added to a budget already strained by depressed income from all sources. Despite Hunter's optimism that a "greater University" could be achieved and that funds for it would be available in due time, it was obvious as early as 1932 that a serious budget deficit of approximately $68,000 existed. Reduced salaries could provide some relief. The faculty met, was apprised of the problems, and voted to create a University Senate—to consist of all full professors, all top administrative officers, and members of the Board of Trustees—to consider problems of salary, tenure, and the like. Despite criticism of the administration for consistently failing to consult with them, the faculty saw no alternative but to make a "collective gift" of $78,000 a year, an amount that could only be considered a salary cut. Those who could not agree to such were notified they could look for another position.

In 1934, after three years of continuing deficits, Hunter launched a campaign to raise $50,000. It was successful enough to reduce the total deficit at the end of the summer to some $1,500, the lowest in many years. Unfortunately, payrolls were met annually by dipping into reserve funds by as much as $56,000 at a time.

In the summer of 1935, Hunter resigned to become chancellor of the Oregon State System of Higher Education, from which he retired in 1946. He later described his first years there as "11 of the most hazardous years of my life," as he had been called to aid a system badly in need of order. He died in Eugene, Oregon, on May 15, 1964, at the age of 85.

The Chancellorship of David Shaw Duncan, 1935–41

This time, the board acted swiftly to fill the vacancy, appointing as their sixth chancellor a man who had been a member of the teaching body for a quarter of a century and who was genuinely respected by students and faculty alike. He was born in Kilsyth, Stirlingshire, Scotland, coming with his parents to Pennsylvania at the age of three. He received an AB from Taylor University in 1901, an MA in 1904. He spent a year as a graduate student at the Free Church College (now Trinity) in Glasgow and became a night school principal, then instructor in Greek at Taylor. In 1906, he came to Denver as instructor in history and political science, later becoming the head of that department. He held a BD degree from Iliff and a PhD from the University. During World War I, he served as chaplain of the Third Colorado Regiment, as chaplain of the U.S. Reserves and an officer in the Student Training Corps for five years, and later the Reserve Officers Training Corps. He was national president of Beta Theta Pi social fraternity. From 1922 to 1935, he was dean of the college of liberal arts, then of the graduate school, resigning to return to teaching. It was there that the board found him. He accepted his new position with reluctance, familiar as he was with the distressed nature of the school, its unbalanced budget, and substantial deficit. His goal was to bring the school out of its financial problems and, if possible, to enhance the very substantial gains Hunter had made in moving it toward genuine university status.

The faculty were with him, and in September 1936 agreed to accept an additional salary cut of 6 percent with the proviso that the amount be reviewed each month by the University Senate. Further austerity proved, however, to be unnecessary when an unsolicited gift of $56,000 was made by the University's great patron Mary Reed (Mrs. Verner Z. Reed). Additional good news was enjoyed that fall when enrollment reached 4,745, an increase of 750 students since 1934. The joint efforts of chancellor, faculty, and board had brought the school out of the worst of the Depression. The great need as always, however, was for endowment, buildings, and faculty. It was possible to reduce scholarship aid for faculty dependents and to increase dormitory rates. The faculty who had asked for a 25 percent restoration of the cut in their salaries in 1933 found that a 50 percent restoration was possible in 1939. More good news came in 1938, when the Alfred P. Sloan Foundation granted $29,000 for the establishment of a Department of Government Management in the Commerce School. The Carnegie Foundation donated $550,000 for the continued endowment of the librarianship school. And Mary Reed, who had already presented the school with more than $675,000, now added another $125,000 to establish an adequate building fund. Even the Department of Electrical and Chemical Engineering was able, despite shortcomings, to secure a two-year accreditation from the Engineer's Council for Professional Development. Finally, on November 25, 1940, Phi Beta Kappa installed its Gamma Chapter (third in the state after Colorado College and the University of Colorado), initiating Duncan as one of its first members.

At the beginning of that year, Duncan asked the board to accept his resignation effective August 1, 1941. He believed he had done as much as he could, and another person should be allowed to approach problems in a fresh manner. He longed to return to teaching, his first love. On September 19, 1940, the board elected Caleb F. Gates, Jr., a member of the administrative staff of Princeton University, requesting him to come and work as chancellor-elect from January 1 to the end of July. But on March 9, 1941, Duncan died, three days after giving a well-received Founders Day address on the history and status of the University.

At Duncan's funeral, the Rev. Frederick J. Cox, pastor of Warren Memorial Methodist Church, of which Duncan was a member, summed up Duncan's contribution: "He was the right man for the task to be done. He balanced the budgets and paid the debts; until today the school is out of debt and has a modest surplus. Moreover, he adjusted difficult problems of personnel with rare tact and wisdom."

Indeed, this speech might have described all the men who headed the school during this period. Harper's dreams of a unified administration and greater involvement with the city and state were in large measure carried out. Two large buildings were completed, and the library collections greatly increased. Student population almost doubled, from 2,780 in 1921 to 5,236 in 1941. There were the frustrations arising from the Depression and the consequent inability to increase the faculty as the level of their remuneration decreased. Most surprisingly, a majority of the teaching staff remained, continuing to conduct research and engage themselves with the community. The budget of 1920, approximately $83,000, was increased to almost $750,000. Barring America's participation in the major wars already under way in Europe and Asia in 1941, there was great hope for even speedier recovery.

Air Corps Obstacle Center

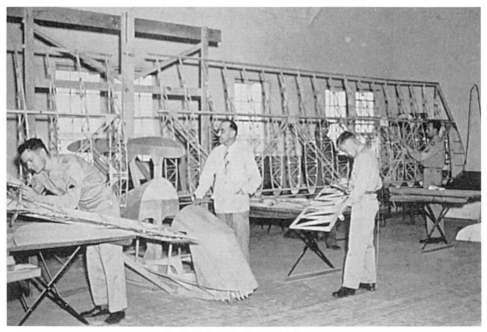

School of Glider Flight and Management

V. The University in the Second World War and Aftermath

In 1936 Chancellor Duncan commented:

> The prestige of a university comes not only from its age, but
> from the careers, reputations, and successes of its students and
> graduates, and its stability from the financial resources it has at
> its command to carry on a program to serve society and meet
> changing conditions.

These words were prophetic, for in the 1940s the University met its greatest
challenge and its finest opportunity to serve the nation, to muster its resources
to meet the challenge of recruitment, wartime austerity, and new ways of
interpreting the world around it. But there followed the even greater problems
of managing a host of returning veterans, the use of large amounts of federal
money, and finally the departure of these veterans with attendant and quite
sudden decline in student population and resources.

When Caleb Gates took office on March 21, 1941, America was already
committed to seeing the European War in personal terms. The previous
October the first numbers were drawn in the draft lottery, and the following
December the country was gripped by the attack on Pearl Harbor. When Gates
joined the Armed Forces during the ensuing war, the chancellorship was filled
by Ben Cherrington until Gates' return. The years between 1941 and 1953 saw
the leadership of the University change six times—Gates for three years,
Cherrington for another three, James Price and Alfred Nelson for a year each,
Albert Jacobs for four years, and finally Levette Davidson who served as interim
chancellor during part of 1953.

Fundamental questions had to be asked and answered in this period. What
contribution could the University make to solving the problems of such
turbulent times? What would be the cost—in people, time, and money? If the
debt increased again, could the school survive? When peace should come, how
could the University cope with returning veterans and a whole new world,
predictably different from that of the pre-war years? Each chancellor had his
own aims and methods. Gates, for instance, with his background in

international affairs and his interest in history, was able to empathize with the concerns of wartime, the arrival of troops, and the interests of students and faculty to participate in the preparations for such events. Cherrington, with a similar background, was faced with the immediate problems of curriculum and staffing. James Price's greatest concerns were for the extension of the school into the urban environment and the need to meet the vocational demands of less traditional students. Nelson followed this pattern while at the same time developing a married-student housing complex on campus. Jacobs' vision was that of a scholarly faculty, a curriculum, and a student body modeled on those of Eastern schools, in which athletics would play a necessary but secondary role. Not all were immediately successful, but elements of all their aspirations appeared later in one form or another.

Caleb Gates, Seventh Chancellor: His First Term, 1941–43

Frank Caleb Gates Jr. was born December 24, 1903, in Istanbul, Turkey, where his father was the distinguished president of Roberts College. His father had been ordained a Congregational missionary in 1881 and sent out to the interior of Turkey, where his experiences with plagues of locusts, inferior educational opportunities, and the great Armenian massacre of 1884 enlivened audiences with frequent telling. He was president of Euphrates College, Harpoot, in central Turkey, before going to Roberts, where he served from 1903 to 1932.

Young Gates was educated first in the preparatory school at Roberts and then for three years at the Hill School at Pottstown, Pennsylvania, before entering Princeton. As an undergraduate, he played tackle on the varsity football team and ran track for three years, becoming an intercollegiate champion hammer thrower. Graduating in 1926 with highest honors in history, he became a Rhodes Scholar at Balliol College, Oxford, where he received a bachelor's and master's degree and, following in his father's chief recreation, was named president of the Oxford Mountaineering Club. Returning to Roberts to be headmaster of one of the preparatory school buildings, Gates then took a year off to conduct research in London. From 1937 to 1940 he was assistant to Christian Gauss, dean of the College at Princeton, and assistant to the director of admissions.

Upon the sudden death of Chancellor Duncan, Gates, then 37, who had been elected chancellor at Denver the previous year, immediately took up the official duties. He set about organizing curriculum and scheduling committees, looking toward greater efficiency and, as he put it, "the gradual adaptation of our curricula to the needs of war, culminating in pre-induction courses designed to meet specific needs of students who have little time to study before being inducted into the military service of the country."

There was a flurry of other activities. The College of Law was moved to temporary quarters in the Mary Reed Building. Helen Bonfils, daughter of one of the founders of *The Denver Post*, donated a building within the block where the University had long planned to build. The block was bounded by the Civic Center and Court Place, 14th and 15th streets. It was understood that this building would be part of the site for a downtown civic theatre. There was a further opportunity to develop the field of music. Although for many years music performance and appreciation had been one of the attractions of the old Seminary curriculum, such offerings disappeared from catalogues between 1912 and 1920, when the Conservatory, located at 15th and Champa, reappeared. Music disappeared again until a department appeared in 1932. In August 1941 Gates, who was characterized as a most culture-conscious chancellor, persuaded the board to purchase the Lamont School of Music. Then financially troubled, the school had been organized by Mrs. Florence Lamont Hinman in 1924. She had been co-founder of The Denver Post Summer Opera, serving as its director/manager for the first two years. She continued to be head of the school until her retirement. Since a proper setting for the school was needed, Mary Reed purchased the Brown-Blayney mansion at 909 Grant for $20,240 and added $7,760 in improvements. Thus ensconced, the school was a success from the beginning.

Not all cultural activities could be continued. The threat of tire and gasoline rationing forced the 11th season of the opera at Central City to be cancelled. But other opportunities were seized. A small contribution from the Rockefeller Foundation made possible the establishment of the Hill-Young School of Corrective Speech, which included the training of speech pathologists. Then there were opportunities for aiding the war effort within an academic environment.

One such opportunity came in August 1941, when the Denver Junior College was created "to supply semivocational courses to meet the needs of young men and women in Denver who are not interested in a four-year program, but who need further training after high school . . . and to offer pre-induction courses." In 1941 the (Marshall) Field Foundation offered to establish a National Opinion Research Center as a non-profit, non-commercial place to measure public opinion, and then to create a research center "to discover, test, and perfect new methods, techniques, and devices for ascertaining the status of public opinion measurement." The center was part of a unified effort to bring together various units whose cause was "to make democratic purposes more efficient." All together, they formed the Government Center, located at 1415 Cleveland Place in the building given by Miss Bonfils. The Center was made up of congruent units: the Bureau of Business and Social Research, the Department of Government Management, the National Opinion Research Center, the School of Social Work, and the Social Science Foundation. As the chancellor saw it,

> The critical time for the University of Denver to educate citizens for the kind of government that is worth the sacrifices of this war is now—during the war. What we can accomplish today in obtaining knowledge and understanding of the ideas that should underlie the functions of free government will to that extent lighten the difficulties of readjustment in the post-war years.

There were immediate needs, of course—one of them to respond to the federal government's urging for the training of troops. One response was the creation of the Department of Glider Flight and Construction, in cooperation with the Post Troop Glider School at Lowry Air Force Base. In the construction classes, four single-seater, all-wood Denver Pioneer gliders were quickly made, in addition to two-seater "cinema gliders." Almost 400 men were trained in the use of these craft in combat.

Social work was also called in service. Such education had become part of the curriculum in September 1931 in the Department of Applied Social Science, which offered from one to four courses for several years, increasing the course offerings in 1942 when the School of Social Work was established. A graduate school appeared in 1960.

But most academic programs awaited better times. Civilian men began to disappear from campus, to be replaced by military units. Aviation students under the 353rd College Training Detachment, as well as members of the Basic Engineering Group of the 4767th Service Command Unit, advanced engineering students of the 4767th Service Command, foreign language students at El Jebel Mosque studying Japanese, Magyar, Bulgarian, French, and German—all appeared to make the campus look much like an army camp. Meanwhile, the enrollment of regular students dropped from 3,277 in the fall of 1941 to 2,329 a year later, to 2,106 in 1943, and finally to a low point that spring of 1,708.

In November 1943, having decided that his knowledge of geopolitics and insights gained from his life abroad made him more fit for the armed forces than for his present job, Gates joined the Army with the rank of major. He was stationed first in England with the American military government and then as assistant military attaché to the American Ambassador in Belgrade, Yugoslavia. Among his duties was the handling of prisoners and displaced persons. Anxious to choose someone familiar with University operations, the board then brought Ben Cherrington, director of the Social Science Foundation, into the office. He came with the stipulation that, in his own words, "I would be chancellor—with all the powers and responsibilities of that office. I knew that to be designated as interim or acting chancellor might suggest a slowdown for the University at a time when present and impending difficulties called for full steam ahead." It was further agreed that he would step down upon Gates' return.

Caleb Frank Gates Jr., chancellor,
1941–43, 1946–47

Ben Mark Cherrington, chancellor,
1943–46

James F. Price, chancellor,
1947–48

Alfred Clarence Nelson, interim
chancellor, 1948–49

The Eighth Chancellor, Ben Mark Cherrington, 1943–46

Cherrington was born in Gibbon, Nebraska, on November 1, 1885. He received his AB from the University of Nebraska in 1911. From there he became secretary of the Young Men's Christian Association (YMCA) of California, and football coach at the University of Southern California, before serving in the Army from 1917 to 1918. He went on to be the national secretary of the YMCA from 1919 to 1926. In 1920 he was organizer of the Students in Industry movement and co-organizer of the first American Seminar in Europe the next year. By that time he earned a master of arts degree from the University of California, Cherrington had already written *The British Labor Movement* and soon after co-authored *Ten Studies in the Sermon on the Mount.* He earned his PhD from Berkeley shortly thereafter. In 1924 he married Edith Harper, sister of Heber Harper, with whom he shared a lasting interest in the movements of people across the world in their economic and social concerns.

Asked to come to Denver from his job with the YMCA, he secured a two-year leave of absence. That leave was extended, with interruptions from time to time until his retirement from the "Y" in 1955. He was to retain the directorship of the Social Science Foundation. As he commented in his *Personal Reminiscence* (1973),

> And so I took over the chancellorship, officially wearing two hats. However, the activities of the foundation and those of the University soon became so integrated that I find it difficult to screen out the former from the latter. By the fall of 1943, our campus was filled with young men, practically all of them in uniform, sent to the University for various types of military training. Many young women were employed in the war effort, resulting in a definite shrinkage in the enrollment of women students.

The University Park campus acquired a definite military aspect as soldiers moved into the fraternity houses and dormitories and drilled on the square between the Beta and Kappa Sigma houses on the east and the land that is now the General Classroom Building, then covered by faculty bungalows. Classes—including mathematics, current history, physical geography, and English—were held in Old Main and Mayo (now Margery Reed) Hall.

The upstairs of the Student Union (Carnegie) was converted into a mess hall. Templin and Schuler Halls were used as barracks, and the residence of former Chancellor Buchtel, which housed the Faculty Club for years, was converted into a dining hall for out-of-town women. Enrollment included a much smaller number of undrafted men, and the campus became predominantly female. The professional schools suffered. For example, the law school moved to the Mary Reed Library Building, where it stayed from 1941 to 1944. This move from 211 15th Street was a mistake. Students were no longer downtown, where most law firms were located, and gas rationing made transportation difficult. The student body shrank to eight students, with some classes having a single member who enjoyed a teaching staff of two professors, including the dean.

Possibilities of Expansion and Development

Cherrington and the faculty saw clearly the need to reshape the curriculum to make the transition from a war-directed series of courses to an integrated one that would educate mature men and women in a changed environment—in a university they knew would eventually have not only a national but a world-wide reputation. But by 1944, the country had been at war for two years, and the loss of students in a school that depended on tuition for almost 78 percent of its revenue was particularly painful. Cherrington then hired the redoubtable Farrington Carpenter as the first director of development. With characteristic enthusiasm, Carpenter visited fund-raisers at Northwestern, the University of Chicago, and the Illinois Institute for Technology. His report of March 15, 1944, urged modernized methods of getting gifts and grants toward a larger endowment. He further encouraged the development of a Civic Center Campus, to enroll students in vocational as well as academic programs, and the formation of the Associates of Denver University to aid in securing gifts.

The board unanimously entered on a drive to buy land across from the Civic Center for an expanded School of Commerce. With president of the United States National Bank Thomas A. Dines' slogan "You can't have a great city without a great university," the campaign quickly raised $2 million. Helen Bonfils donated filling station lots at one end of Cleveland Place, and John Evans donated Mapelli's grocery property at the other end. Eventually the whole of city block 42 was acquired. From then on, Carpenter, Randolph P. McDonough, and Cherrington criss-crossed the state raising more funds.

Carpenter was one of a fair number of people who favored municipal support of independent education by the grant of scholarships to qualified high school graduates, paid for by the city. A call for a revision of Denver's charter, which included such grants but also other more controversial issues, was defeated in November 1947. Proposals for state support came before legislative committees as late as 1988, but were regularly defeated. Another plan had better luck—creating a research division within the University to solicit projects from government and private industry. The plan brought about the establishment of the Institute of Industrial Research, later renamed the Denver Research Institute and recently changed to the University of Denver Research Institute, which, under the leadership of Shirley Johnson and others, acquired an international reputation and brought millions into the University.

In endless meetings with federal representatives, the filing of long reports, and accounting for expenditures, Cherrington spoke of his own feelings on the war years, with their uninterrupted, exhausting activities. With a sense of deep relief, he welcomed the return of Colonel Caleb Gates in February 1946. Cherrington's work had always been on a national and international scale. In 1938, President Roosevelt and Cordell Hull asked him to organize the work of the newly created Division of Cultural Relations in the State Department, and in 1940 he was appointed to conduct preliminary work for what was to become the United Nations Educational, Scientific, and Cultural Organization (UNESCO). From 1946 on, he continued to expand the activities of the foundation until his retirement from government work in 1955 and his death in Denver in 1980.

Caleb Gates' Second Term, 1946–47

The most disastrous war in history came to a slow halt with the unconditional surrender of the Germans on May 7, 1945, and of the Japanese on September 2. By the end of July, the last military students had left campus and the faculty and staff were preparing for what promised to be a vast surge of returning veterans. The enrollment bulge was made possible by the G.I. Bill of Rights, which guaranteed the discharged military man or woman college tuition plus $90 (later $120) per month, in addition to books and other perquisites. Consequently, across the country, 1946 fall enrollments were 57 percent higher than they had been in 1939, more than 60 percent of all students being veterans.

In order to prepare for such an influx, the University organized a coordinated system of student services, including counseling, health education and hospitalization, admissions, registration, student aid, and placements.

Plans for the future of the University Park campus included expanding to some 185 acres, from Buchtel to Harvard and South University to South High. Chairmen of a campaign to raise $15 million for both campuses included Frank H. Ricketson, president of Fox-Intermountain Theatres; Henry C. Van Schaack, realtor; and Thomas A. Dines, president of the United States National Bank and creator of the slogan "You can't have a great city without a great university." The campaign plan called for a new liberal arts building, science and engineering buildings, a fieldhouse and gymnasium, a student union, and religious activities buildings, dormitories, and a clinic and infirmary. Most of these were to wait for partial fulfillment at a later date.

In his public addresses, Gates emphasized a "singularly successful campaign for individualized instruction" and the primary objective of the school as "a liberal education to the end that students may live fuller, more useful, and more gracious lives, and may better shoulder the duties of responsible free citizenship." There would be thorough professional and technical education to round out every student's career. The accomplishment of these goals was more

Temporary buildings after World War II

Another residue of the war

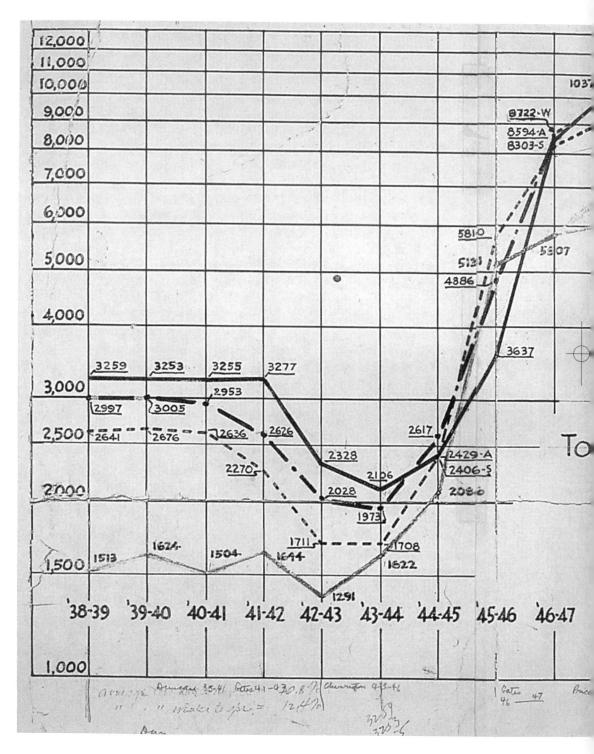

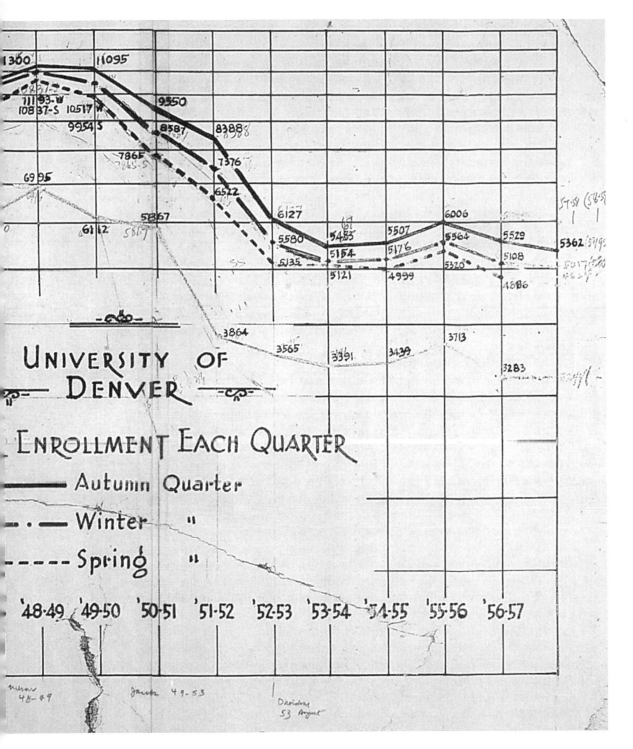

UNIVERSITY OF DENVER

ENROLLMENT EACH QUARTER

——— Autumn Quarter

—·—· Winter "

------ Spring "

'48-49 '49-50 '50-51 '51-52 '52-53 '53-54 '54-55 '55-56 '56-57

141

difficult, in fact. The author remembers teaching three afternoon classes in a row, each with some 200 engineering student-veterans. By the third class, the lecture was well remembered without notes.

There was the further difficulty that the University was becoming all things to all people, as new programs, some of great expense, and new areas of interest became intriguing to various administrators. For example, as a professor walked into his classroom in Mary Reed one day, he found the ceiling painted with stars. The next day, he found a link trainer sitting in the space where students had sat.

In order to assure space for development, the board extended, in its thinking, University Park to include an area bounded by Buchtel Boulevard, University Boulevard, Harvard Avenue, and High Street to permit the purchase of land anywhere within these limits. In addition to purchase, land was acquired in exchange for properties outside these blocks. Temporary buildings began to rise, and 23 buildings were moved, set up, and equipped. They came—old barracks, recreation quarters, and the like—from Camp Hale ("The Pando Gem"), Camp Amache, Fort Logan, and Buckley Field, giving the University more than 115,000 square feet of classroom, office, hospital, maintenance, and dormitory space. An additional 94,000-square-foot building was moved from Farragut Naval Training Base in Idaho to a spot across from the stadium, to serve as a center for recreation and forming the present ice arena and fieldhouse arena.

Housing was a priority for students and faculty alike. Vacant areas near Colorado Boulevard, north of Evans, and south of Mary Reed, were filled with student housing, including some 74 trailers, 160 Quonset huts, and 350 Butler huts. Faculty were housed in two apartment buildings to the south and in a leased apartment building at 14th and Bannock. The newly named College of Engineering, the Department of Science, and the hospital benefited from the donation of $1,317,000 in surplus equipment and supplies from the federal government.

In further anticipation of increasing enrollment, 211 new faculty were hired between 1945 and 1947, of which 141 positions went to the College of Arts and Sciences, 50 to the College of Business Administration, 14 to engineering, and 3 each to law and librarianship. Faculty salaries were increased, although they were still not competitive—the upper limit for a full professor being $5,500, and the beginning level for an instructor, $2,000.

These newly hired faculty represented a trend in scholarship toward publication and a greater concern for national reputation and membership in learned societies.

These were heady days. Some have called the four years after the war "the golden years of higher education." Money was available in quantity, and new programs were started with enthusiasm. A Teaching Institute of Economics was created with money from the Alfred P. Sloan Foundation, and a School of Public Administration started off with 66 students, soon to have some 200. In the autumn quarter of 1946, the University organized the School of Hotel and Restaurant Management, with an enrollment of 74 students from 18 states. It was formed with the idea that on-the-job training in hotels and restaurants would enable students to secure jobs upon graduation, a theory happily fulfilled in the years since that time.

Less successful was the School of Aeronautics, which started off briskly by offering 44 aviation courses, supplemented by courses in numerous other departments. Students participated in "ground training" and agreements with commercial airlines for training in management positions. The school erected a building at Sky Ranch, east of the city, reputed to be "the largest flying field in the country."

Two other additions were made in the summer of 1946. First came the School of Architecture and Planning, which granted a bachelor's degree after five years of study. In the first year, 48 students were enrolled, with expectations of twice that number for the following year. The school was housed on the downtown campus. Most of the buildings on Block 232 across from the Civic Center had by that time been purchased with hopes of acquiring the rest of the block. Here the architecture school, together with other departments, was housed in temporary quarters. All hopes for the arrival of more students were more than amply justified. In 1945, fall quarter registration leaped to 3,637, winter quarter to 4,886, and by spring of the next year to 5,810. The peak was reached in the fall of 1948 when 11,300 students were enrolled.

Gates, reporting to the board on August 31, 1947, commented that "these years have been rich in experience and in personal satisfaction." It was his last report, however, as on that date he resigned his position "for reasons of health." He stayed on for two years as professor of history, then moved to Santa Rosa, California, where he and his second wife operated the Cedar Shake Guest Lodge. There, on the eve of his 52nd birthday, December 21, 1955, he died of a heart attack.

The Chancellorship of James F. Price, 1947–48

In writing about the relationship between the traditional disciplines and vocationally oriented courses in the new curriculum, Joan Beasley, in a 1985 doctoral dissertation on the junior college, commented on the attitude of members of the board of trustees, that they were "split evenly between those who supported a traditional academic school divided into traditional departments and those who supported a vocationally oriented education along with the traditional. The second group supported the less traditionally divided departmental structure." Beasley concluded that this second group prevailed and brought in the next chancellor, this time a member of the current administration.

These two groups represented a continuing tension from the days of the early seminary. On the one side, it had always been axiomatic that one of the

University's fundamental missions concerned service to the community, whether through a manual training school, classes in fine painting for ladies, or a series of professional bodies. The Suzzallo Report of 1928 proposed a junior college with a terminal Associate of Arts degree. This idea was not carried out until 1941, when the junior college came into being with the double purpose of service to the nation and creating new income from large numbers of adults in the area. Thus, when the College of Law left its home at 211 15th, an "Adult Education Center of the University College" was installed to offer adult education for credit at night. In January 1942, the new Junior College, without degrees or credit, was created to offer courses throughout the day and evening. Chancellor Price envisioned an expanded hotel and restaurant management area, an airlines management major, work in real estate development and management, another major in communication, as well as a sales and retail management major. On the other side, traditional courses with a high academic content continued to be taught on the University Park campus and in the College of Business downtown. As the Civic Center campus population increased, these two concepts were blended so much as to distort any sense of focus in purpose and mission.

James F. Price was a Kansan, born of "Republican and Methodist parents, proud that his great uncle was Bishop Matthew Simpson." With a bachelor of science degree from Kansas State College, he received two degrees in law from Stanford University. Then came teaching at Menlo Junior College and the University of San Francisco, where he was responsible for courses in equity, taxation, and trust law. He moved on to become dean of the School of Law at Washburn University of Topeka, Kansas. From 1943 to 1945, he was president of Kansas State Teachers College. Then in 1945, he arrived in Denver to be dean of the Colleges of Law and Business Administration. In 1947, the trustees chose him to be acting chancellor. "After more than 200 candidates had been either investigated or interviewed for the position," they said, "the measuring stick we all found ourselves using was Price." Then 42, Price was a charming man of attractive appearance who impressed his audiences with well-organized speeches. A hard worker, he seemed determined to succeed. His business credentials were sound, and included a seat on the New York Stock Exchange, work with the Chicago Board of Trade, and several years of experience with a trust business in Shanghai.

Furthermore Price had firm convictions that undergraduate courses in law, business, and government should be correlated and that programs should be instituted in real estate development, radio and the print media, sales and retail management—all within the Junior College framework. His own experience was the basis for his interest in securing municipal funding for these programs.

Price was acting chancellor until October 1948. His was the shortest administration in the history of the school—some 14 months—but one filled with numerous creative activities. One was the development (already in progress) of the University of Denver Press. This was the creation of Alan

Swallow, a Wyoming native with a PhD from Louisiana State University. An active poet and anthologist, Swallow had taught at the University of New Mexico and Western State College before serving in the war and coming to Denver to the English department. He created and directed the Press from 1947 to his resignation from the University in 1954 to engage in full-time writing and publishing as the Swallow Press, Sage Books, the Big Mountain Press, and other imprints. Until his death in 1966, he was the only bona fide full-time Denver publisher, at one time or another publishing more than 400 authors. His University inventory, directed from his office in Mary Reed Tower, included now rare books in literature and the history of the American West.

One might speculate on what else might have happened had Price remained. Unfortunately, he was caught up in a situation that caused him to telegraph from San Francisco to Bob Selig, chairman of the board of trustees, on October 2, 1948, that he was resigning "because of health reasons." Sometime later, Arthur G. Coons, president of Occidental College, asked Caleb Gates why such had happened and received the following reply on May 11, 1950:

> His leaving the University of Denver was the result of an unfortunate involvement with a designing woman. This entanglement may have been the result of some emotional immaturity and lack of insight into feminine character on the part of Mr. Price. When the woman in question became publicly objectionable, Mr. Price, in the interests of the University, resigned.

Price settled in California, and practiced law in Barrago Springs and Los Angeles.

Alfred C. Nelson Becomes the Tenth Chancellor, 1948–49

In choosing Price's successor, at least on a temporary basis, the board selected Alfred Clarence Nelson, the only DU alumnus to hold the office of chancellor. Nelson was born in Salt Lake City, graduated from South High School in Denver, and came to the University in 1916, earning a bachelor of science degree in 1920, a master's in 1921, and going on to graduate studies at the University of Illinois, where he received his PhD in chemistry in 1926. From then on, Nelson's career embraced the school, from his professorship in chemistry in 1929, and becoming registrar and recorder of the faculty at the same time, to his assumption of the deanship of the graduate college and leadership of the summer school in 1937. He was always Pete Nelson, a nickname given him in high school when another Pete Nelson, a football player, was making a name for himself. Alfred Nelson, though wiry, had none of the dimensions of a gridiron hero, a fact that made the comparison delightful, and the name remained.

As chancellor, Nelson held strong views about the duty for higher education to be of service to the whole community, in this case, to metropolitan Denver. It would be too much to say that he believed the school should be all things to all people, but he did envision a period in which expansion was needed—in curriculum, program, and buildings. Actions followed words. There was the Junior College, which opened in the fall of 1947 with the expectation that it would be a cost-effective operation that would meet the needs of students not bound for college. Out of this formula came the School of Nursing and the Departments of Photography, Radio Technology, and Sanitary Service.

The programs in dental technology, oil technology, and a multitude of other areas joined programs already in existence, serving more than 450 students in 1948 with expectations of 1,000 within a few years. Indeed, if all the students had been counted, they would have amounted to 14,935 according to one account, most of them coming from Colorado, and a very large part (10,446) from Denver and its hinterland. With 63 percent of all income derived from tuition, endowment income of $119,103 offered too small a base, however, to permit the launching of other significant projects.

The most notable and lasting action of Nelson's tenure came in the building program. A loan secured under the provisions of the Federal Housing Authority enabled seven apartment buildings of 36 units apiece to be built at a total cost of $2.1 million. These new apartment dorms were fully equipped for married students or groups of single students sharing quarters. In more recent times, some of these halls were converted for use as a hotel for the hotel and restaurant management school, as well as departmental and administrative offices. The retention of kitchens and bathrooms made for interesting configurations of work spaces. The Fieldhouse, costing $1,132,015, provided a gym and sports area, a band room, and a swimming pool. And on March 5, 1949, the cornerstone of the Civic Center Campus building was laid.

Against the heady optimism generated by the expansion of the curriculum, however, came the conclusion by examiners of the North Central Association of Colleges and Secondary Schools (charged with the accreditation of all higher education in the region) that the University had lost its sense of purpose. There were insufficient resources for many needed features, faculty, libraries, and laboratories among them. Without adequate funds—and perhaps even with them—the association questioned how the University could do work of college grade and at the same time engage in a proliferation of technical institute courses. There seemed to be no adequate job descriptions for all the heads of operations, nor indeed one for the chancellor's office itself. Having examined the school in 1949, the committee came back in 1952 and continued its accreditation, noting, however, that three years earlier it had found "no evidence at the time of the survey of a definite policy for bringing the scope of the program into line with the available or anticipated resources in such a manner

Civic Center Campus buildings

Business Administration Building, Civic Center Campus

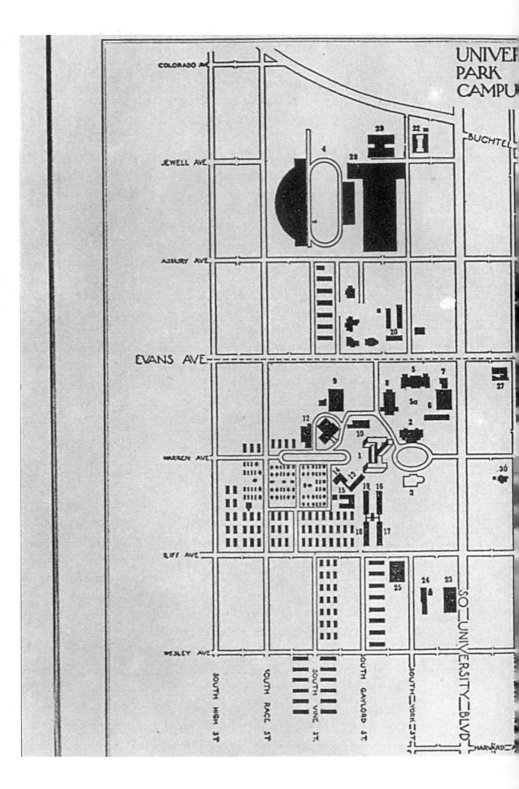

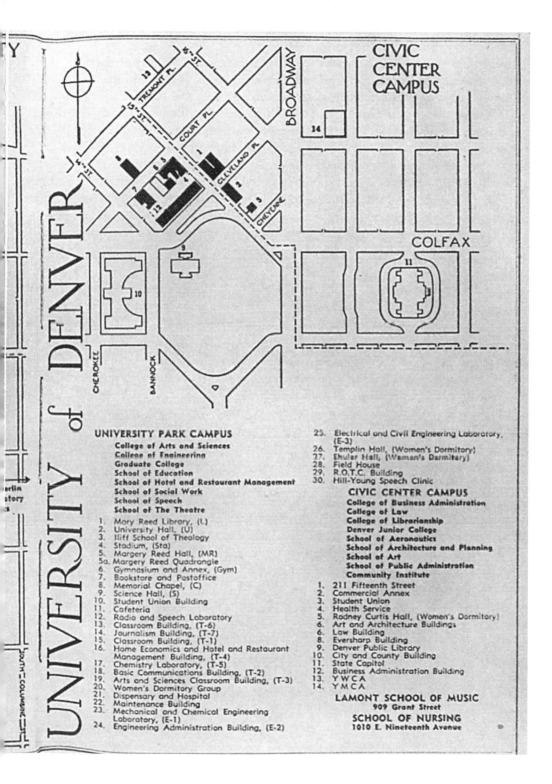

UNIVERSITY PARK CAMPUS

College of Arts and Sciences
College of Engineering
Graduate College
School of Education
School of Hotel and Restaurant Management
School of Social Work
School of Speech
School of The Theatre

1. Mary Reed Library, (L.)
2. University Hall, (U)
3. Iliff School of Theology
4. Stadium, (Sta)
5. Margery Reed Hall, (MR)
5a. Margery Reed Quadrangle
6. Gymnasium and Annex, (Gym)
7. Bookstore and Postoffice
8. Memorial Chapel, (C)
9. Science Hall, (S)
10. Student Union Building
11. Cafeteria
12. Radio and Speech Laboratory
13. Classroom Building, (T-6)
14. Journalism Building, (T-7)
15. Classroom Building, (T-1)
16. Home Economics and Hotel and Restaurant Management Building, (T-4)
17. Chemistry Laboratory, (T-5)
18. Basic Communications Building, (T-2)
19. Arts and Sciences Classroom Building, (T-3)
20. Women's Dormitory Group
21. Dispensary and Hospital
22. Maintenance Building
23. Mechanical and Chemical Engineering Laboratory, (E-1)
24. Engineering Administration Building, (E-2)

25. Electrical and Civil Engineering Laboratory, (E-3)
26. Templin Hall, (Women's Dormitory)
27. Shular Hall, (Women's Dormitory)
28. Field House
29. R.O.T.C. Building
30. Hill-Young Speech Clinic

CIVIC CENTER CAMPUS

College of Business Administration
College of Law
College of Librarianship
Denver Junior College
School of Aeronautics
School of Architecture and Planning
School of Art
School of Public Administration
Community Institute

1. 211 Fifteenth Street
2. Commercial Annex
3. Student Union
4. Health Service
5. Rodney Curtis Hall, (Women's Dormitory)
6. Art and Architecture Buildings
7. Law Building
8. Eversharp Building
9. Denver Public Library
10. City and County Building
11. State Capitol
12. Business Administration Building
13. Y M C A
14. Y M C A

LAMONT SCHOOL OF MUSIC
909 Grant Street

SCHOOL OF NURSING
1010 E. Nineteenth Avenue

that the educational quality of the university would be safeguarded."

Meanwhile, substantial changes had been made. A decision not to pursue becoming a municipal school (and therefore to continue operating a section of the University that would offer open admissions and emphasize a vocational purpose) signalled a turn toward a single mission—academic excellence in fewer fields. The College of Business Administration, for instance, moved to limit itself to four areas of concentration. Aeronautics and the hotel and restaurant school were moved at the same time into that college. The Junior College, a noble experiment, was allowed to die, to be replaced by the Community College in due time.

The argument that the University had an obligation and a remunerative opportunity to offer courses for the general public—ranging from fishing and Oriental cookery to fencing and church ushering—had great appeal. Such courses brought in large revenue and, for a while, served a function taken up only by the Emily Griffith Opportunity School. But as the University of Colorado extension division geared up in Denver, attendance at DU dropped. The attempt to pursue two different goals—academic and vocational—at the same time and place blunted the University's essential mission. In the end, though not immediately, the test of academic excellence was applied in all fields.

Meanwhile, as the trustees began thinking of selecting a permanent chancellor, Nelson affirmed his original intent not to run for the office. In 1951, he became head of the newly created Community College and in 1960 resumed his old post as dean of the Graduate College. A man of many civic interests, he served as national president of his fraternity, Lambda Chi Alpha, and maintained contact with great numbers of alumni through personal correspondence. In all, he expressed the best side of the University—a warm, personal dedication to the continuing cooperation of teachers and students.

Albert Charles Jacobs Becomes the Eleventh Chancellor, 1949–53

The search for a chancellor finally ended with Albert Charles Jacobs, provost of Columbia University. He was born in Birmingham, Michigan, May 21, 1900. After service as a private in World War I, Jacobs received his BA at the University of Michigan, then earned another BA, in jurisprudence, in 1923 as a Rhodes Scholar at Oxford, followed by an MA in 1927. He was the first American to receive a lecturing fellowship, first at Oriel College and later at Brasenose. Returning to America, he joined the faculty at Columbia, teaching family and domestic relations law and writing textbooks on the subject. From 1942 to 1946, he served in the Navy in Washington and the South Pacific as administrative head of the Casualties and Benefits Program of the Bureau of Naval Personnel, and later as director of the Navy's Dependents' Welfare

Division, for which he assisted in the writing of legislation. Back at Columbia in 1946 as professor of law, he became assistant to Dwight D. Eisenhower, in charge of the thousands of veterans then swarming over the campus. Eisenhower, who had confessed before taking the presidency that he knew nothing about universities in general and Columbia in particular, selected Jacobs as provost in 1947. It was a position that entailed the day-to-day running of the university and making contact with the faculty (of whom Eisenhower was somewhat suspicious) and the rest of the administration. At Denver, he found problems.

Just as the University's post-war enrollment increases were higher than those of any other institution in the state, so the decline was equally noticeable. Enrollment in 1949–50 presaged the significant decline that was to come: 11,095 in the fall, 10,079 in the winter, 9,954 in the spring—a drop of more than 1,000 students. By the 1952–53 academic year, the figures reached almost their lowest ebb: 6,127, to 5,580, to 5,135—an almost 50 percent drop in three years. Jacobs saw the problem clearly, but in perspective with other factors. Chief among them was the lack of continuity in leadership, "and this at a time when the finest leadership was of the utmost importance." Further, the decline created a problem "of the utmost magnitude, in view of the dependence financially of the University on tuition income."

Jacobs admired the new Business Administration building on the Civic Center campus, the seven new apartment-dormitories, the new Student Union building, and "the unparalleled Field House with its excellent Ice Arena." But he saw increased financial burdens over a long period to come. His last and perhaps greatest concern was for the improvement of the academic dimension of the school, for which he detected less concern than for construction and athletics. In frequent speeches, he pointed out that "In the final analysis, academic prestige is the sole criterion of an institution of higher learning. Everything else is subordinate to it." However, he found alumni support lacking.

In the frequent turnover of chancellors, Jacobs found the trustees of necessity taking over many of the administrative activities that a regular succession would have assured. He set about with dispatch to establish the confidence of the larger community in higher education in general, and the University in particular. He continued the work of an Internal Survey Committee. He brought George B. Pegram, president emeritus of Columbia University, and Prof. Harry J. Carman of its history department to help in analysis. In searching for substantial funds, he pledged that "not one cent will go into buildings, for capital investment, nor for non-academic purposes," but rather to retain faculty and give them time for research and publication.

In playing down the role of athletics, Jacobs ran into considerable opposition, despite his continuing emphasis on the value of physical training for all students and his personal interest in competitive sports. He was sure the University could not afford to go into athletics "in a big way, even to support

Albert Charles Jacobs, chancellor,
1949–1953

Levette J. Davidson, acting chancellor,
1953

what we are now doing."

By the end of his second year, he had presided over a complete revamping of the educational program and had determined which parts could not be supported. Among the latter was the School of Architecture. It was his painful duty to terminate programs that did not pay their own way, promise to be guaranteed by proper accreditation, or were faced with great competition by the state's public universities. Clearly, the decade of the Forties, which brought great changes—almost always in response to emergencies—was over. Now the choice was urgently at hand—increasing resources dramatically to cover the costs of such experimentation or the understanding of a purpose aligned to available resources. Indicative of the new attitude was the termination of the Junior College and the Community Institute, a successor of the University College. In their place was the Community College, which was organized to conduct a much-modified series of non-credit courses. The Community College in turn was terminated December 31, 1960, in favor of "a more rigorous academic purpose," in which all courses were monitored by academic departments.

In October 1952, Jacobs spoke to the assembled faculty and presented two alternatives for solving "the financial plight." One was a drastic reduction of scale, which would produce a small college "with a reputation for mediocrity." The other was a greatly expanded University, which would, meanwhile, need to balance budgets, cut operations costs, and allow no pay increases during a critical period of some three or four years. There would, of necessity, be a period of deficit financing, as well as some cuts in programs over the next three or four years. The board, however, found itself unable to go along with such proposals. That same month, wearied over the struggle, Jacobs announced his resignation as soon as a successor could be found. The following March, he left to become president of Trinity College in Hartford, Connecticut, where he achieved considerable success.

Levette J. Davidson, Acting Chancellor, March-August 1953

Concerned to appoint a new head only after careful search and to select a scholar-administrator of national reputation, the board turned once again to a seasoned member of the faculty, Levette J. Davidson, professor of English, for an interim appointment. Davidson was an authority in the fields of Western American literature and folklore, in which he had published widely.

Students were concerned with the frequent changes in administration. A headline in the *Clarion* read, "Wanted: Chancellor; Must Be Permanent," and accompanied an editorial that deplored the fact that there had been five heads of the university since the war years. But students remained on, some 5,135 of them that spring, 5,121 the following spring and 5,467 in the fall of 1953. Despite seductive offers from other schools, faculty also remained, as commitments to teaching and interaction with students were still a high priority.

Davidson, then 59, was born in Eureka, Illinois, and received his AB from the University of Illinois, an MA from Harvard, and a PhD from the University of Michigan. After teaching at Michigan State, he came to DU in 1922 to teach Western American literature and folklore and other courses in the English department, of which he was still the head when he died, May 13, 1957.

From Peace to War and Return: A Recapitulation

In the years between 1941 and 1953, the University met a series of challenges that taxed its economic and intellectual resources to the limit. With America's entrance into the Second World War, the administration and faculty responded to a decrease in the number of students and teaching staff and proceeded to create a war-time curriculum for the remaining students and newly arriving troops in training. The end of the war brought veterans in a veritable flood, resulting in dislocations of housing, curriculum, staffing, and all aspects of college life. The steady influx of government payments for tuition, housing, and supplies was balanced by unexpected costs as the ever-increasing complexity of running a university demanded larger outlays.

The inevitable departure of veterans at the expiration of their entitlements brought about a third crisis. Federal funding had enabled experiments into all sorts of operations, some of them of doubtful appropriateness. But with the need to count money much more carefully, serious efforts were made to re-envision the mission of the University at the current time and place. For each chancellor, the challenge had been different, and, in the absence of an agreed-upon job description, each brought his own vision of the ideal school and acted accordingly. By 1953, some of the alternatives had been weeded out, so the time was ripe for the advent of a topflight, fully prepared, dedicated leader who would be in position long enough to make long-range plans and see them through.

VI. The University Enters the Widest World, 1953–89

The 1950s were the turning point at which the great problems of the '40s were finally resolved—problems that resulted from the decline in student enrollment during the war and the great influx of veterans at war's end. In attempting to cope with this rapidly changing situation, the University had committed itself to new programs in every direction, with large sums of money quickly acquired and equally rapidly spent. In short, the school was in danger of falling victim to its own success.

The proposals of Chancellor Jacobs, over-expensive though they had seemed, offered a pattern for the future. He had seen two possibilities. One was an acceptance of small scale and academic content, and consequent mediocrity. The alternative was a greatly expanded school with a vastly strengthened academic program. Further, he called for the development of a master plan, a sound public relations policy, and an enlarged fund-raising operation. Within this scheme, athletics would play an essential but somewhat diminished role.

It was a stiff challenge, one that at the time was regarded as far too costly. The board, in its search for a chancellor who would and could carry out such a wide-ranging and thorough program, cast a wide net. It looked for a seasoned administrator with broad vision who could also inspire the giving needed to pay for that vision and extend it.

Chester M. Alter, Twelfth Chancellor, 1953–67

In 1953, the board moved its focus east to pick their next leader, Chester M. Alter, the dean of the graduate college at Boston University. Alter was born March 21, 1906, on a farm near Rushville, Indiana, some 40 miles southeast of Indianapolis. Having earned a BS degree from Ball State Teachers College in 1927, an MS from the University of Indiana, and done graduate work at the University of Pittsburgh, Alter received his PhD in chemistry from Harvard in 1936. After several years as instructor at Boston University, he became the dean of the Graduate College in 1944. His additional duties included the supervision of academic administration and all research contracts with foundations, trusts, business, and industry. The Department of Defense gave him its bronze medal and certificate of merit. He had successful experience as vice president and director of the Exolon Company, manufacturer of synthetic abrasives. Academic colleagues made him head of the American Chemical Society. Thus, in 1953, he came to Denver with the qualities needed for the development of significant new support from many quarters.

His objectives were clear. In 1954–55, the first year of the University's "Centennial Decade," he saw a sense of "growing hunger to develop for ourselves in higher education more specific standards, more specific guideposts, against which we can measure where we are going and what things we must do in order to make a university what it should be." He knew that "the quality of a university is determined in greatest measure by the quality of the faculty and scholars," but he saw great needs—for classrooms, residence space, teachers, books (the library had some 300,000 volumes). There should be a law building, a science-engineering complex, a cultural center, a mountain conference location, a student union downtown. And all of this was impossible given a total operating income of about $4.5 million, 63.2 percent derived from fees, 25.3 percent from sponsored research and services, the rest from a collection of entrusted funds.

By 1955, student enrollment had increased so The College of Arts and Science had 2,028 students, Business Administration 1,594, and the Graduate College 1,048. Engineering had 310 enrolled, law 218, of whom nine were women, and the Community College offered courses to 1,384 students, making a total enrollment of 6,607. The relationship between the school and the state is symbolized by the fact that 64.5 percent of the student body came from Colorado, and half of the 25,000 alumni lived and worked in the metropolitan area. Half of all Denver Public School teachers had graduated from DU, as had more than a third of all the local lawyers.

Noting that no major buildings had been created between 1950 and 1956, Alter and the board could see some substantial changes in the future. He quoted with approval a report to the president of the United States by the Committee on Education Beyond the High School:

> Revolutionary changes are occurring in America's education of which even yet we are only dimly aware. This nation had been propelled into a challenging new educational era since World War II by the convergence of powerful forces: an explosion of knowledge and population, a burst of technological advance, the outbreak of ideological conflict and the uprooting of old political and cultural patterns on a world-wide scale, and an unparalleled demand by Americans for more and better education.

With an increased and balanced budget and a good year for corporate and individual giving, Alter saw the production of a "margin of excellence" that could provide higher teaching salaries and the beginning of a building program.

Chester M. Alter, chancellor,
1953-67

The first of the new buildings was a $1.7 million dormitory complex along Iliff. It consisted of two separate wings linked by a dining room and lounge facilities for 432 students. Money was provided through the Federal Housing and Home Finance Agency. Johnson-McFarlane Hall, or J-Mac, as the complex is referred to today, honored two long-time teachers, Granville Bradby Johnson and Ida Kruse McFarlane. Johnson, a professor of physical education, came to the campus in time to help wheel Chancellor Buchtel around and stayed to become one of the students' most revered teachers. Likewise, Ida McFarlane, professor of English for many years, was an honored teacher and counselor.

Because the purchase of adequate books for research seemed beyond budgetary means, trustee Marion Gottesfeld met with other women interested in expanding resources for the libraries. She managed to enlist 67 donors in the first year. That program, known as the Women's Library Association, exploded, with lecture series, huge sales of used books, and other organizational techniques used to provide books and money. The names of the founders and subsequent leaders of this group may be found in an appendix.

Buildings continued to rise, among them halls for engineering and research honoring John Greene, Ralph Conrad, and Harold Knudsen. Early in 1959, a decision was made to employ Perkins and Will, a firm skilled in campus planning, to work with the Bureau of Educational Research to create an integrated campus over a period of 10 years.

In 1957, DU's College of Law merged with a proprietary school, which a year before had assumed the title of the Westminster College of Law. Originating in the Westminster Association, controlled by the local Presbyterian Synod in 1912, the law school became a separate institution, functioning under its own board of trustees and offering the only night law school in the West until 1920, with a faculty of some 20 local practitioners of law. Relations between the two schools were universally friendly, so the merger of 1957 was accomplished to the advantage of both schools without great difficulty.

In March 1959, a medieval "livery of seisn" ritual, symbolizing a transfer of title, marked the groundbreaking of a new University Law Center of imposing proportions at 14th and Bannock, across from the City and County Building. More than half of the $1.5 million cost was borne by alumni and friends of legal education. The sale of the old Haish Building at 14th and Arapahoe, in which the law school had its beginning, provided much of the remaining money.

Thus, a building program was coming along, but the thrust of the intellectual and spiritual basis of higher learning was not forgotten. As Alter put it,

> It seems apparent to us that in the flurry of educational activity that has marked our response to Sputnik, too little attention has been paid to the raison d'etre of higher education: the life of the mind, the world of ideas, the growth of honest intellectuality.

Law Center at 14th and Bannock

The Evans Chapel

Curiously enough, this relative neglect has taken place in a world never before so mobile, a world in which intellectual concepts, value systems and ideas, as they emerge from dozens of cultural patterns, exist within easy reach of each other, accessible as never before to every scholar.

Among other activities, 100 Centennial Scholars, those who would graduate in the centennial year of 1964, were selected, thus formalizing an honors program that, under various names, has continued ever since. Another opportunity came with the move of a chapel to the University Park Campus. When the University began plans for a new Law Center, the chapel of Grace Church at 14th and Bannock was scheduled for demolition. The small Colorado-sandstone building was built in 1878 by John Evans to honor the memory of his daughter Josephine, wife of Samuel H. Elbert. John Evans, grandson of the governor, together with his son John, then president of the Board of Trustees, contributed funds to move the building, stone by numbered stone, and re-erect it on an axis between Mary Reed Library and Mount Evans, in an area that later became the Harper Humanities Gardens. Surplus stone was used for parapets, walls, steps, and pools. Regular services by a number of campus religious groups, as well as weddings, memorial, and other services have been frequent since that time.

In January 1960, ground was broken for the Boettcher Center for Science, Engineering, and Research, the result of a gift of $1.25 million from Denver's Boettcher Foundation. The center consists of the first three units of a planned complex of 11 buildings. The east side is a two-story building containing a science and engineering library, classrooms, and conference and office space. The west side contains electrical engineering offices, classrooms, electronics research facilities, and a penthouse and roof for further electronics research. At the south, connected with the other two buildings by covered arcades, is an auditorium adapted to modern technology for teaching.

By this time, funds committed to building amounted to $13 million, 60 percent of which went into student housing, 30 percent into instructional uses, and 10 percent into auxiliary facilities.

But there was much more to think about than bricks and centers. On September 25, 1960, the Ford Foundation announced it was offering $46 million to five "regional center" universities, against which matching funds were to be secured. These schools were Johns Hopkins, Notre Dame, Stanford, Vanderbilt, the University of Denver, and later, Brown. DU was required to raise $10 million by June 15, 1963, in order to qualify for $5 million in Ford funds. Three days later, in responding to this challenge to improve academic programs, Alter addressed the opening convocation of the centennial period and announced a complete blueprint, "New Goals, New Tasks," addressed to "the responsible individual and a free society in an expanding universe." He put the goal before them:

Boettcher Center for Science, Engineering and Research

Ralph Conrad Hall

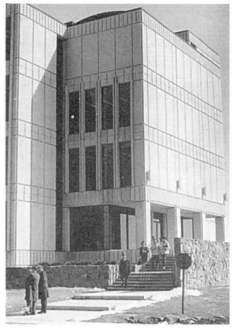

*Clarence Knudsen cuts the ribbon
for a new building*

Space Sciences Laboratory

John Greene Hall

> Our major goal, simply stated, is to develop in this great area of the Rocky Mountains and the High Plains one of the nation's outstanding universities. I say this because, under the opportunities now presented to us, the obligation of high excellence is inescapable. I say it also because our character, that of a private independent university, and our location here at the heart of this great area, surging with growth and promise, impose similar obligations.

In his mind, four general requirements seemed paramount: 1) the liberal disciplines at the core; 2) professional, cultural, and intellectual programs to be undergirded; 3) "peaks of excellence" selected "through a further development of a superior faculty, library, and laboratory facilities, and improved arrangements of our curricula"; 4) more rigorous admissions policy for a medium-sized university.

The shape of the curriculum was controlled by some 31 departments or programs, which offered a standard fare of courses leading to graduation and graduate work. A student elected a major of 40 quarter hours, a minor of 20, or an area major in the humanities, social sciences, or sciences. In a total program of 183 hours, three hours of physical education were required, as well as a distribution of 15 hours each of basic communication, the social sciences, humanities, and physical or natural science. Pre-professional studies, which prepared students for graduate work in medicine, dentistry, law, social work, and librarianship, were also available.

Business administration courses were organized by the theory that such a school should offer "a liberal education for business for positions leading to tomorrow's leadership." Thus, there were 13 programs, including accounting, real estate, management, marketing, and statistics, as well as hotel and restaurant management, business education ("a teaching career is rewarding"), insurance, and transportation. There were combined courses in business and engineering as well as business and law. Of the 180 hours (limitations of space downtown had precluded a program in physical education) fully one third were in the field of liberal studies.

While curricular offerings were quite solid, liberal arts in particular needed a major boost to increase the size and scholarly productivity of a number of departments to greater national recognition. Hence Alter's emphasis on "peaks of excellence."

The peaks included a Center for humanistic studies, the department and areas of history, international relations, physics, chemistry, mathematics, engineering, a School of Communication, a Law Center, an improved library collection, a Chancellor's Venture Fund, and, finally, more buildings. A year later, speaking at a banquet on October 14, 1961, the chancellor announced "A Program for New Resources" in the amount of $25 million. He spoke with confidence:

> The University of Denver stands here tonight, asking for resources to move ahead to greatness. History stands with us; geography speaks in our behalf; the urgency of the world's need pleads our cause; the events of the past year lend to us their voices; the demands of the future can here and now be heard.

By 1963, the program had produced significant gains: the first three units of the Boettcher Center, a new building for the department of radio-television-film at the south edge of the campus, and a science library.

The first endowed professorships in the University's history included the Brainerd F. Phillipson Chair of Metallurgy, given by the American Metal Climax Foundation and the Harold Hochschild and Carl M. Loeb Jr. families. The Lawrence C. Phipps Foundation, named for a man who was a Colorado senator from 1919 to 1931, provided money for a chair in the humanities. Mrs. Phipps, who was president of the foundation, presented to the University the tennis house of the family estate in Belcaro, to be used as a conference center. Two years later, in February 1964, Mrs. Phipps, through her sons Allan and Gerald, donated their 55-room mansion, Belcaro, on the same 10-acre estate, worth more than $1 million at that time.

The Venture Fund was in place, library acquisitions rose from $8,461 in 1960 to $45,000 in 1962. The College of Law acquired the first computer data bank of oil and gas law in the world. The number of areas in which the PhD was conferred was brought to 12 with the addition of six new programs. In April 1963, the Boettcher Foundation gave the six-story Colorado Building at 16th and Champa, worth $1.3 million, presaging the completion of the matching fund drive for a total of $10,048,790. At that point, the second phase of the drive, for a total of $25 million, was also started.

One long-standing activity of the school was terminated, however, when the chancellor announced on January 9, 1961, that football, "being prohibitively expensive" (some $100,000 deficit each year), would be discontinued. Plans were announced to expand the program of intramural sports and participation "in carefully selected sports appropriate to our unique situation." Playing fields were being unduly occupied by football, it was said, so discontinuing the sport would meet the needs of an increasing number of students, both men and women. Student reaction amounted only to an immediate small demonstration. Over subsequent years, nostalgia on the part of some alumni has been of greater duration. For a history of DU sports, the reader is directed to *A Tribute to Champions,* 1985, edited by Eric Prenzler.

The Centennial Year, 1963–64

As Alter put it, "The preparation for a centennial is a university's chance to seek the meaning of its experience and to ask the great questions, regardless of whether there are answers." As director of the centennial, R. Russell Porter brought more than 20 years of experience in both commercial and educational radio and television writing and supervision to the task. The theme, "the responsible individual and a free society in an expanding universe," was developed in a series of lectures, symposia, and seminars by a great array of faculty, joined by speakers from academia, industry, government, and the arts around the world. They included, among many others, Heber Harper, B. F. Skinner, Fred Hoyle, Zafrulla Khan, Barbara Ward, Zbigniew Brzezinski, and U Thant. Three publications should be noted. First came Jim Norland's *The Summit of a Century: A Pictorial History of the University of Denver.* Then in 1964, Michael McGiffert of the history department published *The Higher Learning in Colorado, An Historical Study, 1860–1940.* Finally, in 1964 Russell Porter summarized his interpretation of the year in *The University of Denver Centennial: Its Philosophy, Preparation, Presentation.*

Meanwhile, planning for out-of-town students had been going on since 1961. The enrollment of such students had been limited by the scarcity of adequate housing on campus. Consequently, plans for two large residence halls were begun, with the result that between 1961 and 1965 two large twin-towered structures rose on the northwest corner of the campus, Centennial Halls and Centennial Towers, each with a capacity of 750 students. The total cost for the buildings was $3,686,000.

The campus was further embellished in June 1965 by the completion of the Mary Reece Harper Memorial Garden, given by former Chancellor Heber Harper in memory of his mother. The garden filled a long-felt need for a campus focal point. Four acres, developed with water from three bubbling fountains running toward a reflecting pool at the base of Evans Chapel, were planted with shrubs and trees amid lighted walkways, at a cost of $100,000. In 1966 Harper gave a matching sum toward the establishment of a substantial Humanities Fund.

The face of the campus continued to change. In November 1966, one of the largest of the temporary buildings, just south of Mary Reed Library, was torn down to clear the way for the erection of a building to house the Social Science Foundation and the Graduate School of International Studies. That same month brought the promise of $900,000 from the National Aeronautics and Space Administration for a laboratory building for space-related research. Some 38,000 square feet were allocated to 36 laboratories and 42 office units for 110 research scientists, engineers, and office staff in a structure to the south of Boettcher Center. It was dedicated April 4, 1968. In a different area of the campus, groundbreaking took place in 1966 for a new business administration building along Asbury between Race and Vine, to replace the downtown facilities, which the Denver City Council was willing to buy at the appraised value. The cost of construction was $1.2 million, paid for by the sale or lease of the old property. Part of the basic plan called for this structure to be joined to a

Johnson-McFarlane Residence Hall

Centennial Towers Residence Hall

classroom building to the south and connected to new university center, with a bridge across Evans. Groundbreaking for the business administration building took place May 31, 1967.

The endowment fund was augmented in March 1966 by the sale of the Colorado Building for $1,150,000 in cash. All these elements augured well for a stable university of modest size (8,000 or so students), one increasingly aware of its duty to serve the nation as well as its students. The wider national and foreign interests were increasingly served by the Denver Research Institute (whose income had risen from $1 million in 1953–54 to more than $6 million in 1965–66), the Graduate School of International Studies, and in 1966 by the appearance of a new journal, *The Denver Quarterly,* edited by John Williams, a student of Alan Swallow, and Gerald Chapman, both of the English department. They agreed that it was a period of transition for the arts. As they put it, "To introduce a new literary magazine at a moment when all the arts are tentative in their claims and uncommitted to their ends, as if waiting for a sign, may strike some readers as quixotic and foolhardy." Their better hopes were amply justified.

To provide more adequate facilities for student life and space for the business college on the University Park campus, a vast plan was developed by the architects. It entailed the total renovation of the student union on the south side of East Evans at Race, the creation of a general classroom structure across Evnas, and a second-story bridge between the two. On the north side, and joined with the classroom building, would be the College of Business Administration. All would be built of brick with concrete trim. The total cost of these last two buildings was $6,750,000. The four-story Business Administration Building, a structure of 39,538 square feet, consisted of 30 classrooms, a 500-seat auditorium, and adequate faculty and staff offices. Money for construction came from the sale of the Civic Center campus, the El Pomar and Kresge Foundations, and Title I Higher Education funds. It opened January 4, 1968. The General Classroom Building, 87,500 square feet in size, was designed to match the business building in appearance and function. Paid for in part by funds from the Office of Education, it opened April 2, 1969.

Finally, the news came that the University's twelfth chancellor would ask for a leave of absence as of August 1, 1966, and would retire the following June. For 13 years, Alter had labored with a single goal in mind—to make the University of Denver one of the great institutions of learning in America. His work might be summarized in the words on the tomb of Christopher Wren in the crypt of St. Paul's Cathedral, London: "Si monumentum requeris, circumspice." ("If you seek his monument, look around you.") Alter's monument was more than buildings, budgets, and programs. It involved the force and vigor of new ideas, the convictions that people made a difference and that change could always be brought about for the better. A few statistics will suffice.

For the first time it was possible to earn a doctorate in seven of the sciences (chemical engineering, chemistry, electrical engineering, engineering

Business Administration Building, UPC

mechanics, mathematics, metallurgy, and physics), in four of the social sciences (geography, international relations, psychology, social work), and in five of the humanities (education, English, history, speech, theater). Thus the number of doctoral programs doubled within a decade. But the change was one of quality as well, since the faculty members secured to fill these new positions were geared to a publishing vision and were more demanding of research time to enable the sharing of ideas with a wide audience. Full-time faculty members increased from 180 to 364. Faculty members with a PhD or the equivalent increased from 80 in 1951 to 195 in 1965, and faculty salaries more than doubled, to an average of $10,317. In the last seven years alone, buildings costing more than $19 million had been built. The percentage of out-of-state students increased greatly and, by most indicators, the quality of students overall had increased as well.

From this point on, Alter's advice and counsel was sought by all manner of academic, legal, and other enterprises. Whether focused on Clayton College or Loretto Heights College, Alter always gave a hand to the consideration of the University's future, and remained as urbane and thoughtfully helpful as he had been on the day he arrived in Denver.

Wilbur C. Miller as Acting Chancellor, 1966–67

A nine-member advisory committee of the board had already set about the task of choosing Alter's successor. In the meantime, it chose Vice Chancellor for Academic Affairs and Dean of the Faculty Wilbur Castell Miller, 41, to carry on. Miller was born in Des Moines in 1923 and attended Drake and St. Louis Universities before receiving three degrees from DU—a BSBA in 1946, a master's in 1949, and a PhD in psychology in 1953. After the war, he was a consultant to the Air Force in psychological research and directed grants on juvenile delinquency. He was later described as "an outspoken proponent of top-notch teaching, urging the study of qualities essential to college teaching and the redirection of academic programs to instill such qualities in those who want to teach."

During Miller's term of office, the momentum continued. In November, the Social Science Foundation, in celebrating its 40th anniversary, dedicated a new building to Ben M. Cherrington, co-founder and former director. The three-story building, just south of the Mary Reed Library, was a modern structure with columned facades. It included lounges, seminar rooms, offices, and a large library. The $750,000 cost of the building was paid for in large part with contributions of $250,000 from the May Bonfils Stanton Trust of Denver, $100,000 from the Avalon Foundation of New York, $100,000 from Robert O. Anderson of Rockwell, New Mexico, and $254,000 from the U.S. Department of Health, Education, and Welfare. At its dedication, Josef Korbel, director of the Graduate School of International Studies together with Dean Rusk,

Phipps Memorial Conference Center

Ben M. Cherrington Hall

Chancellor Miller with President Lyndon B. Johnson

U.S. Secretary of State, honored three past directors—Cherrington, Elizabeth Fackt, and C. Dale Fuller. (Korbel's daughter, Madeleine Albright, became the first female Secretary of State in January 1997.)

Elsewhere on campus, plans were under way to develop a chair in Judaic studies to continue the work of Rabbi Charles E. H. Kauvar, which began in 1922 with classes in Jewish literature and religion. Plans also called for a new facility for the Graduate School of Social Work. The College of Law, under the leadership of Dean Robert B. Yegge, was pioneering the study of the relationship between law and society and in developing special arrangements for minority students. In all, things continued to look good.

But as Vice Chancellor and Treasurer Harvey D. Willson pointed out, "The cost of educating a student for one year is approximately $2,000. The tuition is $1,350. The difference is $650 a year. From the University's endowment of less than $12.5 million, the income for each of its students is about $80 per year. This leaves $570 a year that must somehow be supplied by the University from other sources." He concluded that with a full-time enrollment of 6,000 students, the total sum that must be supplied by the University came to $3,420,000 annually. He saw three alternatives: to raise tuition considerably, to "go public," or to secure adequate endowment to care for this and many other pressing problems. Another administration would have to see to them. Miller continued as vice chancellor until 1972, when he became president of Drake University, retiring from there in 1985 to be Chester M. Alter Professor and education administrator at Loretto Heights College in Denver.

Maurice Bernard Mitchell Brings a Different Style, 1967–78

Working with a list of 230 names of prospective chancellors, the board reduced the list to 65 academic administrators and one man who, in his own words, was "one trained in the business world of education and a go-getter." The appointment of Maurice Mitchell was indeed "a break with previous patterns of custom and thinking, a sheer surprise to many," as one journalist saw it. The *Saturday Review* pictured him as "a slight, tense, driving man of formidable energy, with a warm smile and a soft, extremely persuasive voice. He is, in fact, one of the great salesmen in a nation of sellers." Olga Curtis, interviewing him for the *Denver Post,* commented, "He's tall, thin, somewhat stooped, with a lined face, big ears, wide mouth, blue eyes, wiry gray hair." As with all of the University's chancellors, Mitchell's background influenced his style of leadership.

Born in New York City on February 9, 1915, he managed two years at New York University before his father, a real estate developer, was engulfed in the Great Depression. At 20, after a brief stint as night elevator operator, he aimed

Maurice B. Mitchell, chancellor,
1967–78

for better things, "so I ran for my life, dumped my education and grabbed the closest thing to a newspaper job I could find." The *Times* hired him at $10.50 a week to sell classified advertising by telephone. Moving on to newspapers in upper New York, where he set type and wrote articles and news items, he realized that "a New York kid has no roots, no community, and for the first time in my life I discovered that a place was the people in it."

Drafted into the Tank Corps as a radio technician, Mitchell suffered an irreparable back injury when he was thrown off a tank with 125 pounds of equipment during maneuvers. In 1945, he became public relations man for radio station WTOP in Washington, then, three years later, worked for the National Association of Broadcasters of NBC in New York. There, former senator William Benton brought him out of a vacuum and into a brand new world, as vice president of Muzak.

Mitchell made the company its first profits. Benton, who also owned Britannica Corporation, brought him in to supervise the making and selling of films, a part of the corporation that had not turned a profit in 25 years. By 1962, that division was averaging $34 million a year in profits. Films got Mitchell interested in education. For 20 years, he had lectured on broadcasting and communication in frequent, unpaid, and unpublicized visits to the University of Denver, where, he says, "I always had the feeling that I was with good friends." Chief among them was R. Russell Porter, chairman of the Department of Theatre and director of the School of Communication Arts. Porter encouraged him to think about the chancellorship and nominated him to the board. Mitchell was 52, restless, making $300,000 a year, wondering about the future. He had firm ideas about education:

> One thing I sincerely believed, that the place to build the next world is at the universities. The world has to be run by the people who understand its problems. We can't go on running the world like a retail business, with a clearance sale, or a war, to get rid of the obvious mistakes. . . . A university's function is to train the next generation, to give future leaders a chance to think, to develop intelligence.

Mitchell figured he had 10 years of active life left, and he "wanted to use these years to make a major contribution to something important."

He saw the continuing need for a great independent university in the Rockies, the only one of its kind between Chicago and California, on the last Western frontier. In his thinking, it was almost the last place one could build the sort of school he had in mind. His plans were bold—an uprooting of old conventions, the end of the tenure system, greater participation of students in decision-making. One example of this was the replacement of the Office of the Dean of Students with the appointment of a Vice Chancellor for Student

Affairs. Asked if the faculty would be helpful, he was wary, commenting that the teaching body, which had a reputation for liberalism, was a very conservative group of people.

As he commented to Olga Curtis after a year in office, "I came here to make this school something more than a place for the students to visit between ski trips. To do that I'm going to shake up the students, the faculty, the administration. . . . I want to create a situation where change is not only accepted but is a condition of existence."

The board was convinced and prepared an elaborate inaugural for October 20, 1967. The *Rocky Mountain News* noted that "his inaugural set several precedents. He is the first person of Jewish faith to head the University and the first man without an academic degree to become chancellor." He set his style from the modest "administrative building" at South Gaylord and Iliff, saying, "I'm not going to run around the campus, academic gown flapping, and make like a Mr. Chips." An interviewer saw his personality as "part brash salesman, part cool commander, and a large part starry idealist, and it is not easily explained." The first part of Mitchell's administration must be seen against the background of the 1960s. That decade began peacefully enough. Clark Kerr, president of the University of California at Berkeley, commented in 1959 that, "I can just see that they [students] are not going to press many grievances. They are going to do their jobs. They are going to be easy to handle. There aren't going to be riots. There aren't going to be revolutions. There aren't going to be many strikes."

He was proven wrong, of course, by the turbulence, the bloodshed, the angry confrontations of students with the establishment. Certainly the early years can be called an age of innocence, with the election of John F. Kennedy and the spirit of Camelot. Students who heard him say at his inauguration, "Ask not what your country can do for you but rather what you can do for your country" took him seriously at a time when two mighty forces crossed their vision. The first was the Civil Rights Movement, beginning with the sit-in at the lunch counter at Greensboro in 1960 and soon engaging thousands of thoughtful people in redressing grievances. The second equally powerful force was the realization that the war in Southeast Asia would send millions of Americans to the battlefield. The dividing line between innocence and involvement can be placed at Kennedy's assassination, November 22, 1963. The September 1964 free speech movement at Berkeley, which addressed a multitude of student grievances, was followed by sit-ins, stand-ins, and teach-ins across the country. The August 1965 doubling of draft quotas exacerbated the situation. Finally, among many other episodes in academia, the Students for a Democratic Society and others brought Columbia University to a standstill, occupying five buildings from April 23 to 30, 1968, and creating complete chaos for the rest of that semester.

At Denver, a quiet, even somnolent campus, Mitchell's first encounter with student protest came on April 30, 1968, with the sit-in of 39 students in the registrar's office, demanding the implementation of a Student Bill of Rights.

Mitchell acted promptly on his philosophy that "the longest duration of a sit-in should be five minutes," calling in the Denver police to remove the students with force. Later, Mitchell suspended them for a year. Reflecting on the episode, Mitchell later confessed sadness, not that he had acted promptly, but that in the period leading up to the confrontation there had been a failure to understand the whole ethos of the student movement and a lack of negotiation "before it was too late."

As for the events of April and May 1970, it is easy to enumerate the steps by which chaos and total disruption first threatened, then were avoided. It is much more difficult to separate all the various and competing forces at work. There were the genuine reformers, both students and faculty, who found the University too involved in the government and in the support of an unnecessary and unjust war, and who found the work of the Denver Research Institute (DRI) over-committed to the war effort. Others, genuinely puzzled and worried by all the activity, were nevertheless caught up in the sense of movement, the chance to discuss great ideas and enter into dialogue with others. There were others from the outside who arrived to exploit whatever situation might serve their own ends, representing the whole spectrum of political and social beliefs.

Although scattered actions to "off [kill] DRI" had taken place on April 20, three events in the outside world affected students: the killing of two students and the wounding of nine others by local police at Jackson State College on April 28; President Nixon's order to escalate the war by invading Vietnam's neighbor, Cambodia, on April 30; and the killing of four students at Kent State on May 4. The "strike" against the University began on May 6, followed by a huge meeting in the arena on May 8, and the construction of "Woodstock Nation" that same day. The area bounded by Margery Reed, Carnegie Hall, and the Science Building, where Penrose Library now stands, was transformed, first by people lying in sleeping bags, then by an array of tents and shacks in which people ate, slept, argued, and listened to hundreds of speakers, including Colorado Governor and DU alumnus John Love. Evans Avenue was closed off. One poignant memory is that of a man on a motorcycle moving back and forth along the street carrying a huge American flag. The Denver police arrived, and Woodstock was torn down, only to be rebuilt on May 11 amid unsubstantiated rumors that armed vigilantes were on the way and that the police—and later the National Guard—had live ammunition in their rifles. At the request of the governor, the Guard came on May 13 and pulled out the next day, after which Woodstock West was again torn down. A faculty meeting endorsed "the spirit of Woodstock," at the same time deploring most of its physical characteristics. Some students left forever, visibly shaken, while others successfully petitioned to receive their grades on a pass-fail basis. At Commencement, nearly 60 percent of graduates decided not to wear caps and gowns, or to wear peace insignia. Peace returned to the campus, and new projects once more became possible.

Woodstock Nation is proclaimed.

The chancellor is hanged in effigy.

Local police appear with gas masks.

Governor John Love appears.

In 1972, the College of Arts and Sciences applied to the National Endowment for the Humanities (NEH) for a grant to support a truly innovative "block plan," designed to integrate studies at the freshman level. Each course was designed to explore in depth a single place at the zenith of its cultural achievement. The NEH enthusiastically approved this plan, giving its largest grant to date, some $1.2 million. Faculty for these courses were drawn from the humanities, the social sciences, and a few from the sciences. New faculty were added to departments specifically to fill in empty spots in the curriculum.

Each quarter-long course was team-taught, with full-time work by students and faculty. "Blocks" included Periclean Athens, Twelfth Century Paris, Elizabethan England, Sung China, and Weimar Germany. Although highly successful in fulfilling the aims of the program, problems of staffing from contributing departments and difficulty of adjusting to the program of science majors limited the success of the project to some degree. On the other hand, participants felt exhilarated by bringing together ideas from the fields of philosophy, government, literature, language, and the arts. Indeed, although such programs lasted only until 1978, they set significant precedents of the Core Program that was developed almost a decade later.

New Buildings, New Programs, One Demise

In a special convocation in 1975, Mitchell reflected that:

> It seems to me that, during my years here, I've spent a lot of time cutting ribbons and dedicating buildings. I cut the ribbon to open the Space Science Building. I cut the ribbon to open the Business Administration and General Classroom Buildings. I was there the day we opened the new Speech and Hearing Center. I made a personal project of the Penrose Library and presided over its dedication ceremonies, too. We are meeting today in a fieldhouse and arena building that has existed in this form for just a few years, having been saved from utter destruction by some fiscal and engineering heroics. It is another new building, in a sense. Soon we will all go over to Spruce Hall to dedicate the newly remodelled facilities for the Graduate School of Social Work.

Penrose Library, which was dedicated October 12, 1972, was the $4.5 million gift of the El Pomar Foundation of Colorado Springs. It was named in honor of Spencer Penrose, who had come to Colorado in 1892 with his close associate, Charles L. Tutt, and prospered in gold and copper mining. He built the Broadmoor Hotel and the famous highway to the summit of Pikes Peak. The library, one of several funded by the foundation, faces East Evans and was

The General Classroom Building, UPC

Penrose Library

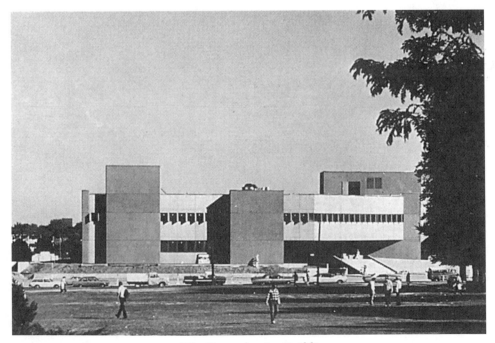

The Shwayder Art Building

constructed of pre-fabricated cast cement in Southwest style of adobe beige color. Consisting of three floors, it offers spacious reading areas and much state-of-the-art technology. Collections include the University's archives, and the remarkably complete Margaret Husted cookbook collection of more than 8,000 volumes. It also serves as a depository for many collections of personal papers.

Just south of the playing fields, the Shwayder Art Building arose along Asbury in 1977. The pre-stressed concrete structure between the fieldhouse and the College of Business Administration, was the result of a $1.7 million gift by Jesse and Nellie Shwayder Inc., a Denver foundation named for the founder of the Samsonite Corporation and his wife. The Shwayders were a pioneer Colorado family, headed by English-born Isaac Shwayder, who came to Blackhawk in 1882 and to Denver in 1888.

It was also announced that Lowell Jackson Thomas would leave his Hammersley Hill estate near Pawling, New York, to his alma mater. Thomas had come with his parents to Cripple Creek, where his father, a prominent physician, had one of the best libraries in the West. Thomas graduated from the University with a degree in speech, and with what he considered its greatest gift, his wife. He became famous as a radio commentator, war journalist, and the writer of more than 50 books, of which the most famous is *With Lawrence in Arabia*. When Thomas died, August 29, 1981, his estate was given to the University along with his books and a large collection of memorabilia. The money was used to fund the Lowell Thomas Building of the new Law Center on the Park Hill campus.

The University had been a pioneer in the development of Judaic studies when Rabbi Charles E. H. Kauvar of B.M.H. Synagogue in Denver initiated a class in Jewish religious literature. His work was continued through a joint appointment by the Departments of History and Religion of a layman, Benzion Netanyahu, a world authority on the Jews of Spain. Netanyahu later left for Cornell, then Israel, where his son Benjamin later became prime minister. His successor was Rabbi Stanley M. Wagner, who came to Denver and the University in 1972 after serving as national executive vice president of the Religious Zionists of America. A highly effective speaker, organizer, and fund-raiser, Wagner founded the Center for Judaic Studies on campus in 1975. From then on, he gathered like-minded people to found a host of related projects, among them the Rocky Mountain Jewish Historical Society and the Ira M. Beck Memorial Archives.

Later came the Israeli Scholar-in-Residence Program and the Institute of Interfaith Studies, through which Judaic courses are offered at the Iliff School of Theology, St. Thomas Seminary (now defunct), and the Denver Seminary. In 1981 came the Center for Publications, which had produced more than two dozen volumes by 1988. It was followed by the Maimonides Institute and the

Lowell Thomas flanked by Ellwood Murray and Paul Wilson

The Lowell Thomas Building of the Law Center

Holocaust Awareness Institute. Public lectures of an ecumenical nature and films on the Jews of western America rounded out a solid program of scholarly and popular activity. On November 7, 1984, Rabbi Wagner became the first holder of the Eva and Emil Hecht Chair in Judaic Studies, endowed by and named for two survivors of the Nazi Holocaust.

Balancing such gains was the disappearance of the College of Engineering in 1973, with Mitchell remarking that "the State had decided to become dominant in that field, and DU simply couldn't compete." Only later was it evident that the College of Arts and Sciences was affected by the departure of numerous instructors in the sciences. Another loss came with the disappearance of an old landmark in July 1971—when the football stadium came tumbling down after much effort on the part of the demolition company.

Aerial view of the Arena and football Stadium

By 1976, the board heard the chancellor commenting on "the scarcity of new funds and greatly increasing competition for those funds available." Consequently, it commissioned Arthur Young and Company to help "in assessing the institution's financial future in light of the proposed $40 million capital campaign and the University's perceived goals and objectives." Thus the Denver Design, 1977–80, came into being. Mitchell pointed to the acquisition of the Forum Building, to become part of the Law Center, and the gift from the Shwayder Foundation as anticipatory parts of the fund drive.

In 1976, a campaign was launched to raise $50 million for programs and structures. In the hands of a fund-raising company, this effort was called the Denver Design. Of the total, $1.6 million was assigned to "program development and the enhancement of professional education." Some $21.7 million was for "facilities and equipment," including an art building ($1.7 million), a University center ($8 million), a biology and chemistry building ($6 million), and an expanded law center ($6 million).

The campus was also to be improved by the renovation of University Hall and Mary Reed Library, as well as the addition of lighting and a new utility system. All of this came to $3.9 million. The Penrose Library collection was to receive an infusion of $2 million, and deserving students would receive scholarships in the amount of $9 million. Finally, annual giving for the following next five years was pegged at $10 million. By the end of 1980, $12.2 million had been raised, of which $977,573 was in "outstanding pledges and estates."

The negative side of all this was illustrated by the board's decision to reduce the budget over the next two years by $1.5 million. Budget year 1977–78 showed 7,877 students, an endowment of almost $16 million, full-time tuition charges of $3,690, and a deficit of $313,265. Having stayed 11 years, a year longer than he anticipated, Mitchell himself was ready to move on. In December 1977, the board of the Center for the Study of Democratic Institutions/Fund for the Republic invited him to become its president the following March. The center had been founded in 1959 by Robert Maynard Hutchins, Mitchell's mentor in Chicago. At the center, Mitchell said, there were "only 30 scholars to keep happy; there are 474 at Denver." He remained with the center until he became chairman of the Pacific Basin Institute, later joining the Annenberg Foundation in Washington, D.C.

Mitchell's contributions to the development of the University were made manifest in his speeches to the faculty, the board, and the public. Pungent, even astringent on occasion, filled with anecdotes, his speeches brought attention to the problems of higher education and to his proposals for their solution. Most notable of his experiences was Woodstock West in May 1970 and his firm solution to a situation that could have destroyed the University. True to his conviction that change was a necessary part of institutional advancement, he encouraged a host of new programs and inspired the gifts that made possible Penrose Library, the Forum Building downtown, the Shwayder

Art Building, and created the Publishing Institute. Mitchell's was a lively mind brought to constructive change and development. He died in Santa Barbara, California, Dec. 1, 1996.

Allan O. Pfnister Becomes Acting Chancellor, March–October 1978

The board was enabled to effect a smooth transition in leadership by appointing Allan O. Pfnister, executive vice chancellor, on an interim basis.

Pfnister came to the job well prepared in the theory and practice of higher education. Born in Mason, Illinois in 1925, he received degrees from Augustana, including an MDiv from that theological seminary, and an AM and PhD from the University of Chicago, before teaching and holding a deanship in Nebraska. From 1963 to 1967, he was dean of the College of Liberal Arts and professor of philosophy at Wittenberg University of Ohio, serving as its acting president from 1968 to 1969. From 1969, he served as professor of higher education at Denver before becoming executive vice chancellor and acting chancellor in 1978. Pfnister was aware of the difficulties of adjusting Alter's idea of the mission of the University (to be a medium-sized research institution of national importance and a school in which the humanities were the center) with the need, in a world of declining enrollments and increased competition for grants and other resources from the public sector, to make some measure of return to a regional stance. In 1974, he and James Davis of the education department prepared a study entitled "Comments on Objectives for the University of Denver for the Next Decade." Events showed the essential correctness of their study. That memorandum to Vice Chancellor William Key predicted that there would be a decrease in the pool of available first-year students in the 1980s and that there would be greatly increased competition with public universities and colleges for students as well as for grants to support research. They also foresaw a decline in liberal arts studies since the demand for vocationally oriented courses increased.

The value of this recommendation lay in their suggestion that the University increase its efforts to produce graduates who not only had the necessary professional qualifications, but were educated in the liberal arts and sciences. One is reminded of Alfred North Whitehead's remark in his *Aims of Education:* "What we should aim at producing is men who possess both culture and expert knowledge in some special direction."

Pfnister and Davis also recommended the forging of closer ties between the University and the Rocky Mountain region, a concept that by no means invalidated the idea of a school with broad national interests and reputation.

After leaving the chancellorship, Pfnister continued to teach courses in higher education, aid in administration, and work on a projected history of higher education in America, tentatively entitled "Challenge and Response."

Allan O. Pfnister,
acting chancellor,
March-October 1978

Chancellor Ross Pritchard,
1978-84

Ross Pritchard, Fourteenth Chancellor, 1978–84

Expectations for the new chancellor ran from, "We ranked them [the candidates] and Pritchard was our first choice. Everyone thought he was outstanding" to, "He has an interesting and broad background." The second indeed hit the mark. Born in the mill town of Paterson, New Jersey, of a divided family, Pritchard studied briefly at Lehigh University at Bethlehem, Pennsylvania, to pursue engineering, a field for which he found he was unfit. On the verge of flunking out when the Japanese struck at Pearl Harbor, he enlisted in the Navy. On his discharge, he accepted one of eight scholarships, this to play wingback for the University of Arkansas at Fayetteville. There he studied political science and history and participated in the Cotton Bowl and the Dixie Bowl. With a BA and MA from the University of Arkansas, he went on to earn an MA and a PhD in international economics from the Fletcher School of Law and Diplomacy. He joined the faculty of Southwestern Tennessee University, where he developed a department of international relations. He left there to be special assistant to Sargent Shriver, director of the Peace Corps. From 1965 to 1968, he was a regional Peace Corps director in Turkey. Opinions of his management style varied, but all who talked about him saw him as a man of contradictions—both aggressive and shy, polite and abrupt, and too aggressive a manager. It was noted that he increased the number of volunteers for his program too quickly, thus exhausting Peace Corps funds for some time.

Pritchard then entered business as vice president of the Development and Resource Corporation and resident manager of the organization in Iran. There, the Pritchards adopted two Iranian children to add to their own five. From 1972 to 1975, he was president of Hood College, a small girls' school at Frederick, Maryland. There, he increased the number of students from 115 to 1,350. It was subsequently shown that such an increase in size and scope was accomplished at the expense of the plant fund and similar financial practices. He then spent 18 months as president of Arkansas State University in Jonesboro, where he struggled with the board and the state legislature over curriculum, finances, and management in general.

He arrived in Denver full of enthusiasm, convinced that he could tackle problems of endowment and enrollment. He was "an athletic-looking man with smooth, steel-gray hair and intense brown eyes," as one interviewer saw him, sockless in sandals. Later, the *Rocky Mountain News,* commented on the divided feelings of loyalty and dislike people felt:

> To some he is ruthless, abrasive, aloof, impatient, shortsighted. Others see a shy, brilliant man who writes poetry, likes Willie Nelson and golden retrievers, reads cheap thrillers, loves to work in his garden, and pushes himself harder than he pushes his employees.

He came as the capital campaign had just started, but with a budget over which Pfnister had labored for months to bring into balance, and which eventually achieved that goal. *Colorado/Business* magazine in May 1979 found that:

> Pritchard claims management as his forte, some of his expertise gleaned, he says, from working with two of the finest examples of exceptional managers, Sargent Shriver, former Peace Corps director, and David Lilienthal, former head of the Tennessee Valley Authority and the Atomic Energy Commission. The analogy he uses is clear and simple: The University is a corporate service industry, with students as consumers. The trustees are a board of directors, and along with the chancellor they "capitalize" the business with funds submitted from other corporations." These remarks are instructive, in considering, for instance, where the faculty (who think of themselves as partners rather than employees) appear in this picture.

The Pritchard years may be considered under five headings: students, campus facilities, income, faculty, and administrative style. As to students, enrollment for 1978–79 was 7,727 and for 1983–84, 8,885, a healthy increase. But first-year undergraduate enrollments dropped 15.6 percent in 1980–81, 13.3 percent in 1981–82, and 15.7 percent in 1982–83. It should be further

The William T. Driscoll University Center

Aerial view of the Colorado Women's College campus

noted that these figures indicated a head count, and increases in graduate studies and specialized areas do not show full-time equivalents.

The first of the campus facilities created during Pritchard's tenure was the new University Center with its bridge over Evans, a long-time dream of the school. It was financed with revenue generated by a separately levied student fee, the revenues from which were pledged to retire $9.5 million in tax-exempt bonds, with the last to be retired in the year 2000. Later, this structure was named for the late William Driscoll, associate dean of arts and sciences, beloved student advisor, and professor of biology.

The other major project was well outside the boundaries of previous campus planning—the acquisition of the buildings, debts, and campus of Colorado Woman's College. The history of that school is recounted in Wallace B. Turner's *Colorado Woman's College, 1888–1982, The Story of a Dream,* which tells of the school until its acquisition by the University of Denver. Conceived as a "Vassar of the West" by its founder, the Rev. Robert Cameron, pastor of the First Baptist Church of Denver, the Colorado Women's College was incorporated in 1888 and finally opened its doors in 1909. Located in Northeast Denver, bounded by 17th and 21st, Oneida and Quebec, the school prospered, creating six residence halls, the magnificent Whatley Chapel, and the equally imposing Porter Library, along with the W. Dale and W. Ida Houston Fine Arts Center. Other buildings—Treat Hall

Treat Hall

and Mason Hall among them—rounded out a compact and restful campus of great beauty.

Under its seventh president, Eugene E. Dawson (1957–1970), the school moved to a four-year curriculum, expanding from 534 to 1,007 students. A "Design for Distinction" was developed to raise $12 million. In 1966, the endowment was only $241,836. Ever since 1941, the school had sought some benefactor who would bring needed resources in return for having the college named for himself or herself. That philanthropist was found in Temple H. Buell, a famous Denver architect. Buell offered to provide an eventual endowment of more than $25 million. Consequently, on July 1, 1967, the school became Temple Buell College. For a variety of reasons, however, since this money was not immediately in hand, the school suffered. There was a downward trend in enrollment, gift income was down because people thought the money was in hand, creeping inflation took its toll, the budget sloped out of balance, and the voices of dissidents who objected to a change of name grew increasingly loud. By the middle of 1972, the debt had risen to $5 million, with debt service at $530,000 a year. Consequently on March 29, 1973, the trustees announced a second change of name, this time to the Colorado Women's College (CWC.) But financial problems mounted as the downward trend of enrollment continued to lead to poor financial support. Realizing that the sale of part of the property would not bring a turnaround in enrollment and funding, the board began

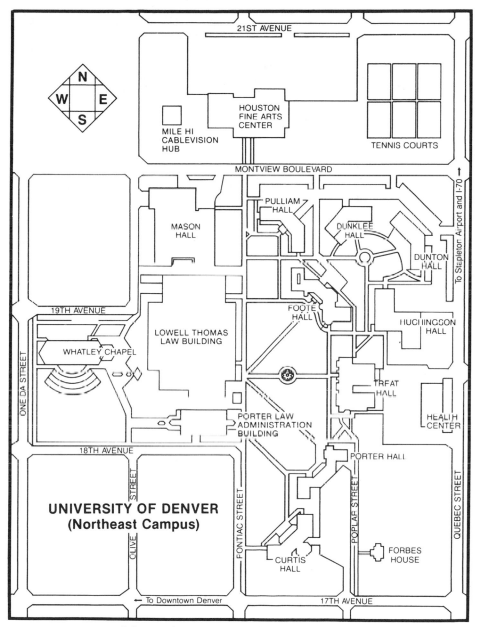

Map of the Northeast Campus of the University, Circa 1988

Treat Hall

Porter Hall

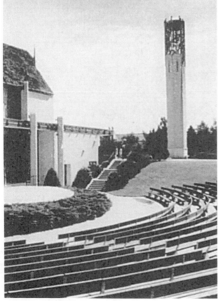

Whatley Chapel

Houston Fine Arts Center

negotiations with the University of Denver, which ended in failure. Finally, however, an agreement was eventually reached between the two boards to merge CWC with the University. Lucien Wulsin, chairman of the DU trustees, wrote Walter Koebel of CWC that the University would receive all of the college's assets in real estate (estimated at $30 million), would take over its liabilities and debts (estimated at $6 million), and would assure and enable all women to complete their education. He gave further assurances that women's studies would be continued on the campus and that the names of all buildings would be retained "to carry out the intent of their donors." The final document of conveyance and transfer was signed February 2, 1982. The Commencement of May 15 ended 94 years of independent undergraduate operations and paved the way for the development of a new law center and a home for the Lamont School of Music.

As to income and expenditures, what had been an operating surplus of $3 million in 1978 was reduced to just more than half a million by 1981. In 1982 there was a surplus of half a million dollars. A $1 million deficit was projected for the following year, and in 1983 Pritchard estimated a $2.5 million drop in tuition, a $1.8 million decline in unrestricted in giving, and another $2 million expense in "interim CWC expenses during construction." In the end, the total deficit was $2.5 million. Obviously, much had gone seriously wrong in planning, oversight, and management. A freeze on faculty salaries did little to help.

The greatest criticism levelled at the chancellor, however, was his style of administration. As one faculty leader put it, "the perception has grown over the years that the chancellor does not keep himself open to information and ideas from people." A case in point was his proposal in 1982 to divide the University teaching and research body into two spectrums, each with a vice chancellor. One would be concerned with science, technology, and management, the other with law, the arts, the humanities, and social sciences. When the faculty pointed out that nothing could be gained, either professionally or financially, from the project (and would have shown that clearly, had it been consulted), the idea was dropped.

Disastrous organization of the admissions operations led only belatedly to the appointment of a qualified man, Roger Campbell, director of admissions at Northwestern. Equally unsuccessful forays into fund-raising led to another appointment of another qualified person, Terry Gibson, director of development at Northwestern. The faculty, which had taken the lead in initiating numerous successful programs (a four-year engineering degree, a greatly expanded computer science program, a joint PhD with Iliff, the New College, and others), found itself increasingly at odds with a chancellor who could not talk with them. The faculty expressed "no confidence." Finally, the Board of Trustees, in the light of all the evidence, voted unanimously to dismiss Ross Pritchard, January 9, 1984. Lucien Wulsin, chairman of the board, took over as acting chancellor. Pritchard left for Arkansas to engage in business.

Seeley G. Mudd Science Building

A final evaluation of the Pritchard years will take account of the positive gains, among them the extensive building projects. There was the acquisition of the Colorado Women's College campus with its magnificent buildings and the new Lowell Thomas Building, part of the College of Law. As Chancellor Dwight Smith later commented, "It is a state-of-the-art facility that will assist the continuing development of that college into one of the premier schools of law in the country. The Inns of Court project is one of the most creative concepts to have surfaced in the University for years. For a lift of spirit, take a tour of the center."

Another development was the creation of the Seeley G. Mudd Building, which provided laboratories and offices for the faculty and research students in the departments of biological sciences and chemistry. Mudd was born in Denver and for 17 years had conducted research in California, dealing with radiation and X-ray therapy. His will provided for buildings such as this, in Denver's case in the amount of $1.5 million. Other funds for the building came from the Boettcher Foundation ($4 million), the Kresge Foundation (a $300,000 challenge grant), and from the Gates and Johnson Foundations. These additions, together with the University Center, were evidences of a sustained vision on the part of board and chancellor.

Dwight Morrell Smith, Fifteenth Chancellor, 1984–89

By the end of 1983, the board was fully aware of the staggering costs of the newly assumed burdens of buildings, a telephone system, repairs to the heating system, and the like. However rosy the future had looked, the hard reality was that it was increasingly difficult to meet even the monthly payroll. Student enrollment was down, a serious fact for a school so dependent on tuition income. Recruitment had, in the past, been poorly organized, with disastrous consequences. Faculty, at odds with the chancellor, felt disoriented. Above all, there loomed the debt, some $40 million, with payment of $30 million due the following December. The perception on the part of many community leaders was that the University needed to demonstrate its ability to manage its own affairs—and soon.

Hence, no small solution was possible. All had to be done in parallel to effect the sort of change that businesses had experienced. The example of the revolution that Lee Iacocca had brought about at Chrysler comes to mind, one that led to the creation of a new product. If any significant change was to come about at the University, it would have to be sharp, painful, and almost inevitably result in some bitterness and alienation.

In view of all these circumstances, the board moved quickly on January 18 to appoint Vice Chancellor for Academic Affairs and Dean of the Faculty Dwight Smith as chancellor for a two-year period. He was born in Hudson, New York, on October 10, 1931, received his BA degree at Central College in Pella, Iowa, in 1953, and his PhD in chemistry at Pennsylvania State University in 1957, the same year he was a DuPont Fellow. From 1957 to 1959, he taught at the California Institute of Technology, then joined the Texaco Research Center at Beacon, New York. Assistant professor of chemistry at Wesleyan University, Middletown, Connecticut, and professor at Hope College, Holland, Michigan, Smith was a National Science Foundation Fellow at Scripps Institute of Oceanography in 1971–72. He was a specialist in analytical and physical chemistry, receiving grants from the Petroleum Research Fund and the Solar Energy Research Institute, and becoming a patentee in selective hydrogenation.

The Reorganization of 1984

Early on, the board commissioned Smith to present within six months a plan "to improve the quality of the University's financial well being." Smith found it necessary to redefine the goals of the University as well. He set up a Select Committee of seven (four faculty members, former Chancellor Alter, the dean of admission, and himself) to supervise whatever reorganization proved necessary. Starting with a favorable faculty (his first appearance had been met with a lengthy standing ovation) and with newspapers interested and benevolent, Smith launched his plans with an all-University convocation on February 16, his address entitled A Great University for a Dynamic Region.

195

Dwight M. Smith, chancellor
1984–89

The Reorganization of 1984

Pulling no punches, he talked of budget deficits and the "morale-destroying salary moratoriums and lay-offs." He found that there had been no concerted effort to formulate operational—rather than vaguely general—goals defining the purpose of the school at that time and place. He did however, point to four buildings already in place and commented on their relevance to this mission. Smith then turned to his plan for change. The mechanisms would be a series of three committees, the Select Committee, a Program Review Committee, and a Blue Ribbon Panel. The second group was charged with analyzing the strengths and weaknesses of all academic programs, to evaluate but not to make specific recommendations. Four questions were to be asked concerning the centrality, quality, demand for, and resources available to each unit. Consultants were sought, among them a group including Richard Chait of Pennsylvania State; Earl F. Cheit, formerly of Berkeley; Harold Howe II of Harvard; Martin Klein, president of Institutional Strategy, Cambridge, Massachusetts; and F. Champion Ward, formerly of the University of Chicago. A panel of students was also invited to share their interests and needs. Meanwhile the board itself raised some $500,000 for faculty salary increases on a merit basis, most of them to be effective September 1. A further sum of $300,000 was made available to be used for development at Chancellor Smith's discretion.

Smith unveiled the reorganization plan on June 22, 1984. The board had approved it the previous day. By its terms, the College of Arts and Sciences, with a single dean, was abolished, to be replaced by four faculties, each with a dean: arts and humanities (William F. Zaranka), mathematics and computer sciences (Herbert J. Greenberg), natural sciences (Gareth R. Eaton), and social sciences (Harold Mendelsohn). A fifth dean, Charles Cortese, headed the College. A Core Curriculum required for all undergraduates was to be fashioned. A new vice chancellor for research and technology (eventually Jerry Plunkett) was envisioned. Balanced against these steps was the reduction of faculty positions by 32. The Graduate School of Librarianship and Information Management was discontinued, as was the Department of Theatre (some portions of which were merged into the English department). The undergraduate major in education ended at this time, followed later by the program in speech pathology and audiology. All these changes brought about a reduction of approximately 50 faculty and 50 staff positions by the fall of 1985. Within 18 months, the full-time faculty was reduced nearly 20 percent, from 450 to 360.

During the summer and fall of 1984, there emerged completely different perceptions of the nature of the crisis and the methods of coping with it, as well as two different perceptions of the role of the faculty in University government. On the one hand was the belief of Smith, the trustees, and others, that they were averting the most serious threat to stability since the collapse of the post-war enrollment boom. The board expressed "complete, full, unanimous, and reaffirmed support for Dwight Smith and for the academic reorganization now in progress." The University was, by these and related measures, saved from financial and academic bankruptcy, and these were pioneering changes which were preparing the school for the difficult years to come—so went one concept. On the other hand, a portion of the faculty (the percentage is difficult to determine) were convinced that they had been bypassed in all the decision-making, that the decisions were hasty, that the new structure was unnecessarily expensive, and that the decisions had, in some cases, a hidden agenda.

At any rate, most of the proposed changes went into effect. The Core program was developed into a new and exciting approach to interdisciplinary learning, and the trustees made a special commitment of $4 million to stimulate community matching funds. In all, the process was much like that of turning a battleship around in stormy seas. For Smith, it was the necessary, difficult, soul-wrenching experience of walking a tightrope between financial needs and the necessity to chart a new course for which not all were prepared. In all this struggle one could observe a genuine devotion on all sides to higher learning in general and to the preservation of its best aspects at this University in particular. By January 1985, it was clear that the University would be "a medium-sized research institution with strong liberal and component studies, a distinctive graduate and professional program, and centralized courses for the non-traditional learner." Asked about the ideal size, the reply would be 4,000 undergraduates and 4,000 graduate students, for a full-time equivalent of some 6,000. An examination is in order then, of the academic and physical environment into which these students were introduced from 1984 to 1989 and of a few of the changes that took place.

The Structure and Appearance of the Campus

Alumni coming back after some absence could note the improvements on the University Park campus. Some 26 temporary buildings were gone, and Buchtel Memorial Chapel, almost completely destroyed in the fire of July 21, 1983, was represented by one tower, now beautifully restored. The Lambda Chi and Kappa Sigma fraternity houses, which had also been struck by arson, were restored. The enclosed bridge across Evans connecting the two parts of the Driscoll Center was in use. One building remained in disrepair—old Carnegie Library, which was given a reprieve after faculty, alumni, and community recommendations were made for its continuance in a number of possible uses. Large photo murals depicting scenes from the past adorned the Center in the Governors Hall (six governors have been associated with DU), the Commerce Room, the 1880s Room, and in other places. Everywhere on campus, sod by the acre was installed, and plants and flowers bloomed in profusion through the summer. The downtown Law Center was sold for $5,874,000, with $2,900,000 at the closing in 1987, $2,374,000 in 1988, and $600,000 in 1989, all to the mutual advantage of the University and the City of Denver. The Law Center

Buchtel Tower and Memorial Garden

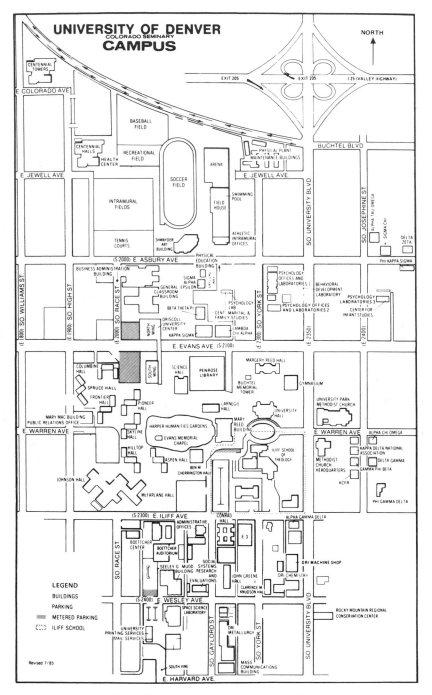

Map of University Park Campus, Circa 1988

and the Lamont School of Music were moved to the former CWC (now known as the Park Hill campus), where the grounds were substantially improved.

New Programs, New Directions

Ernest L. Boyer, president of the Carnegie Foundation for the Advancement of Teaching, commenting on the University's new general education program, said, "As I read your Core bulletin, I would love to come to this campus as a freshman." The Core he referred to was in its fourth year in 1989. It consisted of a series of highly structured lower-division courses, most being a year in length, divided into seven basic areas—English, arts and humanities, social sciences, natural sciences, foreign languages, mathematical and computing sciences, and oral communication—the whole taking about one-third of a student's four-year educational experience. It was a coherent program, designed to replace the incoherence Boyer found in many curricula. Moreover, it was required of all students, regardless of their major fields of interest. Students in the College of Business Administration, the sciences, and engineering enjoyed the same liberal education as those in the arts, humanities, and social sciences.

It was agreed from the beginning that the courses would be taught by experienced faculty, some of them from graduate and professional schools. Four or five options would be available in each area, with each to be a foundation course rather than an introduction to a particular field. It was agreed that there should be regular interaction of the students with faculty and other students in small discussion groups, and that several disciplines should be integrated and taught by teams of at least three to five faculty members. Effective in the fall of 1987, a foreign language course or the passing of a proficiency examination would be required. An unusual aspect of this curriculum was the requirement that natural science courses contain a laboratory experience for non-science students. Two one-term courses were offered: "Oral Communications" and "The University Experience." The latter introduced students to the tradition and culture of higher education, assisted them with their transition to college, and helped them to learn about academic policies and services. A greatly increased advising service was also made available through the College.

Emphasis on women's studies was deepened by the University's commitment to continue courses of a special nature when the school took over CWC. Even earlier, the Rocky Mountain Conservation Center, begun in response to the need for the restoration of fine art and artifacts, was happily in business. The College of Business Administration, celebrating its 75th anniversary in 1984, engaged in a proliferation of programs, including the Center for Management Development and the Institute for East Asian Business and Finance, which became a major player in solidifying trade relations between the Republic of China and Colorado. The College, long known for pioneering new legal areas, created a National Center for Preventive Law. An Institute for the Humanities, along with a Consortium for Human Rights, an Atmospheric Sciences Center, and a center devoted to artificial intelligence emerged. In 1987, the New College, which for four years had been successfully offering graduate degrees at reduced rates to night-time non-traditional students, became University College and acquired a dean.

In March 1987, negotiations were started for the transfer from the University of Southern California of the World-Wide Computer Training Center in Arlington, Virginia, and the Master of Science Program in Systems Management. This program, which the University of Southern California's board of trustees believed no longer fit their on-campus emphasis, seemed to be tailored to DU's interests and world vision. It had an enrollment of 1,800 students at 56 centers throughout the world, 60 percent military, 40 percent civilian. The centers are distributed in four major regions, including Europe, the Pacific, and the western and eastern United States. It was agreed that DU and USC would share the profits for the first five years, to see if the new plan worked, and further to share the costs of phasing it out if it should not. At DU, it became known as the College of Systems Science.

Such programs cost money, for which tuition income was inadequate. But the University was fortunate in acquiring new funds.

Four Significant Gifts

On September 14, 1987, at an All-University Convocation, the chancellor introduced Leo Block, San Antonio businessman and DU graduate of the Class of 1935, who had just presented the University with $1 million to endow a professorship. This, the largest cash gift in the University's history, was designed to bring "highly visible intellectuals and national leaders" to the school for a period of up to two years. The first holder of that chair was Richard Lamm, former governor of Colorado, who came to teach at DU while establishing the Center for Public Policy and Contemporary Issues. Block himself spoke with great warmth of his career at Denver as editor of the *Clarion* during the Depression years. "I really fell in love with this University, and you know how these romances are—unpredictable. One thing led to another, and out of this love came a professorship."

The following February, the chancellor was able to announce that Westminster Law School graduate and long-time loyal DU friend Frank H. Ricketson had provided in his will a sum in excess of $7 million for the capital needs of the College of Law. Ricketson, born in Kansas in 1897, graduated from the University of Kansas and worked his way through Westminster (which merged with DU in 1957) as a reporter for the *Express* and the *Denver Post* before going on to Hollywood and later entering the theatre business in Denver.

Leo L. Block

Frank H. Ricketson Jr.

Bill Daniels

Barton L. Weller

203

In November 1988, the University received $10 million from Bill Daniels to help shape the future of business administration graduate students. Contacting Daniel L. Ritchie of the Board of Trustees, Daniels offered matching funds for the newly designed MBA degree program. Such a program would focus on integrity, ethics, and professional business conduct, enabling students to act responsibly and professionally in dealing with people. The *Rocky Mountain News* called Daniels a "visionary," credited with creating America's modern cable television industry. Born in Greeley, Colorado, 68 years earlier, Daniels was raised in New Mexico, graduated from the New Mexico Military Institute, and served in World War II and the Korean War as a Navy fighter pilot. As *Denver Business* put it, "Then one Wednesday night, he was driving from Hobbs, New Mexico, to Casper, Wyoming, to open an oil field insurance company, a branch of his family's business, when he stopped at Murphy's and saw his first television program. Then and there his cable television empire was born."

In December 1988, it was announced that Barton L. Weller, a bachelor of science graduate of the Class of 1938, had presented the University with the gift of $1 million to aid programs in the natural sciences and the Department of Engineering.

A Janus-Look in the 125th Year

A report to the Board of Trustees in October 1986 succinctly spelled out the situation in 1984, and pointed to the progress made in two short years:

> Two years ago, the University of Denver was experiencing a crisis that threatened its academic credibility and financial survival. Administrative mistakes, trustee inaction, program deficiencies, marked declines in traditional enrollment, liquidation of assets, and increased indebtedness had combined to generate a very tangible sense of internal malaise. The community perceived the University as increasingly unstable.

By this time, however, the turnaround had been accomplished, at least in its initial stages:

> Fortunately, our University was able to respond positively and begin the process of building new strength. This response took the form of new leadership, an aggressive reappraisal of personnel requirements and nonessential costly programs, and of the planning and immediate implementation of new academic experiences designed for its future. We have sought to reaffirm our mission as a prestigious independent university,

one which provides a classically rigorous education for contemporary professional careers.

From the beginning of his administration, Smith had stressed the absolute need for "a sufficiently focused sense of mission to differentiate our institution from those with whom we compete for students, [to eliminate] one of the root causes of the admission decline during the past five years." While acknowledging resource problems, he pointed to the new focus on academic programs as essential for continued progress.

Before considering the vision and planning of the chancellor and board at the beginning of 1989, one should know the financial position of the University as expressed in a report from Elizabeth C. Williams, vice chancellor for business and financial affairs, June 30, 1988:

> Last fall, the University refinanced virtually all its existing debt and took advantage of the opportunity to lower the interest rates on our bonds to obtain additional funds for campus renovation projects. Over the summer, several of these projects were completed, and students returned this fall to find new laboratories for Core science courses, completely remodeled office and classroom facilities for the School of Hotel and Restaurant Management . . . and 39 brand new apartments in Curtis Hall on the CWC campus.

As to financial stability, the report was equally positive:

> From a financial perspective, the University experienced some important gains during FY '88. It ended the year with an operating surplus of $109,705. The University's overall net worth rose by more than $6 million, primarily as a result of new gifts that were placed in the endowment and the sale of non-campus real estate. Finally, during a year when many investors saw the value of their holdings decline, the value of the University's endowment investments increased and stand at $41.4 million. The increase of the year in market value was almost $8.6 million; about $2.4 million of this gain was due to the appreciation of investments.

Often, the chronicle of this long history has seemed to point to events that presaged the beginning of the end. Once more it is possible and enormously encouraging to point to the end of the beginning. The regaining of stability had taken hard work, good thought, and great commitment to the institution on the part of all those in positions of leadership—faculty, administration, and trustees.

Stability had been regained, and thoughts could turn to planning for the qualitative improvement of the programs and structures created during the period of reconstruction.

Fund-raising was obviously advancing on all fronts. Alumni support, for instance, was at 9 percent in 1981–82, rose to 21 percent in 1985–86, and was expected to reach 35 percent in 1990–91. A balanced budget, reduced expenses, and major additions to the endowment permitted increased attention to the quality of Denver's educational experience.

In September 1987, Smith announced the appointment of Roy V. Wood, dean of the School of Speech at Northwestern, as the first provost in the history of the University. In this position, Wood would be second in command, uniting the responsibilities, hitherto divided, for the formulation and implementation of academic and budgetary policies. As the appointment notice read, "he will be charged with all internal management and overseeing DU's academic environment, including student affairs, admission, financial aid, and athletics. . . . Dr. Wood will administer all those areas that shape the academic environment."

Wood earned his BA, MA, and PhD degrees at the University of Denver, becoming assistant professor of speech communication at DU in the mid-1960s. He joined the faculty of Northwestern as an assistant professor in 1967 and remained there for 20 years before arriving in Denver and taking up his duties in January 1988.

As the College continued to structure and streamline its academic format in producing a distinctive program of liberal arts education through the Core program, it offered a real distinction between DU and those schools that competed for students and funds. It was a new world in student perceptions of higher education and the growing attractiveness of life at the university.

As the pool of students ready for college shrank from 1.8 million in 1968 to 1.2 million in 1988, and as the steady movement of population from Northeast to West and Southwest continued, the strategic position of a Western school (one of only three independent schools in Colorado) was greatly enhanced. It was further increased by a vigorous and intelligent approach to student recruitment. The twin thrusts of increasing international recognition and a developing sense of the Western heritage of which DU was so much a part came together in making high school and transfer students more aware of the University's mission. Roger Campbell, dean of admission, found that such people came in greater numbers and were far more satisfied if the reality they found here matched their realistic expectations, if they found lively and coherent courses taught by vigorous faculty, if personal advising was regularly available, if, in sum, the University was a caring place. That this sense of satisfaction was growing was demonstrated by the fact that 63 percent of those who entered in the fall of 1985 were still enrolled, ready to graduate in 1989. If one added those who would spend an additional year here, the percentage

The world of tomorrow: University of Denver students

Denver's skyline, 1989

A composite of University of Denver athletes: Oil by JuLee Simmons

would be about 68 percent, an unusually high number for an urban university. The increase in the number of non-traditional students, both those who sought degrees and those who did not, was also substantial.

Dwight Smith, in a report marking his fifth anniversary as chancellor, summed up his experience of those years and his thoughts for the future:

> The past five years have seen the restoration of institutional stability, as reflected in a demonstrable improvement in confidence by our constituent groups, a measure of financial integrity, and a more focused academic mission. New leadership at all levels has resulted, or is resulting, in programmatic redefinition, increasing philanthropic support, a healthier enrollment picture, and sound financial management. While I am proud of these achievements, and of my administrative and faculty colleagues who have brought them about, I believe that our greatest challenges lie just ahead.

His perception of the problems faced by higher education both nationally and at Denver led him to observe:

> Higher education today is overbuilt, underproductive, and in intense competition for human and material resources. This University's apparently increasing price sensitivity, because of more critical consumers of our educational product, can be diminished only through improved quality and its accurate perception in the marketplace. We still are vulnerable to external economic forces and demographic change. Our image must be sharpened, and the DU story requires communication, particularly in specific markets, with greater precision and continuity. The University's historic undercapitalization, relative to its principal competitors, must be remedied through significant endowment growth. We must maintain our independence, which, in my view, is one of the major characteristics setting us apart, and assures our ability to create and innovate.

On the eve of Founders Day 1989, it seemed that the University better understood its purpose and mission and was prepared to carry out the dreams and aspirations of chancellor and board. Some of those dreams included the building of a much-needed science complex and the renovation of Carnegie Library, University Hall, and the Mary Reed Building among others. Other plans included the improvement of the academic environment, the enhancement of curriculum, the improvement of the library collection, and investment in research, creativity and scholarship, financial aid, student activities, and communications.

The University and the Widest World

Another look at this story, one that is symbolic of the extent of the change, shows a picture of Dwight Smith addressing the faculty and students on scientific education at Lioaning University in the People's Republic of China. In Beijing, Smith and Dean Elliot Kline spoke to an audience of graduate students at the People's Bank graduate school. The story could be reinforced with accounts of faculty and administrators intimately knowledgeable about and concerned with affairs in Great Britain, Europe, the Soviet Union, Latin America, and Africa. An odyssey through the history of the University travels not only through time but in space, from that small building on Arapahoe in downtown Denver, out into Colorado and the Rockies, and across America—to the world beyond.

The DU Delegation to China

VII. Reinvigoration and Expansion, 1989–97

The history of the University, like that of most institutions of higher learning, is the record of alternations between periods of slow growth and cataclysmic changes, and redirection in purpose and programs. Some years have been painful, others hearteningly creative and rewarding, opening into the broad vista of a new era. The record of the last eight years, from July 1989 to the conclusion of 1997, points to a new world of systematic development on many fronts. That new landscape ranges from new organizational patterns to changed curricular arrangements, from a new financial structure to highly successful fund raising, as well as the creation of new structures and the renovation of existing ones on both campuses. Change began with an election.

Daniel Ritchie Becomes the Sixteenth Chancellor, 1989

On June 30, Chancellor Dwight Smith announced his retirement effective July 1. During his five and a half years of service, he had overseen an almost complete reorganization of the University. He commented:

> I believe that one of the unfortunate syndromes of the typical university president is that he stays on too long. From such stimuli as a new research grant, the constant reminder that I am not getting any younger, and the general feeling that it's time for someone else to pick up the mantle, I will be spending the rest of the summer months doing research and seeking some new horizons.

After commenting on the remarkable effectiveness of Smith's chancellorship during difficult times, Edward Estlow, chairman of the Board of Trustees, announced a year's leave for Smith to travel and conduct research. Smith became president of Hawaii Loa College at Kaneohe from 1990 to 1992, returning to DU and his position as professor of chemistry after that school merged with another nearby.

Chancellor Daniel Ritchie

Daniel Ritchie Becomes the Sixteenth Chancellor, 1989

At the same time, Estlow announced the appointment of Daniel Lee Ritchie as the next chancellor, effective July 1. Estlow characterized Ritchie as "an outstanding manager, a strategic planner, and an excellent communicator who has raised millions of dollars for this school as a board member these six years."

Ritchie, son of a North Carolina businessman, was born in Springfield, Illinois, September 19, 1931. As a Harvard undergraduate majoring in literature and Russian, he spent a summer in Boulder reading economics and "fell in love with Colorado." After earning his degrees from Harvard, a BA in 1954 and an MBA in 1956, he began a two-year stint as securities analyst with Lehman Brothers on Wall Street. He moved west again in 1960 when entertainment conglomerate MCA of Los Angeles sent him to run its newly acquired Columbia Savings and Loan Association in Denver. During his service there, from 1960 to 1967, he increased company assets from $43 million to more than $200 million. Over the next three years, he served as founder and president of Archon Pure Products Company, dealing in natural foods and food supplements. The firm eventually became a $40 million enterprise.

In 1974, Ritchie joined Westinghouse as executive vice president of the Learning and Leisure Time Industries division. He retired only briefly to his 160-acre avocado farm, Rancho Cielo, near Santa Barbara. In 1978 he joined giant Westinghouse Broadcasting Inc., also known as Group W, which operated radio and television stations, to distribute programs and supervise numerous other activities as president and chief executive officer. Citing his dedication and integrity, *Channels* magazine (May–June 1984) hailed Ritchie as "TV's Moral Minority" and "an unusually long-term thinker in a business obsessed by the short-term problems of an unpredictable marketplace." They also saw him "like a circus acrobat astride two horses (broadcast and cable), one young, the other established." For his leadership, Ritchie and his company garnered substantial awards. Throughout his career there he held a conviction that "what holds us together, what makes the society work, is a respect for human beings."

In the spring of 1987, after 13 years with Westinghouse, Ritchie stepped down from his chairmanship to devote time to his Colorado ranch and California avocado farm. He had served on the University's Board of Trustees since June 1983, and at that time he was vice chairman and head of the development committee. During his tenure, the University raised more than $14 million.

Throughout the difficult days of reorganization in 1983–84, Ritchie worked tirelessly with the board and administration to help maintain faculty and staff morale as entire programs were eliminated and departments trimmed or eliminated. But his vision was not limited to survival; rather, he saw the inherent possibilities for a great school, providing that funds could be secured and the proper policies put into place.

The problems were enormous—a substantial number of the 400-member faculty were laid off and property in the amount of $20 million sold off. In

1985, the University's deficit grew to $8 million, the long-term loss more than $30 million.

In January of that year, Ritchie persuaded the trustees to pledge an unprecedented $4 million of their own funds over a two-year period and challenged the University to raise another $5.3 million over the following four years. For the most part, these goals were met. Under Ritchie's leadership, total giving in 1986 reached $7.8 million. In 1988, Bill Daniels made the first of his donations—some $10 million in matching funds for the College of Business Administration. As Chancellor Dwight Smith perceptively pointed out, "Ritchie constantly touted the positive changes taking place at DU to members of the Denver community. As a result, people who had never before been involved became interested in the University."

With business acumen honed sharp over a long and successful career and a rapidly developing love of the school and its history, Ritchie was ideally suited in 1989 to assume charge of yet another gigantic enterprise—a fine but troubled university. The first of several problems he confronted was financial stability and health.

Solving the Problems: Fiscal Responsibility, Planning, and Budgets

Chief among pressing matters was the absence of a coordinated budget-making process. Department heads, faculty, and staff assumed the budget would be prepared by Provost William Zaranka. Their duty, as they saw it, was to spend their allotments within the year and forfeit any unspent funds or write off any deficit at year's end. Academic quality lay in one realm, fiscal responsibility in another unrelated sphere. The response to these assumptions came in a paper, "A New Model for Resource Management in Higher Education," and the appointment of a new vice chancellor for business and financial affairs. James Griesemer arrived in 1990 with a doctorate in public administration and experience in heading two communities, one of which, the neighboring expanse of Aurora, is the third-largest city in Colorado. The team thus formed— Ritchie, Zaranka, and Griesemer—proceeded to direct the creation of a new financial and academic pattern.

Hitherto, it had been almost impossible to predict the outcome of policies and to know what the real liabilities were, since final operating costs were not available until a considerable time after a particular commitment was made or a problem encountered. The new model envisioned two radical solutions—up-to-the-minute reporting and decentralized responsibility. Monitoring procedures were established, with monthly recapitulations made possible through on-line computer accounts. Long-term variable-rate debts were consolidated at a single stable rate. Elsewhere, immediate savings were effected in workers' compensation, air travel, food, and telephone service costs.

The second reform came in the creation of a bottom-up approach, bringing an end to the spend-it-or-lose-it process and rewarding departments for exceeding revenue expectations and for year-end savings by forming "gainsharing" accounts. Fifty percent of excess revenues, and 100 percent of expenditure savings remained with the academic units; one third of the banked total could be spent on equipment, expansions, and the like, in any one year. Since each department had previously had a share in shaping the original budget, based on factors including the number of hours taught, each department had a primary interest in the educational and financial success of the University as a whole. As a writer in the *University of Denver Journal* (Autumn 1993) stated, "In effect, DU has become a network of 88 small entrepreneurial businesses called 'responsibility centers,' which are groups under divisions that parallel the academic units." In two years, nearly $4 million were made available for new ventures. The University College, which had experienced phenomenal increase in enrollment, could buy its own building, the old Kappa Delta house at 2111 South Josephine Street.

All-University committees on marketing, recruitment, and retention began exploring creative planning procedures. One such committee proposed getting faculty involved in recruiting students and in greater interaction with all undergraduates.

An argument voiced by some members of the community asserted that such bottom-line decision-making diminished those scholarly activities that were not, by their nature, geared to financial evaluation and success. The reply came that, inasmuch as high-quality education and financial stability were essential for the health and survival of any institution of higher education and were not mutually exclusive, the measures taken were far from drastic and could accommodate a number of variations.

Indeed, stability was assuredly achieved by 1993. Enrollment in a highly competitive market reached 8,200 students. The debt had been significantly reduced, and the endowment, although still precariously low, stood at $62.5 million. Between 1990 and 1993, some $12.3 million in operating surpluses had been accumulated. The campus had received $8 million for the improvement of landscape and buildings. Moreover, great changes had been taking place in organizational patterns and academic planning.

Solving the Problems: Strategic Planning, Initiatives, Action

Colleges and universities are visited regularly by a variety of accrediting bodies. While some are broadly based, most are concerned with the operation of a single program, such as law or engineering. In all cases, a judgment is made whether the program or institution is given full approval, placed on probation, or listed as non-accredited. One such body concerned with an entire university, the North Central Association, scheduled its visitation for February 1990, at which time a team of administrators and faculty from comparable institutions would begin a thorough analysis of DU. The survey would analyze administrators, faculty, students, alumni, and all operating activities, from libraries to budget-making, as well as the sense of purpose and mission. A positive rating would bring another visitation a decade later.

In preparation for this visit, a detailed self-study was begun in 1989, the first of a series of plans that evolved into the Capital Campaign of 1994–2000. A favorable visitation report came in May, listing numerous strengths including the Board of Trustees, the Core Curriculum, improvements in affirmative action and faculty involvement, a dedicated and capable faculty and staff, high scholarly and creative activities, financial control, and non-traditional student initiatives.

The accrediting board also voiced concerns, which paralleled those of the self-study—the lack of a clear sense of mission and goals, inadequate financial strength, and less-than-adequate faculty salaries. With these assessments in hand, a second step was initiated. This formal strategic planning process lasted from 1990 to June 1992. A 42-person coordinating committee led by Provost Zaranka headed a series of task forces that produced working papers on the most significant areas of concern—financial management, quality assessment, interdisciplinary programming, student life, undergraduate mentoring, lifelong learning, and internationalization.

In 1992, an Academic Mission Task Force produced a concise statement of the mission of the University (see Appendices), along with a "strategic goals" series of proposals for restructuring a multitude of operations, all aimed at an educational enterprise of highest quality. To that end, there would be more interdisciplinary Core program and majors, greater support for graduate and undergraduate research, mentoring, and an honors program. Innovative and socially responsible curricula were not only to be envisioned but created and effectively monitored. The broadest international and multicultural approaches were to be put in place. Above all, lifelong learning found a focus in this proposal.

The final goal was a restructuring of administrative and academic units for greater efficiency and coherence. A system of budget accountability and responsible accounting methods was to be balanced against academic priorities, with neither being sacrificed. "The College," after eight years of experimentation, was to be dissolved and the duties shifted to the provost's office, with the addition of vice provosts as appropriate at the undergraduate and graduate levels. Another vice provost would be in charge of all internationalization activities.

These initiatives were then developed and shaped throughout the University community. In November 1993 the third stage, or active phase, of the process began with the creation of a Strategic Initiatives Committee. All interested faculty and staff were invited to submit proposals—for programs, for Centers, for facilities, for infrastructure, and so on—that would advance the mission and goals of the University.

Solving the Problems: Strategic Planning, Initiatives, Action

In the end, 193 specific proposals were submitted. Forming three bulky volumes, these proposals represented the aspirations of the University for the 21st century. The reports, divided into 14 areas, were made available in April 1994 for discussion and eventual decision.

The first committee studied a variety of proposals under the heading of "Teaching and Learning." Among them were endowed chairs in the Core curriculum and women's studies. An international house and an arts and creativity house were high on the list, as was the field of student-faculty collaborative research and a summer science field project. The "Research and Scholarship" committee reviewed more endowed chairs and recommended projects for seed money for new faculty, post-doctoral fellows, greater support for the library, encouragement for undergraduate research excellence, an environmental institute, and geographic information systems. The committee on "Social Responsibility" favored urban social work initiatives, a center for career research, and enlargement of the West High School VIP program. "Information Technology" saw the need for an "institute to transform learning," as well as a host of initiatives to produce a "library for the year 2010," create a center for "future media studies," and increase technological literacy on a large scale. The committee on "Internationalization and Multiculturalism" envisioned a center on human rights, the formation of many international linkages, and scholarships for students from abroad and for DU students studying overseas. The area of "Support Services" recommended a new building for the College of Business Administration as well as the renovation of the General Classroom and Business Administration buildings for programs in arts and humanities and communications. The committee on "Centers and Institutes" found it advisable to define these two terms, which had been appearing with increasing frequency on campus. Their conclusion read "Centers and institutes represent one vehicle for a university to highlight and support its chosen areas of distinctiveness. They are particularly appropriate in special areas of expertise for the publics we serve." The committee found value in an expanded center for international business education and for centers on the environment, transportation, tourism, and telecommunication.

Although expectations were high and campus-wide planning was enthusiastic and widely published, the success of this work was dependent on a much larger financial base. The bridge between planning and monetary support was found in "A Vision for the University of Denver: Outcomes from the Strategic Planning Process," issued by the provost in September 1994. The plan was clear:

> The University seeks funding to enhance its distinctive mission and to build the physical facilities and the technological infrastructure to support this vision. Whether these measures are supported externally, with the anticipated Capital Campaign, or internally, is a decision that defines our direction for the future and reflects on how best to get there.

That December, the chancellor publicly shared the news that the Board of Trustees had authorized a five-year campaign for $140 million, not only for bricks and mortar, but for a sizable expansion of programs and support services. "Our goal is to do what we do with the highest quality," he said, "and, in touching many lives, to create a student-centered environment within a community of scholars, scholars who are engaged in the generation and communication of knowledge to produce an informed citizenry and to benefit society."

Ritchie communicated his enthusiasm and shared his vision of long-range planning:

> The University is on the threshold of greatness. We've been talking about this as a University community for months, and enthusiasm has just been building. Our goals are not modest. They will transform the University in profound and enduring ways. Our goal is the highest-quality education for our students, an education that will blend academic and non-academic life into 'total education'—a seamless learning experience that encourages development of the whole person.
>
> Our goal is to become one of the finest independent universities in the world. I think that being clear about what we intend to accomplish—and how we will do it—has convinced people to join in. We are gratified at the level of support from alumni and friends across the country, and from our own students, faculty, and staff.

The goal of the Capital Campaign, later increased to $150 million, continued to attract donors who enthusiastically offered funds, not only for buildings but for scholarships, faculty, and programs.

In January 1997 it was announced that Sam, JD '29, and Freda Davis had established a number of charitable trusts in the amount of $3 million to fund many activities of the College of Law, including scholarships for law students. Dedicated contributors for many years, they had helped in the construction of the Lowell Thomas Law Building. "Through their devotion and generosity, Sam and Freda have left a permanent legacy at DU," said Dean Dennis Lynch in the campaign's *Chronicle*. "They will forever change the lives of our students."

The *Rocky Mountain News* of April 25, 1997, announced that real estate planning pioneer Franklin L. Burns and his wife, Joy, had pledged $5 million to the Daniels College of Business, thus bringing the total receipts and pledges of the University's Capital Campaign to $132 million. The money would be used to support and enhance faculty and programs in what is now called the Franklin L. Burns School of Real Estate and Construction Management. Joy Burns, who had helped found the Women's (now Colorado Business) Bank and the Burnsley Hotel near downtown Denver, chairs the DU Board of Trustees.

The University as Community: Administration

The charter of 1864 set up a board of 28 elected members. Their powers included the appointment and dismissal of a president (after 1880, a chancellor) and the financial operations and organization of the school. A survey of the activities of chancellors and boards through the years shows a wide variation of activity, some people giving only perfunctory attention, others a totally dedicated and focused concern for the total health of their charge. These latter characteristics define the members of the board just before and during the Ritchie years. Time, talent, and treasure were given generously to underline the conviction that this University was a great enterprise.

The chancellor and the team he organized (Provost William Zaranka, the vice chancellors, and other heads) demonstrated four characteristics early on: (1) a clear view of the shape of a great university; (2) a willingness to expend great effort to achieve that goal; (3) a business-like approach to that achievement, and (4) an eagerness to share with the University community the authority to help create and develop plan after plan as the vision enlarged.

As the organization tables show (pp. 294-297), the chancellor is aided by a provost as chief executive officer for academic affairs, and by vice chancellors for business and financial affairs; institutional advancement; communications; sports and wellness; and University technology services. In the spring of 1992, the decision was made to create two vice provosts, one for graduate, the other for undergraduate studies, designed "to enhance the quality of existing programs and explore creative initiatives at each level." Barry Hughes, described as a "futurist," and author of a book on "choices in the creation of a new world order," was appointed to the graduate studies position in March 1993. His mandate was to chair the graduate council, integrate graduate teaching and research, and help develop the annual budget, including decentralized budgeting, recruitment, and the exploitation of the World Wide Web.

In August of that year, Sheila Wright of the University of Hartford became vice provost for undergraduate studies, responsible for developing a distinctive and powerful undergraduate experience. She would implement recommendations of the undergraduate council, oversee the Core Curriculum, the honors program, advising, and the integration of non-traditional offerings. Looking at a total undergraduate experience, she saw that "by placing student life and athletics in a structural or functional relationship with academics, DU sends a strong message that student life and athletics are an integral part of undergraduate studies."

The University as Community: Colleges and Programs

Students entering the University during this time—both undergraduates and graduates—found themselves members of one of nine bodies, each headed by a dean. At the heart of the University's commitment to liberal studies was the formation of three faculties, which together have the largest number of departments, faculty, and scholarly activity. The first two, Arts and Humanities and Social Sciences, have been headed since 1990 by Roscoe E. Hill. A listing of departments shows the broad range of their disciplines: The School of Art and Art History, the Center for Judaic Studies, the Lamont School of Music, and the Departments of English, Languages and Literatures, History, Philosophy, Religious Studies, and Theatre. Their vision "is to educate students in the best our culture and other cultures have to offer. Courses help the students not only to develop tools for aesthetic and ethical discrimination and the refinement of taste but also to use these tools in the context of the best that has been thought, spoken, and created."

The faculty of Social Sciences see their goal as being "to work toward a better understanding of human behavior, the development of research and analysis strategies that will yield that understanding, and the application of the resulting knowledge to social issues." Units involved here are the School of Communication (including Human and Mass Communication), the Departments of Anthropology, Economics, Political Science, Psychology, Public Affairs, Sociology, and programs in public policy and women's studies.

The Division of Natural Sciences, Mathematics, and Engineering, noted for active involvement in research, found itself "able to offer students stimulating, intellectually challenging courses and to undertake independent research or design projects under the guidance of faculty members active in research at the frontiers of their disciplines." Departments include Biological Sciences, Chemistry and Biochemistry, Engineering, Geography, Mathematics and Computer Science, Enviromental Sciences and Physics and Astronomy. Led by Deans John L. Kice and later Robert Coombe, these areas have produced one of the great success stories of the past few years, largely due to the quality of faculty and faculty recruitment efforts. Their work has led to substantial grants and to the erection of the magnificent F.W. Olin Hall.

A fourth faculty, the Daniels College of Business, is headed by Dean James Griesemer. Here units include the Schools of Accountancy, Hotel, Restaurant, and Tourism Management, The Franklin L. Burns School of Real Estate and Construction Management, and the Departments of Finance, Legal Studies, Management, Marketing, and Statistics and Operations Technology. Faculty members see their mission as "to enhance the practice of management in the areas of technical competence, creative leadership, professional behavior, social responsiveness, and global awareness through effective teaching, relevant scholarship, and meaningful professional and community service."

Other graduate programs include the Colleges of Law, Education, the Graduate Schools of Professional Psychology, International Studies, and Social Work, as well as University College and The Women's College. All of these will be examined in more detail later in this history. In all, there was considerable curricular change, as well as success in money-saving and money-raising activities. A sense of increased interdependence and greater participation in the welfare of the whole community was increasingly apparent, here as elsewhere in the University.

Joy and Franklin Burns

Changes in the Undergraduate Curriculum

Students considering the University found a rich but confusing diversity of independent introductory courses, each ultimately leading to some profession or life-interest. To bring order and meaning to the first two years of the undergraduate experience, DU always offered some program of required courses, not usually integrated with one another, but serving departmental needs. In the reorganization of 1983–85, the College was created along with the Core Curriculum, which produced a set of common requirements that would, its designers hoped, support the development of "the educated person" and provide the "skills and sensibilities" such a person would need in a rapidly changing and challenging world. A parallel set of course offerings, the Coordinated Humanities series, was in successful operation since the late 1970s.

Crossing between departments and divisions, the Core required first-year English, mathematics and computer science, oral communication, and a variety of options in arts and humanities (with course titles such as "Making of the

221

Modern Mind," "Civilizations Compared," and "Multiple Voices of America," among others). In social sciences, four departments offered introductory courses. Students could meet the natural sciences requirement from a menu including such courses as "Theory of Everything: Cosmos and Creation" and "From Molecules to Humankind." A foreign language and a "Freshman Experience" requirement were also added.

These efforts at integration won recognition across the country. It was no small achievement, given the nature and complexity of the undertaking. As a 1993 report on the Core commented,

> It has become an integral part of what is presented to parents, students, high school counselors, the trustees, and the general public about what the undergraduate experience as a whole is here. It represents a huge investment of faculty time, administrative and staff supervision and coordination, financial investment, and focus in admissions and public relations.

The first substantial revision came after nine years of operation. Students were interviewed by the Center for Academic Quality and Assessment of Student Learning, among other groups. A 1994 report pointed to the need for smaller lecture sessions, in some cases better teaching, and greater emphasis on "a general education," with requirements perhaps spread out over several years. Consequently, students entering as the Class of 1999 received a booklet detailing new requirements for the Core, including some 8 to 12 hours of upper-division courses still to be designed.

In February 1984, the Faculty of Natural Sciences, Mathematics, and Engineering was created, bringing together biological science (which administered sport science and physical education), geography, physics, mathematics and computer science, and engineering, which had been a college until it was dissolved in June 1975, and was recreated as a department in September 1982. In 1990, after four years of curriculum-building and documentation, all four departmental programs of electrical and mechanical engineering were approved by the Accreditation Board for Engineering and Technology. A vigorous campaign to increase enrollment included visitations to high schools, faculty members offering personal responses to enquiries, and a summer course for high school students called "The Making of an Engineer." As Chairman Al Rosa commented, "People at DU didn't realize there is a department of engineering," but he believed that a clearer profile resulted from the recognition of the interdependence of all the sciences and the new technologies.

A new vision for the College of Business Administration came in the fall of 1986, with the work of a faculty committee that proposed a wholly new and challenging curriculum, one that, with its emphasis on ethical standards, social responsibility, and contribution to community welfare—ran directly counter to the prevailing business climate of the time. The proposal was, in fact, created in response to the changing needs of corporate executives, who found students lacking the ability to integrate their technical skills with management and leadership demands in a rapidly changing world. From the beginning, cooperation between faculty and a wide variety of business leaders led to the formation of a truly unique design. In addition to standard degrees in management, finance, accounting, marketing, and taxation, a new graduate degree included an "enhanced laboratory requirement," a three-day Outward Bound experience, "transitional leadership exercises, workshops, required community service projects, all interlaced with an ethical thrust, emphasis on creativity, and an understanding of cultural diversity." All the elements of a standard graduate program were included, but newly organized in meaningfully integrated patterns.

When this proposal was shared with Dan Ritchie, then a member of the Board of Trustees, he was so intrigued with it that he asked the faculty to prepare an extended report for "a potential donor," later revealed to be Bill Daniels, Denver cable pioneer, who shared their vision. In the next several years, Daniels gave $11 million for the program and another $11 million for an imposing building. The new curriculum was introduced in January 1994. Daniels remarked, "My challenge grant may be one of the most significant decisions I've ever made to help our city, state, and nation. I'm beholden to the many individuals, corporations, and institutions that joined me in this grant." As Dan Ritchie saw it, "We are the Pioneer University, and Bill is a pioneer in the most important and revolutionary business of our time." The school became the Daniels College of Business September 13, 1994.

In the process of redesign, the five-quarter-long MBA degree reached a new stage in curricular reform, one that was unique in the country. Here was an integrated seven-course core that modeled the world of business in all its decision-making processes as reflected by the course titles: "High Performance Management," "The Foundations of Business Decision," "Managing in the Global Century," "Values in Action," "The Quest for Quality," "Integrative Challenge," and "Positioning in the Competitive Environment." Master's degrees in the traditional fields of business administration were still available, thus making the college highly competitive among the nearly 600 schools offering the degree. Meanwhile, other areas of the University were moving steadily forward.

In October 1992, the College of Law celebrated a century of legal education in Colorado. Dean Dennis O. Lynch commented:

> It opened its doors on October 3, 1892, to one woman and 57 young men . . . Today a century later the college has 1,058 JD students—45 percent women—and 8,000 living alumni. The college is proud of its leadership in government, industry, and the legal community.

Faculty and students were justifiably proud of the school's pioneering work. African American Robert Hayes had been a member of the first class, while women, including Ann Hunt and Mary Lathrop (the first woman admitted to the American Bar Association) were early graduates. Making a legal education available to minorities, especially Hispanics, was a deep commitment. Other advances included a degree in legal administration, as well as cooperative degrees with business, international studies, and the social sciences.

A thoroughly modern law library operation, including print and computerized access and audio-visual components, supported the fields in which the law school was especially strong—international law, natural resources, jurisprudence, conflict resolution, regulated industries, and legal thought. The 34-acre Park Hill campus included the Lowell Thomas Law Building, which opened in 1984. In 1987, a gift of more than $8 million to the University and the College of Law by Frank W. Ricketson Jr. was the largest individual gift in DU's history at that time. The gift was recognized by the renaming of the entire law complex in his honor. To make the campus an ideal environment for all three schools—the College of Law, the Lamont School of Music, and the Weekend College—and for visitors, a major renovation of Mason Hall was undertaken. Plans called for a new student center, fitness facilities, and a dining room. At a dedication ceremony in August 1995, the center was named for former law school dean Robert B. Yegge, who serves as a director of the legal administration program at the time of this writing. The Weekend College, which offered a business administration degree emphasizing management training, attracted women of all ages, a quarter of them minority students. In July 1993, it was renamed The Women's College.

Courses in the training of educators also underwent substantial change during this period, with the College of Education moving to the newly named Ammi B. Hyde Building at the south end of the University Park campus and receiving the designation of a college and the appointment of its own dean, Elinor Katz. Undergraduates were offered teacher certification, which required an academic major. Professional courses were available only at the senior or graduate level. The University also began offering programs for administrators, as well as students who could attend classes on weekends, high school mathematics and sciences students, and Rocky Mountain Talent Search students. DU extended its reach to establish relationships with schools such as West High, Remington Elementary, and the Pioneer Charter School, a partnership with Denver Public Schools.

The University had always been among the foremost in providing teachers for the Rocky Mountain West—among them the author himself. But there had always been a lack of full cooperation between town and gown. During this period, however, a bright new understanding opened up due to the driving interest of the chancellor in all community affairs. The business community demonstrated a vastly increased interest in participating in attractive projects sponsored by the University. Ritchie made creative proposals to the Colorado legislature, for example, in showing the advantages of aiding independent schools in the area of scholarship aid. He participated as an active consultant in the development of the Denver Public Schools and wrote persuasively in the press about educational and related matters.

An engaging opportunity for educational cooperation opened up in November 1996, when the Denver Public School Board enthusiastically accepted a proposal for the establishment of the Pioneer Charter School, to be housed in Harrington Elementary School at 3230 E. 38th St. in Northeast Denver. Extended school days and school years, advanced teaching methods, and mutual oversight by DU and the Denver Public School Board all promised success in improving education in an often-troubled school system. In addition, the College of Education established the University of Denver High School. Its philosophy was to focus on students who benefitted from a high degree of independent learning. With this program in place, the University now offered opportunities for young people, starting at age three at the Ricks Center, to senior citizens who could audit University classes at little or no cost.

Ammi Hyde Building

The Ricks Center was built in 1994 for elementary- and middle-age students.

The Center expanded in 1996 to accommodate burgeoning classes.

Changes in the Undergraduate Curriculum

Another educational dimension was added with the creation of a program for gifted and talented youngsters, which had begun in 1984 as an experimental half-day summer class organized by Norma Hafenstein. When the program moved on campus, it expanded, eventually occupying its own building at the corner of Evans and York, with a full complement of full- and part-time teachers. Now, enthusiastic parents came to the administration with proposals for a grand new building. Subsequently, funds were obtained from the Temple Hoyne Buell, Kenneth Kendal King, and Gold Crown foundations and individual donors Alta Merle Ricks and Ruth O. Johnson. The substantial complex named "Ricks Center" was dedicated on November 14, 1994, in honor of Alta Merle Ricks' husband and son. This innovative program, which allows each child to proceed at his or her own pace in small classes, was highly successful from the beginning.

Across the hall from the College of Education, the School of Professional Psychology, which opened in 1976, acquired Dean Peter Buirski and by June 1995 had enrolled 90 students, of whom 53 earned the PsyD degree. In this student body, ranging from 22 to 56 years in age, 76% were male, 24% female, 16% minority. Job prospects were strong for those students, and the U.S. Department of Labor reported, "Employment of psychologists is expected to grow much faster than the average of all occupations through the year 2005." The report went on to explain that the demand stemmed from societal problems requiring professional intervention—such as alcohol abuse, drug dependency, and family violence—as well as the need for services for children and mental health maintenance.

Graduates of the school are now licensed in 36 states, Puerto Rico, Canada, and Israel, and are employed in mental health centers, hospitals, clinics, health organizations, group private practice, and the armed services. The movement toward full- or part-time practice became a trend.

As previously described, the Social Science Foundation was founded in the 1920s by James H. Causey, Ben M. Cherrington, and Heber R. Harper. In 1964, under the leadership of Josef Korbel, its (largely *undergraduate*) international relations department expanded into the Graduate School of International Relations (now the Graduate School of International Studies) established in Cherrington Hall, south of the Mary Reed Building. As a commentator remarked,

> During the years since its establishment, GSIS has grown in both size and reputation, becoming the major source for international studies between Chicago and the West Coast, graduating hundreds of MA and PhD scholars into responsible governmental, academic, and independent positions around the world.

The accomplishments of the faculty and staff of the school have been numerous in research, publication, and the widest community involvement. GSIS has sponsored the journal *Africa Today* as well as the *Monograph Series in World Affairs,* the Center for Teaching International Relations, the World Affairs Challenge, faculty exchanges abroad, and support for Hispanic cultural studies. All contributed to a sustained focus on the enlargement of consciousness of 20th century global problems and their solution. Dual programs with the College of Law, the Graduate School of Social Work, and the Daniels College of Business are examples demonstrating an interest in interdisciplinary research and teaching. Dean E. Thomas Rowe was succeeded in 1996 by Tom J. Farer, then director of the joint degree program in law and international relations at American University in Washington, D.C.

The Graduate School of Social Work, housed in Spruce Hall, continued a long tradition of response to local and national demands for highly trained workers in a challenging and difficult field of operation. The school has almost doubled in enrollment since 1988, from 242 to 430 students, including 390 MSW candidates and 40 doctoral students. More important, a major curriculum revision extended completion of course work to four quarters rather than three, and created dual degrees with GSIS, the School of Communications, and the Iliff School of Theology.

In 1991 the school was again nationally accredited, this time for the longest period in its history, eight years. The report endorsed the dedicated work of dean, faculty, and staff, and underscored the success of its innovative curriculum. For example, in 1995, GSSW played a key role in community outreach in establishing the Colorado Human Services Research, Education, and Training Center of five universities to secure substantial funding for stipends and faculty acquisition to aid child welfare training and research.

Thanks to the long overseas experience of former Dean John F. Jones, who is particularly well-traveled in Eastern Asia, the school has become involved in international projects, most recently in the U.N. Center for International Development in Nagoya, Japan, and the China Youth College of Politics in Beijing. In response to local needs, in October 1991 the school initiated its Bridge Project in Denver's North (and later South) Lincoln Housing Project. In an area in which the high school dropout rate had reached almost 90%, GSSW set up a store-front center to provide numerous programs including tutoring, pre-school reading, and DU scholarship assistance. Major grants from government and private sources allowed continuing success in the Bridge and many other projects. Jones was succeeded as dean in 1996 by Catherine Foster Alter, former director of graduate social work programs at the University of Iowa.

In the fall of 1995, University College celebrated a decade of phenomenal growth in the highly competitive area of non-traditional education with the production of numerous programs leading to a new definition of certificate and master's degree education. The College had its origin in the thinking of Arts and

Changes in the Undergraduate Curriculum

Sciences Dean Ken Purcell, philosophy Professor Roscoe Hill, and mathematics Professor Peter Warren. Termed The New College, it opened as a subdivision of the Division of Arts, Humanities, and Social Sciences, with Roscoe Hill as dean. The A & S College was dissolved in 1984, the New College became University College, and in 1986 Warren became dean, bringing his experience in energy policy research and the creation of the Denver International Film Festival. From the beginning, the school's premise was to provide working adults with an education through immediately applicable, up-to-date, quality curriculum—guided by industry, professional, and personal goals.

This new curriculum was designed by a combination of faculty, corporate executives, regulatory agents, consumer advocates, and adults looking for self-improvement and new jobs—in short, people deeply aware of and affected by the profound changes in the world around them. The college's response to these needs was a dazzling array of invigorating new courses in interdisciplinary form, at a lower tuition rate, offered in the evening and on weekends, available on-campus and in corporate headquarters and other spots in Boulder, Longmont, and elsewhere. The view was global as well, with study opportunities in more than 10 countries, a variety of seminars and programs presenting the University as an excellent place for overseas companies to send executives for further study through an operation entitled Understanding America.

Formal classwork was divided among five divisions, each comprising a number of related departments. The first division, Communication and Cultural Studies, involved topics such as "Great Ideas of the World" and "Liberal Studies." The division also offered study of 15 languages and Hispanic studies, as well as a certificate program in the Native American experience. The Division of Health and Environmental Studies designed a master's degree and seven certificate programs including one in ecotourism management. The Division of Information Technologies, with its master's degree and accompanying certificates, offered courses including one in artificial intelligence. A cooperative program with the Department of Geography offered "Information Technology Update." Those who saw the lamentable demise of the School of Librarianship were especially interested in the appearance of a cutting-edge master's degree in librarianship and information management, particularly considering the substantial initial enrollment in fall 1995. Offerings were also made available in the burgeoning field of health care management, with courses covering managed health care, ethics, eldercare systems, and telemedicine.

A special program, the Institute for Strategic Studies, was conceived to be flexible enough to accommodate individual students or entire organizations, linking engineering science and managerial disciplines in fields from global business and cultures to dispute resolution.

By all measures, the record of University College is impressive. In 10 years, the number of degree-seeking students has increased from 15 to well over 1,000;

from 10 graduates in the spring of 1986 to some 250 in 1996 (1,756 to date); from three to eight master's programs; from a staff of five to 53; from a faculty of 150 to 451; and from revenues of $330,000 to more than $5 million. More than 35 national programming and marketing awards testify to this progress.

In 1987, the Center for Public Policy and Contemporary Issues was founded by Richard D. Lamm, three-time Colorado governor (1975–1987), to make a major contribution to regional and national policy dialogue through a variety of presentations. Among these were conferences, seminars, a lecture series, a substantial monograph series, and a quarterly newsletter—all made possible by numerous foundation grants. The public affairs program, headed by Richard Caldwell, was integrated into the University's curriculum and offered courses aimed "to create analytical skills that can be applied to public policy questions."

Publications produced by the center, written by Lamm, Caldwell, and a variety of invited experts, explored a vast array of problems and possible answers. Readers were invited to explore "The Uncompetitive Society," "What's Wrong with American Schools," "A Vision for Our Nation in the 21st Century," and "Rethinking American Security." A series of highly controversial and stimulating columns in the press resulted in a book *America in Decline?,* which explored dysfunctional institutions, health care woes, "debtquake," immigration, health, racism, day of reckoning—to use terms found in the book. Another publication, *The Competition Time Bomb,* outlined 25 threats to American survival. In sum, the center's work in research, publication, and teaching presents a view of the hard choices confronting America in an era of heady and rapid change and suggests viable solutions.

Envisioning "a commercial republic, but an enlightened one," their advice was clear: "Americans must stop defining the world purely in terms of cash flow and start thinking about the ingredients for long-term success—namely motivation, savings, investment, education, delayed gratification, and quality."

The Center for Judaic Studies builds on a long tradition, initiated by the teaching of Rabbi C. E. H. Kauvar of the B. M. H. Synagogue in 1924. He was succeeded as Kauvar Professor by Benzion Netanyahu, renowned authority on the Jews of medieval Spain. He finally settled in Israel. His eldest son, Jonathan, was killed leading the rescue mission to Entebbe, July 3–4, 1976. His second son, Benjamin, became prime minister of Israel in May 1996. With the arrival in Denver of Rabbi Stanley Wagner, a vast undertaking was launched—the Center for Judaic Studies, to be devoted to teaching, research, and community involvement.

Wagner saw the mission as one "to enrich the intellectual life of our University and to build bridges of understanding between all segments of our community." To this end, a substantial Solomon Shwayder Memorial Library, the Ira M. Beck Memorial Archives, and the Rocky Mountain Jewish Historical Society were developed, as was a publication program. To these were added the Institute for Interfaith Studies and Social Concerns, the Institute for Islamic-

Changes in the Undergraduate Curriculum

Judaic Studies, and the Holocaust Awareness Institute. Courses in Hebrew, Jewish history, and related topics were shared with three Christian seminaries in the area—Iliff, St. Thomas (defunct as of 1995), and The Denver Seminary. Among other programs was the Institute for Israeli Culture. An autonomous and self-supporting institution, the center had by the end of 1996 an endowment of over $2.5 million.

In 1993–94, the Lamont School of Music significantly reorganized its curriculum, enlarging its bachelor of music degree into a rigorous conservatory-style program and offering a fifth-year certification program in music education. The program thus presented four directorships: conservatory, university (theory, history, core, music education, and the like), jazz and commercial (including music technology), and an ever-evolving "community program," which brought the school back to Florence Lamont Hinman's original concept. These certificate degrees offered work with children and adults. A special dimension was the emphasis on volunteerism. As Director Joe Docksey put it, this was "a chance to instill values in our University students by offering free music lessons to public school students who would not otherwise be able to afford them." While the location of the school in the Houston Fine Arts Center on the Park Hill campus made relationships with academic programs on the University Park campus a bit difficult, the problem was offset by the excellent facilities and opportunities for community involvement.

The School of Art has likewise undergone significant changes, both physical and intellectual, since 1989. The gallery and studios received new lighting and equipment, a state-of-the-art computer imaging and graphics laboratory was instituted, the slide collection was increased to more than 121,000 slides, and a new pottery kiln was completed. As professor and sculptor Maynard Tischler commented, "renewed emphasis was placed on the recruitment of talented prospective students" by the addition of a recruitment specialist and additional student scholarships. Already solid community relations were strengthened by a unique, ongoing exchange of curators and faculty programs with the Denver Art Museum as well as the creation of DU Art!, a group of prominent supporters of the arts in Denver who worked together to bring in visiting lecturers, provide scholarship assistance, and support special gallery exhibitions. In 1994, as a result of this growth and development, the Board of Trustees agreed to change the name to the School of Art and Art History.

During this period, the University was engaged in a significantly large number of interdisciplinary programs, sometimes leading to departmental mergers, as in the case of communications. A coming-together of the speech communication and mass communication departments in 1991 resulted in the School of Communication, which had two departments, human communication studies and mass communication and journalism studies. A complete reconstruction of the undergraduate and graduate curricula of both departments resulted in a core of undergraduate courses shared by students in both departments. Another such merger resulted in the joint graduate degree program shared by the departments of history and religious studies and the Iliff School of Theology. Likewise, the Department of Management works with other professional units to offer the MS in management with concentrations in engineering, health care, and sports management.

Allied Enterprises in Research and Social Exploration

The organization of the University involved far more than academic divisions. A number of University-related organizations had a somewhat different focus, including the Denver Research Institute. Sponsored research on any scale has been a component of the University since 1946, when John Greene and Ralph Conrad organized the Bureau of Industrial Research, later named the Industrial Research Institute, and eventually taking the DRI title. From relatively modest beginnings, it became "the largest university-affiliated diversified research organization between the Midwest and the West Coast." Originally comprised of five divisions—electronics, physics, chemistry and chemical engineering, metallurgy and mechanical engineering—the institute expanded into nine divisions by 1970. With 486 employees, it had attainined a research volume of more than $6 million.

Unfortunately, with the closing of the College of Engineering in 1975 and the lost ties with University departments in science and mathematics, the institute suffered grievous losses of staff, although the research volume stayed high for some time. By 1989, the staff had been reduced to 50, working in two laboratories of the old mechanics division— Ordinance Research and Development (ORDL), and Target Vulnerability and Survivability (TVSL)— still housed in the west wing of the Boettcher Center. By 1990, a 20 percent increase in employees enabled research to reach a volume of $4 million.

In 1990, the chancellor appointed a study group to examine the problem, giving members only two constraints: The plan "must involve interaction with academic departments and look beyond the immediate needs of the institute to longer-term evolution." Another group, the Task Force for Research and Scholarship, was able to recommend an ambitious long-range plan for all research, sponsored and non-funded. The plan would increase the visibility and quality as well as the volume of such enterprises. Specifically, it called for the appointment of a vice provost for research, a new chair for DRI, the reinvigoration of the institution, a substantial increase of cooperative ventures between industry and faculty, and the introduction of DRI research into the classroom. As Provost Zaranka saw it, "We are creating an environment in which funded research, applied research, and traditional scholarship are equally encouraged and supported." The results of these efforts were immediate and positive. Joint appointments were made in DRI and the sciences. Research expanded beyond defense work. For example, in 1994 the University and the

Buchtel Tower

National Institute of Justice established the Regional Law Enforcement and Corrections Technology Center at DRI, one of four such centers in the country.

The institute saw two major changes in 1996. A new partnership between DRI, the U.S. Department of Justice's Office of Technology, and the Sandia National Laboratory in New Mexico initiated work on a number of research and development projects. One project called for the design and production units, or "portals," that could detect small quantities of explosives residue in large amounts of air. The portals could operate in airports and elsewhere as easily as metal detectors. Feeling the need to realign the institute more closely with the University and its overall goals, the administration appointed a new director, Carl Lyday, and changed the name a final time, to the University of Denver Research Institute.

The University as Community: the Faculty

As the University's reach broadened in this decade, the concerns of professors and administrators alike were intensified in almost all areas—appointment of new faculty, increased representation of women on faculty, tenure and its acquisition, the relative value of teaching and research, relations with students and the community, the share of faculty in all-University decision-making, the very organization of the faculty and its mission. To these points, the conclusions in the report of the Carnegie Foundation for the Advancement of Teaching, *Scholarship Revisited: Priorities of the Professoriate* (1990), offered a pattern for judging faculty performance. As Ernest L. Boyer pointed out, "It is toward a shared vision of intellectual and social possibilities—a community of scholars—that the four dimensions of academic endeavor should lead." These dimensions were the scholarship of discovery or basic research, and the scholarship of integration, of application, and of teaching. "We believe the time has come to move beyond the tired old 'teaching versus research' debate and give the familiar and honorable term 'scholarship' a broader, more capacious meaning, one that brings legitimacy to the full scope of academic work," Boyer explained.

The issue of a full scope was at the heart of much academic debate in those years, particularly as it related to the professional rewards attached to each activity. The Conference on Faculty Roles and Rewards in 1995 was a watershed. *Scholarship Revisited* was distributed to all faculty by the provost, and the book's major principles were discussed and debated during the conference proceedings. Another arena for this discussion was the Faculty Senate. In the reorganization of 1986, this body, which had been a combination of administrators and teachers, acquired its present status. With presidents serving two-year terms, a permanent office location, departments sending one or two representatives each, the Faculty Senate reached approximately 50 members and provided a forum for discussion of issues, publications of importance, and eventual action. Their studies included faculty evaluations of administrators; comparisons of the compensation structure; a review of sabbatical policies; and an examination of equal opportunity and sexual harassment policies and procedures.

The University as Community: the Faculty

The Faculty Senate took on a greater role in University governance. Faculty Senate presidents became more instrumental in developing University policy and governance. Jim Walther from the Department of Finance and Bill Burford from the Department of Economics helped the senate transition from a University Senate to a Faculty Senate with a new constitution and operating system. Joe Szyliowicz from the Graduate School of International Studies worked to improve communication with the central administration. During the four years Gordon Von Stroh was president, a higher level of interaction between faculty and administration was developed. For example, a new Faculty Appointment, Promotion, and Tenure Policy strengthening professional standards was approved, a new model for the Office of the Provost was developed, and faculty were given greater roles in University policy-making and governance. Linda Cobb-Reiley, the second woman to serve as president, further strengthened the role faculty played in University agenda-setting and helped raise the visibility of equity issues while getting more younger faculty into decision-making roles. Keith Harrison, the first African-American to serve as senate president, continued this effort, serving to expand the role of faculty from all units.

With the new Faculty Senate model, the Faculty Senate president now served ex officio on the Board of Trustees, while other faculty served on the trustee Committees of Budget and Finance, Faculty and Educational Affairs, Student Affairs, and Buildings and Grounds. The changes taking place in the University with faculty involvement mirrored what was happening in business—greater participation in policy and financial decision-making and higher expectations for individual involvement in the organization. For example, with all-University committees, 25 to 50 percent were to be composed of faculty appointed by the Faculty Senate. More than ever, faculty were involved in the future destiny of the University.

It was an increasingly younger faculty. Of the 389 members in 1995, 23 percent (89) were of the so-called Silent Generation, born between 1921 and 1939; 255 (more than 65 percent) were born between 1940 and 1959; and 45 (almost 12 percent) were born between 1960 and 1970. Both the small numbers, whose memories included the 1920s, the Great Depression, even the Second World War, and the large number of those who experienced the 1960s and were part of the Baby Boom generation had demonstrable impact on the University's view of curricular and social concerns.

In an increasingly evaluative world, the search for new faculty involved higher expectations and an elaborate selection process. Annual reviews, printed student evaluations of each course, faculty evaluations of administrators, additional compensation for merit, and a steeper road to tenure—all became a normal way of faculty life. The size of the faculty, however, remained about the same—120 full professors were male, 23 female; 78 associate professors were male, 40 female; 50 assistant professors were male, 37 female. One male and one female instructor, 18 male and 15 female lecturers made a sum of 273 male and 116 female faculty, for a total of 389. Length of service illustrated the stability of faculty and staff. In fact, 93 people had served more than 25 years, 72 between 20 and 24 years, and 125 between 15 and 19 years.

The measurement of teaching effectiveness and its improvement was admittedly a difficult task. In 1990, to help solve the problem, the Center for Faculty Development was created and directed by Special Assistant to the Provost Jim Davis, author of *Better Teaching: More Learning* (1992). Originally designed to help faculty improve techniques, the center offered workshops and planning seminars and provided videotaping and individual counseling. In 1992, it expanded to become the Center for Academic Quality and Assessment of Student Learning, and its new direction included curriculum planning, standardized assessments, workshops in curriculum improvement, and systematic interviews of graduate and current students. Provost Zaranka remarked that "in the context of the mission and goals of the University's strategic plan, this center will become central and crucial to our effort."

The University as Community: Students and Alumni

The student population changed significantly in overall numbers between 1989 and 1997, rising from 2,765 traditional undergraduates in 1989 to 3,456 in all undergraduate programs in 1997. The number of graduate students rose from 4,501 in 1989 to 4,729 in 1997. Students came from all 50 states, with percentages of domestic students as follows: Colorado (43%), the West and Southwest (25%), the Midwest (15%), the Northeast (12%), and the South (5%). Some 15 percent were minorities: Hispanic 6%, African American 4%, Asian and Pacific Islander 4%, and Native American 1%. A full 15 percent of the total enrollment was international representing 92 countries. The top 10 countries were Japan (71), Thailand (39), South Korea (34), Indonesia (33), Malaysia (33), India (28), Taiwan, R.O.C. (27), Canada (25), China, P.R.C. (19), and Kuwait (18). Of international student enrollment, some 26 came from Africa (3 percent), 423 from Asia (55 percent), 135 from Europe (17.5 percent), 31 from Latin America (4 percent), 124 from the Middle East (16 percent), and the remainder from Canada and Oceania.

Across the nation, observers noted that students and faculty alike found the world of the 1990s at once exhilarating and frightening because of new global challenges, new methods of instant communication, a dismaying proliferation of data and choices, change overriding continuity, challenges to old values, and above all the rising cost of everything. These and many other factors greatly affected the behavior of students, both in and out of class. To meet tuition and living costs, many students worked at least part time. Many came with unresolved problems, and all appeared more sophisticated, showing a surprising awareness of the greater world and a distaste for the traditional humanistic approach to learning, an almost unfriendly attitude toward print media, and a determined individualism against the idea of community. The University's response in this period was dramatic and successful.

The University as Community: Students and Alumni

In 1994, more than a dozen programs were centralized in the Center for Academic Resources. For example, the Student Orientation, Advising, and Registration program (SOAR) was designed to bring prospective students and their families to the campus in the summer to explore the nature of a liberal arts education at DU and initiate them into the values and practices of academia. Once on campus, students had the assistance of a professional central advising system, named "best in the nation" by the American College Testing program. Another resource, termed Total Excellence in Academic Management (TEAM), offered "an interactive forum designed to help students become active, successful learners" through workshops, centralized computer experiences, and the like. For international students, the Learning Transitions program offered a wide variety of assistance in adjusting to American life. A comprehensive support program for students with special learning disabilities was made available through the Learning Effectiveness Program, a one-on-one program focused on crucial areas of skill development. The center's responsibilities included publication of course description booklets and student evaluations of courses, as well as a "stopout and withdrawal" counseling service, retention initiatives, and the initiations of a highly successful mentoring system.

A new and innovative mentoring program, the University of Denver Campus Connection, was designed to get students involved socially and academically by matching them in their freshman year with faculty in the area of their greatest interest. This year-long mentoring experience generates opportunities to share in campus activities and mutual research interests. In 1994, in another mentoring effort, the Career Center began making connections between business leaders and potential graduates. Two years later, the alumni association began producing a register of thousands of members across the country who were interested in helping students with their job search. Special programs in the law school linked second-year students with practicing attorneys. Mentoring programs in the graduate schools of business, social work, international studies, and elsewhere placed equal emphasis on community assistance.

Another example of mentoring is found in one of the strategic initiatives of 1995, namely a Partners in Scholarship program to improve the quality of undergraduate education by supporting research partnerships between students and faculty mentors. The partners typically work one-on-one on research projects of mutual interest, with each student receiving a $500 merit award. In the winter of 1996, eight projects were selected, three each in social sciences and mathematics and computer science, two in the humanities. This early pilot program gave way in 1996 to a funded program that has expanded to nearly 50.

Meanwhile, the physical environment for all these endeavors received scrupulous attention, ranging from a dramatic improvement of flower beds and lawns to the renovation of all living areas. All students except Denver residents were required to live in residence halls or one of the Greek houses for two years. In 1996, the latter consisted of nine fraternities—Alpha Tau Omega (which had no house), Beta Theta Pi, Chi Phi, Kappa Sigma, Lambda Chi Alpha, Phi Kappa Sigma, Sigma Alpha Epsilon, Sigma Chi, and Theta Chi. Sororities included Alpha Gamma Delta, Alpha Xi Delta, Delta Gamma, Delta Zeta, and Gamma Phi Beta. These houses continued to contribute to campus leadership, even though their numbers declined from a high of 50 percent of the student body some years ago to less than 30 percent in 1996.

Student living quarters on both campuses received dramatic improvements in the '90s, as did the areas of recreation and conviviality in the Driscoll University Center and Yegge Center. These and other changes added to the growing sense of community, always a difficult achievement in an urban setting. Future plans called for a major modernization of residence halls and the apartments in the heart of campus to provide a thoroughly modern complex of shared living accommodations reminiscent of those of an earlier era in Britain and America.

In 1993, the reorganized alumni association stated that its mission was "to maintain, enhance, and perpetuate a mutually beneficial and enduring relationship among alumni, the University, and their communities." The year-and-a-half hiatus in the association's directorship ended in 1992 with the appointment of Sue Goss and signaled a revitalization and redirection of the program. Initial concentration in five cities—New York City, Washington, D.C., Chicago, San Francisco, and Los Angeles—was assured by the formation of councils in each, with later expansion to Denver and other areas. Alumni who had graduated 50 or more years ago were presented with Pioneer Legend medallions. A dues-paying membership program was established to help fund more extensive offerings.

Of special interest to undergraduates, a student alumni council—Advance—came into being "as a link between past, present, and future students to increase pride in the University and to encourage active participation in the alumni association after graduation." Distinguished alumni were brought back to campus to lecture as part of the Alumni Masters Program, and reunions of the 10th, 25th, 40th and 50th years were invited to each commencement. The *University of Denver News,* the alumni magazine, was revamped into a more attractive, colorful, prize-winning *University of Denver Journal.* And after years of wandering around campus, the alumni association acquired a permanent headquarters at 2000 South Gaylord Street. Generous donations from alumnus Leo Block and others allowed the old Alumni House to be refurbished and expanded to host a variety of alumni activities.

Athletics, Recreation, and Wellness

In 1995, a new vice chancellor, Bernard Mullin, was chosen to lead the Division of Sports and Wellness. The name of the division was appropriate for a wholly new approach to the total student. Athletics had always been part of the University's mission, albeit not often well-funded or organized, from the baseball teams of the Colorado Seminary onward. Intercollegiate athletics developed slowly—baseball (1867–1997), football (1885–1961), basketball (1904), track and field (1912–1971), tennis (1917), golf (1924), hockey (early 1930s) swimming (1947), skiing (1948), ice hockey (1949), gymnastics (1950), soccer (1961), women's basketball (1969), women's field hockey (1974), women's volleyball (1983). Although the proportion of women to men has always been about even, only $15,000 was allocated in 1975 for women in five sports. Change came with Congressional passage of Title IX, requiring equal support for men's and women's sports. This change was welcomed and changes were instituted at DU.

Traditionally, a department of health, physical education and recreation had staffed a three-hour freshman course required of all freshmen except business majors. It included field sports, gymnastics, and some lectures on health and fitness. By the mid-eighties that requirement had been dropped, and in the crisis of that time its successor, the department of sports sciences, was terminated. A new voluntary program of sports activities was then created, termed "Recreation for Life."

The advent of Dan Ritchie as chancellor in 1989 brought a completely new perspective. He early showed the keenest desire to improve and expand all these programs and their surroundings as well. "It is time that we do something major in our facilities, something that will be architecturally and structurally extraordinary." At the same time, he saw the possibility of returning all varsity sports to the NCAA Division I level. But important as he saw this return to tradition and an improvement thereon, he saw it only in the context of the broadest sort of fitness for the whole student body:

> I view athletics as a central part of our mission, and athletics are important for every student. It's not just for the great athlete. We really want to encourage every one of our students to get involved in some way in this, not only as spectators but as participants.

The beginning of this reinvigoration occurred with Title IX and with the formation of a task force on gender equity, with an aim to put women's sports on par with their male counterparts with an initial investment of $200,000. Athletic achievements since that time have been spectacular. With national visibility in athletics being in large part dependent on membership in Division I of the NCAA the University had much ground to regain. Denver had been a member of Division I until the 1978–79 season, after which time only ice hockey and women's gymnastics (1983) participated at the Division I level.

*Athletes representing each sport at the University of Denver
prior to the transition from Division II to Division I.*

Athletics, Recreation, and Wellness

From 1990 onward, plans were underway to return to Division I in all sports. It was agreed that participation at this level would make the varsity athletic program consistent with the University's commitment to overall excellence. Consequently, in 1995 a task force of faculty, coaches, and students was directed to assess DU's record and current achievements in athletics. The record showed that DU athletes had won 20 national championships at the Division I level, and the school had produced 22 All-Americans and nine coaches of the year, and had won 73 first-team all-conference championships. All national requirements appeared to have been met, and all board members and senior faculty were in support. Funds were available to support high competitive standards, an athletic director and coaches were coming on board, and there was significant work in progress toward a great new facility. While the problems, especially funding, were indeed daunting, an anonymous donor offered to underwrite any losses. In 1996, the University applied to the NCAA to play all varsity sports for both men and women at the Division I level by the fall of 1998, assuming a two-year compliance review by the association. It was assumed that the program would be in the black in seven years, with additional money generated through community use of the new facilities as well as increased attendance and broadcast revenue.

In all this planning, both sides of the coin were kept in mind—athletics on the one side, "wellness" of body and mind on the other. To head this second program, Diana McNab, an internationally recognized sports nutritionist and psychologist was recruited. This was the first post of its kind at any college, aimed not only at helping sports teams to improve their performance, but also at encouraging all students to improve their individual health and shape their development as individuals and leaders. On December 20, 1995 the *Denver Post* quoted McNab as saying,

> Dan Ritchie wants to change the world in which we live by creating a new vision and reality for the university student, to nurture personal development through self-care and self-responsibility. I came here to manifest that vision.

The new Department of Wellness offered academic courses, organized a residential learning program known as the Wellness House, sponsored a National Outdoor Leadership School (NOLS), and took part each fall in Pioneers in the Rockies at the YMCA camp at Estes Park.

Students of the Nineties: Varied Backgrounds

VIII. A New World Emerges: Investing for the Future

At the heart of any great enterprise lies financial support to initiate change and to continue advancements once begun. In academia, such support has usually come from a major campaign. In the University's history, one campaign, The Denver Design, produced meager results in earlier years, in large part because it had been handed over to a professional organization. However, in the Chancellor's mind, a totally different approach, to be planned and carried out at home with talent and organization already on board, would be far superior. He took the first bold step himself. The announcement was made June 8, 1994, that he had given $15 million to the University, setting a record in the Rocky Mountain area by outdistancing any previous gift to higher education, regardless of source. His donation of 19,600 acres of Western Slope ranch land was expected to sell for more than the $15 million pledged, with the University to receive the full selling price. At the same time, Ritchie challenged the Board of Trustees to match that sum. They responded by committing $30 million of their own money. All this played out within a positive financial frame. The University had been in the black, and the total annual gift level had increased from $7.9 million to more than $12 million in the previous three years. Overall management of these fund-raising enterprises had been led by the vice chancellor for institutional advancement, first LaRue Boyd, then Jack Miller.

Such incentives led the board to announce on November 10, 1994, a five-year capital campaign to raise $140 million. At the Chancellors Society dinner, a vast scroll was unrolled, showing that $61,201,101, or nearly 43 percent of the total needed, had already been pledged, including more than $1 million from the faculty, staff and students.

Surveying these results, Ritchie mused, "Is it too much to hope, just maybe, that 100 years from now people will look back and say the real foundation for greatness at the University of Denver was laid at the end of the 20th century?" The plans for the outlay of money were indeed impressive. A full 21 percent, or a total of $32 million, was planned for scholarships, endowed chairs, and professorships. Another 29 percent, or $41.4 million, was slated to enhance student life through a wellness and sports center, student residences, and an international program. Partners in Scholarship and faculty research and

Joy Burns

development was allocated 5 percent, or $7.5 million. Resources for learning, including buildings and endowments, were given $45.1 million. These resources included a new science hall, a new Daniels College of Business building, a consolidated home for the three faculties and the School of Communication, and a University high school. Plans also included money for technological resources and a technological information center for the disabled. Underlining DU's commitment to industry and the community, the sum of $8.5 million (5 percent) was to be spent on the creation of Centers for Academic Distinction, with selected initiatives to include the environment, telecommunications, transportation, tourism management, and social responsibility. The campaign's $140 million total also included the College of Law Campaign of $8 million (6 percent) and annual support for current programs (4 percent), at $7.5 million.

The continuing success of this campaign encouraged the trustees to increase the campaign goal by another $10 million, with the closing date remaining at the end of the century. By this time, the whole process of determining how these funds could best be used was sufficiently under way for specific proposals to be presented. The planning process had begun with the formation of a Strategic Initiatives Committee to formulate a statement of mission and goals and to review proposals aimed at propelling the University successfully into the next millennium. The committee took these 193 initiatives, submitted by 170 faculty, and organized them into a coherent series of proposals. When the major capital campaign was announced in November 1994, the provost invited participation in a series of working groups to move the recommendations forward as academic realities. In January 1995, more than 160 faculty and administrative staff members began the academic strategic initiatives consolidation process. By the end of 1995, eight specific proposals had been endorsed by the trustees, with another seven approved the following November. For each, a strong case was made for timely necessity, appropriate resources in the area, and academic preparedness to initiate the program.

The five Centers for Academic Distinction received attention. An Environment Institute would be created, comprised of Centers for Montane Studies, for Sustainable Development, and for the Urban Environment. A second center, the Institute for Future Media, was comprised of the Center for Cable and Telecommunications and a Center for Digital Media Studies, the latter using campus-wide installations for exploration. A third center, one that had been in operation for several years, was renamed the Intermodal Transportation Institute. A new Tourism Management Center was established under the auspices of the School of Hotel, Restaurant, and Tourism Management. Finally, an Institute, or consortium, for Ethics, Values, and Social Responsibility was created, to include a Center for Professional Ethics, particularly concerned with law and business, a Diversity Institute, and a Community Outreach Center. For many, the establishment of these centers called to mind how much John Evans had supported Denver as a great hub, and how clearly he had seen the University's role in creating the great city of Denver.

Proposals were advanced for endowed chairs and professorships, as well as for scholarships for undergraduates and fellowships for graduate students. A substantial proposal was made for converting residence halls into "living and learning communities," much in the style of medieval and later housing arrangements. Support would be given to the Partners in Scholarship project and to endowments of faculty research and a more creative use of faculty time as related to the introduction and use of new digital media techniques. Another endowment would greatly increase resources for and the acquisition of printed journals and books, even though many speculated new technologies would seem to be ready in some distant future time to replace them. The proposal was made to create classrooms and offices as well as geographically distributed multimedia centers to benefit individual students in the quest for technological literacy. The systematic entrance on the Information Superhighway had been greatly expedited by a gift from the chancellor in February 1995 of $1.5 million over three years. The gift would enable a fiber-optic spine to be laid on both campuses as a high-tech foundation to which all areas would be linked. One part of this transformation was a Center for Adaptive Technology, designed to establish and equip a centrally located, easily accessible laboratory in Penrose Library aimed at providing teaching, learning, and research resources for the disabled in an academic environment. Another working group proposed plans for the complete renovation of the General Classroom and Business Administration Buildings to house Arts and Humanities, Social Services, and the School of Communication. This building will be renamed Sturm Hall.

During these years, the University became home to a number of national groups whose programs coincided with DU's overall goals. One such was the First Amendment Congress, a group of 17 national media organizations that carry on a continuing forum for dialogue and debate, primarily in community outreach. They arrived from the University of Colorado at Denver in February 1995. That same year, the trustees of the National Cable Television Center and Museum at Pennsylvania State University announced they would be moving to Denver. On the DU campus, they planned to erect a building costing $22.7 million and establish their operation with an annual budget of more than $1 million. One other example was the Interstate Commerce Commission, which, when it was disbanded in Washington, left a library of more than 70,000 items of great value. The University offered to take the archive and use it as a centerpiece of the institute. The offer being accepted, a group of rail and trucking firms subsidized the transportation first to Pueblo, then to Denver, at a cost of $100,000. Other arrivals included the Colorado Alliance for Asian Studies, from Colorado College, and the American Center for International Leadership.

The Face of the Campus

The ongoing transformation of the physical appearance of the school during these years was spectacular by any standard, beginning with the improvement of lawns, the addition of flowers and trees, the updating of tennis courts and parking lots, and of the signage designating buildings and the east entrance of the campus. The first structure to receive massive refurbishment was University Hall, beginning with a new copper roof and steel casements, with improvements paid for in part from surplus funds. In June 1995, a $3.5 million renovation was begun with reconstruction of the entire interior, to bring together admission, registrar, and financial services, and provide offices and classrooms on the upper levels. A completely new entrance on the north with ground-level approach and elevator, and a new south entrance and hallway, affording historical exhibits, would make the building more functional as well as more impressive and pleasing to the eye.

A gift to benefit astronomy and astrophysics came from an unexpected source. William Herschel Womble, a 1934 graduate in anthropology and an amateur astronomer, served in World War II and mined in Central America, then moved to Newport Beach, Calif., where his mother, Cora Taylor Womble Fowler, sold tract houses. Unmarried, Womble died there January 27, 1989, leaving a will

William Herschel Womble

247

Womble Observatory, just off Mount Evans summit

that included a gift of $3.753 million to the University for astronomical research. The use of these funds allowed the Department of Physics to reenter that field by creating an endowed chair. Physics also renamed the department, added an action component to its work, and after years of neglect, once again looked to the stars from Mount Evans. At the top of this peak, the University had had a laboratory since the Depression years. In 1972 it erected a building containing a 24" optical telescope. Located 50 miles west of Denver at an elevation of 14,264 feet, above 40 percent of the atmosphere (including 90 percent of its water vapor), Mount Evans was a perfect site for infrared imaging, planetary spectroscopy, the search for new stars, and the observation of comets. The construction of a new observatory began in October 1995. To this observatory, Eric and Barbara Meyer of the Meyer Foundation in Chicago contributed the optical elements, worth $1 million. They brought them from Chicago personally, just as Herbert Howe had done for the great refractor more than 100 years earlier. State-of-the-art technology would make communication with campus, schools, and the Gates Planetarium instantly available.

On campus, the historic Chamberlin Observatory and the small student observatory to the east had received grants of $100,000 from the Historical Society of Colorado and $8,000 from the 1772 Foundation, which, together with matching funds from the University, brought these facilities back to their earlier grandeur.

Meanwhile there was the inescapable impression of a somewhat incongruous collection of buildings, ranging from the massive stone structures of Old Main and the Iliff School, to Mary and Margery Reed's pillared halls, to modern slab construction. Many questioned whether they could be brought together in some happy and companionable conformity, while preserving their integrity. A solution became imperative with the promise of a string of new edifices. To help solve this problem, the University appointed a full time University architect, Cabell Childress. Childress, a 1954 architectural engineering graduate of Georgia Tech, left his highly successful business in 1992 to set up shop on campus. Early on, it was agreed that a unified approach was possible, and that the use of the pattern of brick and limestone in the Reed buildings offered the best visual approach for buildings best suited to the highly inventive mission of the school at the end of this century.

In 1994, construction was begun on a $1.5 million facilities management building at the corner of East Wesley Avenue and South Race Street, to house paint and general shops, administrative offices, a garage, and work space for the University architect. What would have been a solid but unedifying block was enhanced with copper trim and designed to echo the brick and limestone facades now appropriate for much of the campus. East on University Boulevard, one could see an open space extending from Iliff southward and could imagine here sometime in the future a performing arts and music center, a rendering of which was already on the drawing board.

Cabell Childress and Mark Rodgers

Facilities plant

The Face of the Campus

At the corner of South Gaylord Street and East Iliff Avenue is the imposing edifice of the new F. W. Olin Hall, a copper-roofed neoclassical building to house the departments of biological sciences, chemistry, and environmental science, previously located in 11 different buildings. This 44,000-square-foot structure is the result of a donation by the F. W. Olin Foundation of New York, with the original cost of $6.5 million augmented by an additional gift of $560,000 to complete construction. Chancellor Ritchie commented that the success of the University's application for the gift was due to "the quality of our faculty, our students, our programs for teaching and learning science, and the sound thinking that has gone into planning the future of science education and research." The new edifice became the cornerstone of science education facilities, including the Boettcher Center and the Seeley G. Mudd Building.

Just south and around the corner of the Mary Reed Building, stands a 70-foot-bronze flagpole with a limestone base, the gift of the Class of 1995, which raised $10,000 to meet a matching gift of $10,000 from an anonymous donor.

But at present, students of the Class of 2000 can remember a September evening in 1996 when they walked in procession between lines of luminaria in front of Margery Reed to participate in the initial Pioneer Passage ceremonies. Standing there, they could see all stages of development around campus. The ground on which they stood had been given by Rufus Clark to John Evans and the board before 1890, to create a new venture beyond Denver's city limits. Behind them was the first building, University Hall, opened in 1892. Before them was Mary Reed's 1928 gift of one of the two Collegiate Gothic buildings that set the pattern for the buildings of the 1990s. To their left was all that remained of Buchtel Chapel, one of the two north towers, which now contains a victory bell, the gift of the Class of 1992.

To their right stood the Alumni Gym. Built with $25,000 in subscriptions from alumni and students, it opened in the fall of 1910. It was demolished in 1997 to make the way for a new home for the Daniels College of Business, now under construction and slated for completion in the summer of 1999. Like Olin Hall and the new wellness and athletics center, the new business building was designed to embody not only state-of-the-art technology and the finest architectural details, but the creation of a new model of faculty and student learning. Here, as the chancellor pointed out, students "will learn to be team builders, leaders, and valued members of their communities in surroundings whose quality matches the curriculum that Bill Daniels' philosophy has helped shape."

In 1995, Bill Daniels made a second gift of $11 million, this one toward the $22 million needed to complete the building. The plans called for two interlocking edifices, one three stories, the other six, for a total of 100,000 square feet with two levels of underground parking. Of specially fired brick to match the Reed buildings, cut limestone trim, and finely detailed adornments, the new business college would contain a Great Room, a two-story atrium, the latest in technology classrooms, and break-out rooms—all speaking of excellence in thought and operation.

Science Hall, 1912–1997

University Hall renovation

F. W. Olin Hall

Leo Block Alumni Center

Jay G. Piccinati

*Carl Williams (right), Joost Eijsbouts, and the bells of DU's carillon
at the Royal Eijsbouts foundry in Asten, Netherlands.*

Across Evans, an addition to the Ricks Center was completed in 1996, part of a plan to make South York Street a cul-de-sac opening on Asbury Avenue, with new playing fields at the north end and a reworking of the parking lots. The price for all this would be $2.5 million, with costs to be borne by donations, University contributions, and foundation money. West along Asbury, space was allocated for the University of Denver High School. Meanwhile, the high school opened in 1995 on the second floor of Margery Reed.

At 2000 South Gaylord Street stands the headquarters of the alumni association. At the south end is a recently completed two-story addition, containing offices and conference space. The costs, including gardens next to the house, amounted to $550,000, and were covered by alumni and University contributions. Alumni and friends purchased inscribed brick pavers that line the garden paths. In 1996, the edifice was named the Leo Block Alumni Center, in recognition of a generous donor who also funded an annual lectureship attracting controversial and cutting-edge faculty.

In March 1996, it was announced that Donald and Susan Sturm had donated $5 million to restructure the business administration and general classroom buildings completely. Donald Sturm, a Denver banker, is a trustee and 1958 graduate of the DU law school. Susan Sturm is a member of the Ricks Center board. Sturm Hall will bring together all the humanities and social sciences departments, currently housed in six separate buildings. The building will feature "smart classrooms," the latest in video and computer equipment, laboratory spaces, a news writing lab, and a facility for student television production, with office space for about 100 faculty.

The Daniel L. Ritchie Center for Sports and Wellness, slated for opening in 1999, will be, upon completion, the most imposing structure on the University of Denver campus. The center was named by a unanimous decision of the board in January 1996 "in recognition of the chancellor's extraordinary dedication and vision for the future of all aspects of DU's life. Naming the premiere campus center for him lets the community know what his leadership means for us." Ritchie's remarks at the time were to the point: "The broad definition of wellness is central to the future of quality education. We think of it in the balanced development of the physical, emotional, intellectual, and spiritual self—the 'whole person.'"

Extending all the way from Buchtel Boulevard to Asbury Avenue, the complex includes the following:

Magness Arena. Located in the center of the facility, the arena features up to 6,200 theatre-style seats for hockey, 7,200 seats for basketball, and 6,000 seats for concerts, gymnastics, and volleyball. When configured for hockey and skating, the ice surface has an 85 x 200-foot surface for North American rules play. The arena was named for the late Bob Magness, a cable television executive and industry pioneer in Denver, founder of Tele-Communications, Inc. in 1956, and for his wife Sharon, who in 1995 gave $10 million for the facility. Magness died in 1997.

Donald and Susan Sturm

Sharon and Bob Magness

Hamilton Gymnasium. The northwest corner of the complex houses a gymnasium with seating for 2,800. This venue features retractable seats, allowing for diversified use of the facility and creating space for three basketball or volleyball courts. Designed primarily for varsity, intramural, and recreational athletics, the gymnasium will also serve community youth athletic leagues. The space and its equipment were the gift of $3.5 million from Frederic C. and Jane M. Hamilton, he a business executive and she a trustee since 1975 and a founding member of Pioneer Sportswomen, leaders in the development of women's sports on campus.

Gates Field House. At the south end of the center, a 41,000-square-foot field house invites students, faculty, staff, and members of the Denver community to participate in programs to improve and maintain good health and physical well-being through exercise and other stress-management programs. The field house contains three courts for basketball, volleyball, and badminton, a squash court, and two racquetball/handball courts. A 10,000-square-foot gymnastics center, at the south end of the field house, is the practice site for the women's varsity team and an extensive junior program. The Gates Foundation made the largest single gift in its history—$3 million—for the facility.

Coors Fitness Center. Featuring a 10,000-square-foot space for weight training, cardiovascular, and conditioning exercise, the fitness center has 20,000 square feet of exercise rooms for dance aerobics, martial arts, yoga, and similar programs. Classrooms and offices finish out this first-class fitness and wellness facility for $2.5 million.

El Pomar Natatorium. The 30,000-square-foot state-of-the-art natatorium forms the center's southwest quadrant. The primary pool is a 50-meter by 25-yard handicapped-accessible Olympic-length pool with two 3-meter and two 1-meter spring diving boards. Permanent seating for 300, with room for more temporary seating, completes this $2 million facility, funded by the El Pomar Foundation of Colorado Springs, established in 1939 by Spencer Penrose, who years earlier gave the lead gift on the University's Penrose Library.

Joy Burns Arena. A second North American-sized rink was constructed to the north and east of the Magness Arena. Completed in 1997, the arena accommodates varsity practice and most needs of the youth hockey and figure skating programs. The rink seats 300 and shares a food court and lounge with the Magness Arena. The interior includes some spectator seats from the old arena, a lobby with vending area, customer counter, and offices. Burns, a prominent Denver business and civic leader, avid sports enthusiast, and chair of the DU Board of Trustees since 1990, contributed $1.5 million toward the overall cost. Inducted into the DU Sports Hall of Fame in 1997, Burns helped establish DU's Pioneer Sportswomen in 1976.

Rising above the center is a 218-foot carillon tower. The $1.5 million cost will be covered by a gift from Trustee Carl Williams. The tower will contain 66 bells, the largest of which is to be the Chancellor's bell, weighing 11,684

Frederic and Jane Hamilton

pounds. A brick structure with an exterior of Utah sandstone and limestone and a gold roof, it will match the rest of the Ritchie complex. A spiral staircase will lead to the bell level, while the third level, with access from the spine, will feature a meditation room. The tower will be illuminated at night, with special lighting for athletic victories.

Other gifts benefitted the center. When in March 1996, the Boettcher Foundation announced a gift of $2.5 million "to expand and improve services for students," the Board of Trustees added this sum to the total working capital for the center. The Boettcher Foundation and others were particularly impressed with the determination to make athletics and wellness available not only to athletes and students, but to the public—as participants as well as spectators.

The University's tennis courts received a $2.4 million renovation to create the Benjamin F. Stapleton, Jr. Tennis Pavilion. It has six top-quality outdoor courts for game competition and varsity practice. All courts have flood lighting, and there is grandstand seating for 300 on court one, above the locker rooms, pro shop, and concession stands.

The University plans to construct a 2,000-to-4,500-seat soccer/lacrosse stadium to the west of the Ritchie Center. It will have a sand-based drainage system similar to the city's Coors (baseball) Field and is planned to be one of the finest soccer/lacrosse surfaces in the western United States.

On the northern boundary of the campus is a 3.5 acre site for the National Cable Center and Museum, a free-standing institution that will lease the land for $1 per year. Facing Buchtel Boulevard and open to the public, it will also be open on the south to all the intellectual resources for education, research, and training the University has to offer. This two-story building of about 40,000 square feet, designed by the firm of Rogers, Nagel, and Leinhart, will conform to the other buildings in the area. Cost is estimated at $15 million for the facility and equipment, with $10 million in in-kind contributions and another $20 million for endowment. Plans for this center, which was at Pennsylvania State University until 1995, call for groundbreaking in April 1999 and opening in the year 2000.

Goals of the center are threefold—to educate the widest public, to ensure the preservation of the heritage of communication, and to promote professional training in cutting-edge technologies. The institution would have five major components, beginning with a library, embodying not only a large, traditional collection but also the use of innovative technologies to distribute digital material on the Internet and by multimedia. The center will provide training and education as well as curricular services for colleges and universities with management to be by contract with the University. A third component, the museum, although modest in size will be global in scope, as a "virtual museum" concentrating on outreach enabling it to educate a vast audience through traveling exhibits and other offerings. Within the museum will be a Cable Television Hall of Fame, celebrating industry pioneers and inducting laureates. The center's Demonstration Academy, with an executive briefing room, will be

Architect's original rendering of the Daniel L. Ritchie Sports and Wellness Center

Joy Burns Arena

used by industry members, professional organizations, and trade associations. With the goal of reaching millions rather than thousands, the center will be dedicated to producing programs, updating an enhanced World Wide Web site, and producing educational products on CD-ROM for retail and institutional sale.

On the southeast corner of Evans and Columbine is the Buchtel Bungalow, one of the many rare gems of University Park. Here Chancellor Henry Augustus Buchtel lived with his family from 1905 to 1924 while simultaneously serving as governor of Colorado from 1906 to 1908. Thanks to the efforts of the University Women's Club, a restoration is underway, aided by a grant from the Colorado Historical Society. Two upstairs bedrooms are available for visiting professors and guest lecturers, and extensive landscaping, including the planting of the rare crimson and yellow DU rose, is in the planning stages. This building provides a continuous memorial to the University's highly creative and much beloved third chancellor.

Toward a Wider World: Denver and Internationalization

Although the University had been involved with the world outside academia for a long time, particularly through the Department of History and Graduate School of International Studies, recent systematic efforts, beginning with projects and programs to relate the school to its neighborhood, have been highly successful. It has been said that "one third of the University's mission and goals statements demonstrate one important fact: With increasing momentum, we are opening our doors to the community." That relationship has always been present, but now it is being woven into the fabric of the strategic plan.

Efforts to relate the scholarly pursuits of the Faculty of Arts and Humanities with the broader Denver community resulted in the creation of the Humanities Institute in 1991. This format provided a forum for local and national speakers on crucial issues and sought to encourage a stimulating public dialogue among faculty. In addition, so-called salons provided evenings of conversation between town and gown on topics as varied as democracy and violence, poetry, and music and theatre. In May 1997, the institute co-sponsored the fifth Norwest CultureFest, "a place of discovery, where people of all ages and backgrounds can come to appreciate the uniqueness and difference of many cultures." The institute is also regularly involved with the Colorado Symphony, the Colorado Ballet, and the Denver Art Museum.

The Bridge Project, initiated in 1990 by the Graduate School of Social Work, sought to help improve the lives of children in Denver's Lincoln Park housing project, offering peer tutoring, daycare, mentoring, and scholarship aid. The project was successful from the beginning. The Community Action Project (CAP), working on a variety of long-term activities from tutoring to aiding the homeless, enlisted a thousand DU students, whose reports described the values

International House

they had discovered in such service. That same year, the University adopted West High School, working with the Denver Community College to tackle the problem of reducing the drop-out rate of students and increasing the number of students who would be college bound. A high degree of success is being achieved in both areas. Chancellor Ritchie, despite a busy schedule, became a consultant to the Denver Public School system. As he said, "We must substantially improve the Denver Schools. If we do not, and soon, our city will be in serious difficulty within a generation. A large number of our people will be economic burdens, not economic contributors."

DU's commitment to community involvement was underlined in the requirement of community service for graduation, most notably in the "ethical MBA" degree of the Daniels College of Business.

In the fall of 1989, the thinking of chancellor and provost turned to the relations of DU with the rest of the world. Acknowledging that Denver had always been a pioneer in international studies, they asked whether the entire University, working together, might make an even more significant contribution to world awareness and understanding. Consequently, the International Studies and Activities Task Force was activated. A white paper in 1992 outlined the strengths and weaknesses of all present efforts, and came out strongly for definite action. The University was ready to embark on the greatest program of internationalization in its history. As Ritchie pointed out in his 1993

Commencement address, "Our mission is to prepare all of our students for life and work in our global community."

To coordinate all the activities in this area and to recommend further expansion, Ved Nanda, internationally recognized lawyer-activist and director of the international legal studies program at the College of Law, was appointed vice provost for internationalization. Acting as a catalyst, he brought together a staff and responsibilities from hitherto-scattered areas, including the the study abroad program and international student advising into one location, a former sorority house at 2200 S. Josephine Street. From this office, a vast array of new enterprises could be formulated. The critical roles of the Graduate School of International Studies, the Daniels College of Business, and University College in all these activities could receive further University-wide support.

Denver's outreach encompassed a large variety of governmental and educational enterprises throughout the world. Working partnerships have been established with schools in Costa Rica, Italy (the University of Bologna and John Cabot University in Rome), China (the People's University and Beijing University), England, Japan, Spain, and elsewhere. The business college, with its degree in international business and interdisciplinary graduate programs, created the Center for Brazilian-American Business and Social Research.

Joining the University in these years were a number of organizations, including the Colorado Alliance for Asian Studies and the American Center for

University College

International Leadership, whose aim was to "give emerging and established leaders from America and other countries opportunities for ongoing dialogue through talks, conferences, and training in leadership skills."

Thus the University opened its doors to the community, strengthening its ties to the new world of global business and intellectual activity. This concerted effort, building on long-continuing participation in world affairs, was deepened and widened by incorporation into all strategic planning, and advanced by the infusion of increasingly adequate financial support.

The Knowledge Revolution and Physical Change

In April 1994, the strategic initiative subgroup on information technology concluded that "a technological revolution is sweeping the U.S. and world economies and totally transforming the social world of learning and teaching." Seeing a tidal wave of new technology, it proposed steps to increase technological literacy among faculty and students and recommended state-of-the-art facilities to satisfy these imperatives. To this end, the subgroup examined more than 60 proposals submitted by faculty and staff members. The recommendations included the establishment of a permanent information technology task force, a series of strategically placed laboratories, and the development of Penrose Library as the nerve center for all these operations. Recommendations also called for a panorama of "networking" operations that would make on-campus communication easy and bring the widest world into classroom and office alike.

With Chancellor Ritchie's $1.5 million donation, such networks would "provide our students with access to the most advanced online resources in the world, from laboratories and classrooms to their own residence halls. It will transform their learning environment," according to James LaVita, chair of the Department of Mathematics and Computer Sciences. Additional sums, from the Johnson Foundation and other donors, were available for the improvement of library activities. A substantial sum went to improving technology and the creation of a Center for Teaching and Learning.

Penrose Library was now fully recovered from the frustrating "reorganization" days of the mid-'80s, when staff morale had been at a low ebb, and new acquisitions severly reduced. Now with its own dean, Nancy Allen, the first systems librarian head, important technological improvements began to take shape. The card catalogue gave way to CARL, the Colorado Alliance of Research Libraries, an electronic search tool that gave access to other libraries on the screen. Penrose had more than 2.9 million items, including some 5,000 subscriptions, a substantial new video collection, and thousands of microforms and documents. With this rapidly expanding collection, the addition of a copy center, and an array of computer terminals, the library was running out of space. Systematic weeding-out of excess materials and the introduction of movable compact shelving for special collections brought some relief. Other problems included the rapidly accelerating costs of accessions, especially serials, somewhat alleviated by the continuous creative financial assistance of the Women's Library Association. Particularly strong collections have included those on Judaica, especially the Ira Beck Archives, the Civil War, railroads, and Colorado history, as well as the Husted cookbook collection, and the Carson-Brierly Dance library.

In their search for the best electronic cataloguing system, the librarians decided to continue the use of CARL, but in 1997 opted to join Innovative Interface Incorporated (Triple I) in an alliance with the University of Colorado, the CU Medical Center, and Colorado State University. The Denver Public Library, Regis University, University of Wyoming, and Colorado School of Mines remain on the old system. However, despite the use of different on-line systems, all library users can connect to any of the catalogues. Thanks to major grants from the Helen K. and Arthur E. Johnson Foundation, the University library system participates in a global on-line catalogue, where searches are made easier with the use of point-and-click graphical screen design and the World Wide Web.

The Tradition Is Deepened and Enlarged: A Summary

Within all this change came a deeper appreciation of the University's history and a systematic attempt to make the past more real to all those interested in its progress. In a 1994 speech to the Newcomen Society, Chancellor Ritchie prefaced his remarks by commenting that

> It is not a story about a university in Denver, but rather the University of Denver because the personalities who shaped and sustained us are, in many cases, the same people who built the city of Denver. These names march through the generations, an impressive testament to the pioneers who settled this land and who even today contribute to its character. Names like Evans, Loveland, Warren, Elbert, Moffat, Byers, Cheesman. Names in more recent years like Boettcher, Phipps, Daniels, and Coors.

In the names of buildings and programs and in many other ways, memories of the past have been preserved. The Buchtel Bungalow is a focal point of homage to the third chancellor. University Hall, now handsomely restored, will contain historical exhibits. And the DU rose will one day bloom again on campus. The story goes that Chancellor Buchtel, in a visit to the Western Slope in 1913, obtained cuttings of an old-fashioned Austrian Copper, red and yellow in color. Back in Denver, botany professor Ira E. Cutler propagated new plants and gave them to colleagues so that the rose was found on campus and in gardens all over University Park, blooming for only a few weeks around commencement time. They gradually disappeared, leaving only three healthy bushes by 1992. These were turned over to Denver Botanic Gardens for propagation and eventual return to the campus. Blooms of an Austrian Copper were used in the first Pioneer Passage in the Margery Reed Quadrangle in September 1996 to commemorate the arrival of the Class of 2000.

Another tradition involved the now-famous red vest. At a breakfast long ago, Chancellor Buchtel once donned a heavy red wool vest, flecked with gold and decorated with agate buttons. He came to wear it on special occasions to symbolize joy and pride and hopes of gridiron victory. One year, after defeating the University of Colorado, victorious DU quarterbacks received similar vests. More recently, Chancellor Alter took to wearing such a vest; then Chancellor Ritchie revived the custom and placed Buchtel's original vest on display in his conference room. The 1996 Founders Day ceremonies honored recipients of various awards with red vests, thus inaugurating yet another custom with venerable roots.

The remarkably clear and succinct statement of mission and goals reflects the University's underlying purposes of higher learning (see Appendix). The mission and goals have undergirded all programs, the raising and spending of money, particularly by the capital campaign, and the relations with the world outside.

To bring home to the academic community the necessity of and opportunity for carrying out these goals, Chancellor Ritchie presented his annual Convocation addresses, commented to the press, and lectured to a variety of audiences. He articulated his firm convictions on leadership, values, research, and internationalization, quality and curriculum, and above all, on the purposes and results of a high quality education here and now. In responding to criticism that today's higher education in general is less meaningful and rigorous than yesterday's, he replied, in an editorial in the *University of Denver Journal* in the spring of 1996:

> The University of Denver, with its agenda firmly centered on students, has a clear vision of what constitutes a well-rounded, educated person. Quality in every respect is our measure and our goal. I hope you will agree that we are holding the line on a rigorous and thoughtful undergraduate experience.

Marion Gottesfeld and Bill Coors
chaired the highly successful University of Denver Capital Campaign.

Buchtel Bungalow

Understanding that the University was at "a defining moment in history," he summed up his beliefs:

> Our mission is to prepare all of our students for life and work in our global community . . . to provide the intellectual means and the moral support to develop leaders of tomorrow who can take us to a prosperous, just, and purposeful world.

Underlining all these projects, he saw the need for "emphasis on quality and its value in the education of our students, in the interaction of our students and faculty, and in the way we plan for the future. . . . People want to give to a great program, not something ordinary."

As the University prepares for the next century, Ritchie's concluding thoughts in the 1993 Newcomen address bring together the past, the present, and the future in perspective:

> Looking back across 130 years of boom and bust, glory and struggle, incredible energy and devotion to our mission, our challenge is clear: to provide the financial means and management systems so that the University of Denver can achieve the potential that is here, the potential to be a world class institution.

The vision is clear:

> We have in the University of Denver a venerable and magic place where the Pioneer spirit burns brightly and faculty and staff care passionately about their students. In today's "Profscam" world, that is a precious heritage. Do we have the courage and the financial and managerial savvy to let it soar to its potential and not crash? Stay tuned.

The man who shared those thoughts was described by Chancellor Emeritus Chester Alter in these words:

> A wise, caring, and generous man; an astute manager and entrepreneur with a great civic purpose; a man of vision tempered with a sense of what is possible; a leader as well as a servant of society. He cares for the soil as well as for the soul of America and Colorado.

The Tradition Is Deepened and Enlarged: A Summary

Those who tuned into the University history at the end of 1997 saw the promise not of a crash but a boom. Campus construction proliferated. Progress in building was somewhat hampered by the building boom in the Denver metropolitan region, as concrete was in short supply.

In November 1997, the annual Chancellor's Dinner was the occasion for a special announcement: The University had reached its $150 capital campaign goal, just three years into the five-year campaign. The chancellor announced an expansion of the campaign goal to $200 million, and enthusiasm and support were almost euphoric.

Thus this period in the history of the University comes into clear focus. The vision and determined hard work of the sixteenth chancellor and those of a dedicated administrative staff and faculty, are combined with evermore involved students and alumni, as well as generous supporters, all engaged in a great endeavor. They show that the University has reached not the sad beginning of the end, but the glorious end of the beginning.

Renaissance Reading room in Old Mary Reed Library

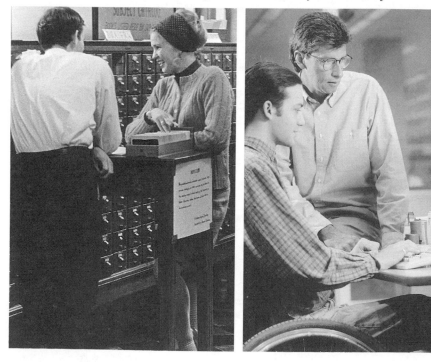

Card Catalogues in Hallway, Mary Reed

*A Student of the Nineties Using
Electronic Technology*

A Bibliographic Note

Since this is an informal chronicle, designed for general use rather than formal history, the usual footnotes have been dispensed with. Full documentation, however, is available. The source of most of the references is obvious from the text. I am indebted to the many people who have offered personal reminiscences from the 1920s to the present. The University is rich in archival material, both in manuscript and printed materials as well as a veritable host of photographs. Two other collections, the Western History Division of the Denver Public Library and the State of Colorado Historical Society, have been abundantly helpful, particularly for newspaper sources.

On his retirement as professor of history, Leslie Wiles Scofield organized and copied materials concerning the University and made them available to researchers. After him, George Snyder became director of archives and further organized the holdings; he was succeeded by Steven Fisher, the present director of Archives and Special Collections.

Michael McGiffert's *The Higher Learning in Colorado: An Historical Study, 1860–1940* (Denver, Sage Books, 1964) is of continuing value and importance. McGiffert also directed three useful master's theses.

In 1961, Donald E. Angel wrote "A History of the University of Denver, 1880–1900," and Donald E. Connor covered "The History of the University of Denver: The Buchtel Chancellorship, 1900–1920." In 1963, Gerard Eugene Mayer produced "A History of the University of Denver, 1920–1940." In 1985, Allan O. Pfnister directed a doctoral dissertation by Joan H. Beasley, "The University of Denver Defines Its Purpose: A History of the Junior College and the Community College, 1940–1961." For academic lists, see Phyllis Bay's "Degrees Conferred, University of Denver, 1882–1995" and "University of Denver, Departments and Courses, 1881–1946."

Unfortunately, no manuscript sources have survived from the period of the Colorado Seminary, but Jeannette Joan Dunleavy's master's thesis, "Early History of Colorado Seminary and the University of Denver" (1935) collected all the newspaper articles connected with the school during those years, 1860–1884. For more on the life of John Evans, see Edgar C. McMechan's *Life of Governor John Evans* (Denver, Wahlgreen, 1924) and Harry E. Kelsey Jr.'s *Frontier Capitalist: The Life of John Evans* (Denver, State Historical Society of Colorado, 1969), originally a DU dissertation, as well as Robert B. Rhode's "Governor John Evans, Builder of Two Universities," a master's thesis, 1952. Bernard Knittel's "John Evans, Speaker and Empire Builder," a doctoral dissertation from 1950, deals with Evans' public personality. For personal reminiscences, see Susan Riley Ashley's "Reminiscences of Colorado in the Early Sixties," *Colorado Magazine* 13 (Nov. 1936): 219–30; George C. Anderson, "Touring Kansas and Colorado in 1871, the Journal of G. A. C. Partane," *Kansas Historical Quarterly* 22 (Autumn 1956); Rezin H. Constant, "Colorado as Seen by a Visitor of 1880," *Colorado Magazine* 12 (May 1935): 103–16; William Crawford, "Colorado as Seen by a Home Missionary, 1863–1868," *Colorado Magazine* 12 (March 1935): 60–69; Robert Latta "Denver in the 1880s," *Colorado Magazine* 18 (July 1941): 130–36; George Richardson, Diary, 1861–1864, manuscript deposited at the Iliff School of Theology; Louis L. Simonin, *The Rocky Mountain West in 1867* (reprinted, 1966).

Thomas R. Garth published *A Life of Henry Augustus Buchtel* (Denver, Peerless, 1937). See also Allen D. Breck's *William Gray Evans* (University of Denver, 1964) and *John Evans of Denver* (Boulder, Pruett, 1972). For Methodism in Colorado, see J. Alton Templin and Allen D. Breck, eds., *The Methodist, Evangelical, and United Brethren Churches in the Rockies 1950–1976* (Denver, Rocky Mountain Conference, 1977).

The chief sources for this history, in addition to printed materials, are the detailed reports of the Board of Trustees and those of various colleges and programs. The student newspaper, *The Clarion,* the University annual, *Kynewisbok,* the faculty-staff newsletter, *The Source* and its predecessors, and the *University of Denver Journal* have all been of great value.

Some beginnings have been made on departmental histories. These include: Cecil L. Franklin, "History of the Study of Religion at the University of Denver," *Iliff Review* 34 (Winter 1977): 3–18; Bernard Spilka and Sabre J. Brown, "A History of Psychology at the University of Denver 1864–1930" (April 1976), mimeographed, 22 pages; Ben M. Cherrington, *The Social Science Foundation of the University of Denver: A Personal Reminiscence* (The Foundation, 1973). See also Alton Barbour's "A Brief History of the School of Communication."

Manuscript histories of the early years of the College of Business Administration were compiled by Deans Frank C. Onstott (1949) and Theodore H. Cutler (1958, 1979). Alton Barbour, chair of human communication studies, has given us a manuscript account of that area.

The College of Law has produced *Lawyers from Denver, A Centennial History of the University of Denver College of Law, 1892–1992,* the work of Philip E. Gauthier, in 1997.

Scholarly journals include *The Denver Journal of International Law and Policy, The Denver Law Review, Preventive Law Reports,* and the *Transportation Law Journal,* all produced by the College of Law. The English department is responsible for another established journal, *The Denver Quarterly.* From the Graduate School of International Studies we have, among others, *Africa Today. Foundations of Physics* is published from Physics House at 2408 S. Gaylord.

See also Harold B. Secrist, "With Eyes on the Stars: How the Spirit of Chamberlin Observatory Inspired 1953 Student Custodian to Develop Apollo Simulator" (MS March 1997).

Charter of the Colorado Seminary
An Act to Incorporate the Colorado Seminary
Approved March 5, 1864

> *Be it Enacted by the Council and House of Representatives
> of Colorado Territory:*

Section 1. That John Evans, Samuel H. Elbert, W. N. Byers, H. Burton, A. B. Case, J. G. Vawter, A. J. Gill, W. D. Pease, Edwin Scudder, J. H. Morrison, Warren Hussey, J. W. Smith, D. H. Moffat Jr., R. E. Whitsett, C. A. Cook, John Cree, Amos Steck, J. M. Chivington, J. B. Doyle, Henry Henson, Amos Widner, John T. Lynch, Milo Lee, J. B. Chaffee, Lewis Jones, O. A. Willard, W. H. H. Loveland and Robert Berry be, and they are, hereby constituted a body politic and corporate for the purpose of founding, directing and maintaining an institution of learning, to be styled the Colorado Seminary, and in manner hereinafter prescribed to have perpetual succession, with full power to sue and be sued, plead and be impleaded, adopt and alter at pleasure a seal, acquire, hold and convey property, real, personal and mixed, to the extent they may judge necessary for carrying into effect the objects of this corporation, and, generally, to perform such other acts as may be necessary and proper therefor.

Section 2. Said Trustees, at their first meeting, shall be divided into four classes of seven in each class, which class shall hold office for one, two, three, and four years, respectively, dating from the first day of July, 1864; their successors shall be appointed whenever terms expire, or vacancies for any cause exist, by the annual conference of the Methodist Episcopal Church, within whose bounds the City of Denver may be included, but all of said Trustees and their successors shall continue in office until their successors are elected.

Section 3. No test of religious faith shall ever be applied as a condition of admission into said Seminary, but the Trustees shall have power to adopt all proper rules and regulations for the government of the conduct of teachers and pupils, and the management of all affairs pertaining to said institution.

Section 4. They shall have full power to confer all degrees and emoluments customary to be given by similar institutions.

Section 5. Such property as may be necessary for carrying out the design of the Seminary in the best manner, while used exclusively for such purposes, shall be free from all taxation.

Section 6. In all cases, a majority of the Board of Trustees shall constitute a quorum for transacting any business, or said majority may vest the power of the Trustees in an Executive Committee, or agent of their number, at pleasure.

Section 7. This shall be deemed a public act, and be in force and take effect from and after its passage.

Mission and Goals

The mission of the University of Denver is to provide education of the highest quality. We define quality in education through

• **Fostering Values.** A campus culture in which ethical behavior and individual, social, and environmental responsibility are integrated into our educational enterprise.

• **A Global Perspective.** Internationalization of our curriculum, faculty, and student body to prepare students for life in our global community.

• **Diversity.** Unity and understanding in a community of diverse faculty, students, and staff.

• **Scholarship and Research.** The highest quality scholarship, research, and creative activity by faculty and students.

• **Undergraduate Distinctiveness.** A distinctive undergraduate program, based on the traditional values of liberal learning, with mentoring by faculty, an emphasis on interdisciplinary learning, and the integration of scholarship and research into the undergraduate experience.

• **Talent Development.** Pedagogical innovation that emphasizes and encourages active and experiential learning.

• **Technological Literacy.** The effective use of learning and information resources and computer technology.

• **Rigorous Self-Assessment.** The assessment of learning outcomes to sustain the highest quality of instruction.

• **Professional Leadership.** Regional and national leadership in selected areas of specialized professional education.

• **Lifelong Learning.** A commitment to education for life and to the values of lifelong learning for both traditional and adult learners.

• **Community Commitment.** Student, faculty, and staff involvement in the community and the use of the University's creative energies to address cultural, social, technological, and economic issues in the region and the nation.

• **Responsible Management.** Efficient, responsible and careful stewardship of all resources in our University organization and management practices.

Presidents and Chancellors of the University of Denver (Colorado Seminary)

Presidents of the Colorado Seminary

1.	George S. Phillips	October 24, 1864–March 30, 1865
2.	George Richardson	March 1865–June 1866
3.	Bethuel Thomas Vincent	September 1866–June 1867
4.	P. D. Barnhart	August 13, 1867–May 22, 1868

Chancellors of the University of Denver

1.	David Hastings Moore	October 4, 1880–June 1889
	Ammi Bradford Hyde, acting	1889–90
2.	William Fraser McDowell	1890–June 1899
	Herbert Alonzo Howe, acting	July–December 1899
3.	Henry Augustus Buchtel	December 1899–September 1920
	Wilbur D. Engle, acting	September 1920–November 1922
4.	Heber Reece Harper	November 1922–January 1927
	Wilbur D. Engle, acting	January 1927–July 1928
5.	Frederick Maurice Hunter	July 1928–September 1935
6.	David Shaw Duncan	September 1935–March 1941
7.	Caleb Frank Gates Jr.	March 1941–November 1943
8.	Ben Mark Cherrington	November 1943–February 1946
	Caleb Frank Gates Jr.	February 1946–August 1947
	James F. Price, acting	August 1947–April 1948
9.	James F. Price	April–October 1948
10.	Alfred Clarence Nelson, interim	October 1948–November 1949
11.	Albert Charles Jacobs	November 1949–March 1953
12.	Chester M. Alter	August 1, 1953–July 31, 1966
		(on leave, August 1, 1966–June 16, 1967)
	Wilbur Castell Miller, acting	August 1, 1966–August 31, 1967
13.	Maurice Bernard Mitchell	September 1, 1967–March 10, 1978
	Allan O. Pfnister, acting	March 10, 1978–October 4, 1978
14.	Ross Pritchard	October 5, 1978–January 7, 1984
15.	Dwight Morrell Smith	January 18, 1984–July 1, 1989
16.	Daniel L. Ritchie	July 1, 1989–present

Board of Trustees, 1997

Members

Morley Ballantine	1983–present
Patrick D. Bowlen	1987–present
Joy S. Burns, chair	1981–present
William K. Coors, vice chair	1978–present
Edward W. Estlow, vice chair	1976–present
Steven W. Farber	1997–present
Nathaniel R. Goldston III	1989–present
Leo K. Goto	1991–present
Marion S. Gottesfeld	1953–present
Jane Hamilton, secretary	1976–present
Phillip J. Hogue	1990–present

Provosts and Vice Chancellors of the University of Denver

Student Affairs

Barbara Mertz	1968	John L. Blackburn	1969–74
Frank J. Vattano	1968–69	Tom Goodale	1981–88

Deans, Directors, and Chairs

Directors and Chairs of the Denver Research Institute
(became the University of Denver Research Institute, 1996)

Shirley Alonzo Johnson	1957–84	Samuel R. Freeman, chair	1994-96
Jerry Plunkett	1984–89	Carl Lyday, chair	1996–present
Larry Brown	1990–94		

Deans and Directors of Graduate Studies

Herbert Alonzo Howe	1913–17	Robert C. Amme	1975–80
David Shaw Duncan	1928–33	Mary Kime	1981–86
Wilbur Engle	1934–36	Robert D. Coombe	1986–87
Alfred Clarence Nelson	1937–47	Eric Gould	1987–92
Nathaniel Evers	1970–74		

Librarians, Library Directors, and Deans (Penrose Library)

Ammi Bradford Hyde, honorary	1909	Stuart G. Baillie	1953–65
Linda M. Clatworthy	1921–33	H. William Axford	1965–67
Malcolm Glen Wyer	1933–46	Melvin J. Klatt	1967–69
Joe Hare, assistant	1934–46	Morris Schertz	1969–90
John Van Male	1946–48	Sallye Smith, interim	1990–92
Donald E. Strout	1948–52	Nancy Allen, dean	1992–present

Directors of the School of Librarianship and Graduate School of Library and Information Management

Malcolm Glen Wyer	1931–48	Lucille Hatch	1966–68
Harriet Howe	1948–50	Margaret Knox Goggin	1968–79
Donald E. Strout	1950–53	James K. Foyle	1979–80
Leslie Post	1953–55	Ben Franckowiak	1981–84
Stuart G. Baillie	1955–66		

Deans of the College of Arts and Sciences

Joseph C. Shattuck	1885–88	Malcolm A. Love	1948–50
Ammi Bradford Hyde	1888–92	Frank A. Dickenson	1950–53
Herbert Alonzo Howe	1892–1926	James E. Perdue	1953–65
David Shaw Duncan	1926–30	Edward A. Lindell	1965–75
Roland J. Walters	1930–40	Robert C. Amme	1975–76
Edward J. Allen	1941–47	Kenneth Purcell	1977–84
James E. Perdue	1947–48		

Deans, Directors, and Chairs

Deans of the College of Law

Albert E. Pattison	1892–1902	Harold E. Hurst, acting	1952
Lucius W. Hoyt	1902–10	(3 months)	
George C. Manly	1910–26	Harold E. Hurst	1958–65
George E. Tralles, acting	1926–27	Robert B. Yegge, acting	1965–66
James Grafton Rogers	1927	Robert B. Yegge	1966–77
(6 months)		Lawrence P. Tiffany, acting	1977–78
Roger H. Wolcott	1928–44	Daniel S. Hoffman	1978–84
Alfred Clarence Nelson,	1944–45	William M. Beaney, acting	1984–85
administrator		Edward A. Dauer	1985–89
James F. Price	1945–47	William M. Beaney, acting	1989–90
W. Gordon Johnston	1947–58	Dennis O. Lynch	1990–97
Frances H. Schalow	1949	Robert B. Yegge, acting	1997–present
("in charge" for 3 months)			

The Directors and Deans of the Graduate School of Social Work

Florence Day	1931–1931	Laverne McCummings, dean	1978–85
G. Eleanor Kimball	1931–34	Kay Vail, dean	1985–87
Florence Hutsinpillar	1934–47	John F. Jones, dean	1987–96
Emil M. Sunley, dean	1947–71	James Jorgensen, interim dean	1996
Kenneth W. Kindelsperger, dean	1971–78	Catherine Foster Alter, dean	1996–present

Deans of The College

Charles Cortese	1984–89
Judith Snyder	1989–93
Joseph Hornback, interim	1993

Deans of the Graduate School of Professional Psychology

Peter Buirski	1995–present

Deans of Mathematics and Computer Sciences

Herbert J. Greenberg	1984-1986
William Dorn	1986-1990

Deans of Natural Sciences

Gareth R. Eaton	1984-1986
John L. Kice	1986-1990

Deans of Arts, Humanities, and Social Sciences

William Zaranka	1984-1989
Roscoe Hill	1990–present

Deans of Social Sciences

Harold Mendelsohn	1984-1985
Carl Larson	1985-1986
William Zaranka	1986-1989

Deans of the Faculty of Natural Sciences, Mathematics and Engineering

John L. Kice	1990–95
Robert D. Coombe	1995–present

Deans of College of Business Administration
(became Daniels College of Business September 30, 1994)

John B. Geijsbeek-Molenaar	1908–13	Ronald R. Gist	1979–80
George A. Warfield	1913–36	Richard Brandenburg	1980–86
Clem W. Collins	1936–45	Leon Giles	1986–87
James F. Price	1945–47	Elliot H. Kline	1987–89
Cecil Puckett	1947–55	William F. Ford	1990
Theodore H. Cutler	1955–66	Bruce Hutton	1990–93
Arthur W. Mason Jr.	1966–74	Glyn Hanbery, interim	1994
Peter A. Firmin	1974–79	James Griesemer	1994-present

University College
(formerly The New College)

Peter Warren	1986–present

Dean of The College of Education

Elinor Katz	1995-present

Deans of the Graduate School of International Studies

Ben M. Cherrington	1926–51	Michael G. Fry	1977–81
Elizabeth Fackt	1951–53	Bernhard Abrahamsson, acting	1981–82
C. Dale Fuller	1953–59	James Middleman	1982–87
Josef Korbel	1959–69	E. Thomas Rowe	1987–96
Robert C. Good	1969–77	Tom J. Farer	1996–present
David Bayley, acting	1976–77		

Board of Governors as of 1996

Robert Albin
Chester M. Alter
Sonia Barnes
Paula Bernstein
Eda Brannen
Allen D. Breck
Alvin L. Cohen
Peggy Crane-Epand
David V. Dunklee
Walter C. Emery
Dorothy Goodstein
Marion S. Gottesfeld
 (Trustees' liaison)

Rachel Harper
Patricia Jean Harrington
Richard D. Heiserman
William C. Kurtz Jr.
John A. Love
Edward Lehman
Joseph McGarry
Stephen L. McNichols
Myron Miller
John C. Mitchell II
Richard N. Olson
Lenore Ott
Allan R. Phipps

Charles M. Schayer
Fay Schayer
Ruth Silver
Elio Stacey
Leonard v. B. Sutton
Robert K. Timothy, chair
Frances Z. Webster
William Weil
George M. Wilfley
Lucien Wulsin
J. Louis York
Ruth York

Award Recipients

The Evans Award

Mary Lathrop	Frank H. Ricketson, Jr.	William T. Driscoll
Clem W. Collins	Shelby Harper	Thompson G. Marsh
John A. Hill	Wilbur Castell Miller	William D. Ford
Evelyn Hosmer	Francis S. Vanderbur	John L. Kane, Jr.
Cleo S. Wallace	Alfred Clarence Nelson	Pete V. Domenici
Ralph B. Mayo	Randolph P. McDonough	Edward Lehman
Alberta Iliff Shattuck	Wayne E. Shroyer	Jay G. Piccinati
Frank J. Johns	John E. Gorsuch	Jean Joliffe Yancey
George Johns	Lowell Jackson Thomas	W. Porter Nelson
Joseph D. Lohman	Charline Jackson Birkins	Leo L. Block
Abraham White	Edward W. Estlow	Richard Schmidt Jr.
Robert W. Selig	Charles F. Brannan	William B. Collister
Rollie W. Bradford	Maurice Bernard Mitchell	Leo K. Goto
Reuben G. Gustavson	Allen D. Breck	Otto Tschudi
Chester M. Alter	Allan R. Phipps	Roscoe L. Davidson
Donald H. Menzel	John A. Love	
Walter K. Koch	Paul D. Laxalt	

Professional Achievement Award

Wayne N. Aspinall	Thompson G. Marsh	Elliot E. Martin
James H. Binns	Louis W. Menk	Michael J. Grisanti
Ruamie Hills Binns	Howard H. Jenkins Jr.	Ann Spector Lieff
Anne Roe	Paul F. Cornelsen	William T. Diss
Frank E. Evans	Lewis F. Kornfeld Jr.	Asa C. Hilliard, III
Donald H. Menzel	Richard H. Harris	Gerald F. Groswold
Clem W. Collins	Richard C. Webb	Abraham J. Kauvar
Harold M. Agnew	Anthony F. Zarlengo	June E. Travis
Robert G. Bonham	Mark Harris	Lloyd G. Chavez
Howard P. James	Cleo Parker Robinson	Frederick Downs Jr.
Robert O. Bass	Fred Michael Tesone	

Randolph P. McDonough Award for Service to Alumni

J. Glen Arko	John H. "Jack" Deeter	Betsy C. McGee
Richard G. Arnold	Robert A. Fitzner Jr.	William E. Mitchell
Ann Zegob Hoffman	Elaine Parker	Robert R. Swenson Jr.
Phoebe Anne Ellis Smedley	Patricia J. Dublin	

Distinguished Scholar Award

1990–91	Joyce Goodfriend	1994–95	E. Spencer Wellhofer
1991–92	not given	1995–96	Peter Golas
1992–93	Hugh N. Grove	1996–97	R. Buck Sanford
1993–94	J. C. "Chuck" Wilson		

Community Service Award

Edward Hirschfeld	Earl R. Rinker	Peter H. Coors
Frank H. Ricketson Jr.	Lois Rinker	Elaine Brown Jenkins
Sebastian C. Owens	Alexander B. Holland	Leo K. Goto
Jack C. Hunter	Clara M. Humphreys	A. Barry Hirschfeld
William Thayer Tutt	Dorothy V. Lamm	Arlene Friedman Hirschfeld
Ann C. Brown	Myron Miller	Harry H. Ruston
Raymond A. Kimball	Polly Grimes	Florence Ruston
Paul D. Ambrose	Carneice Brown-White	Swanee Hunt
Fred E. Holmes	Franklin L. Burns	Lafawn Hall Biddle
Ruth Haines Purkaple	Gene Amole Jr.	Helen N. Driscoll
James H. Binns	Grant Wilkins	Merry C. Low
Ruamie H. Binns	Richard L. Gooding	Georgia R. Imhoff

Distinguished Service to the University Award

Allan R. Cohen	Stanley M. Wagner	Edward W. Estlow
Ann D. Love	Edith M. Davis	Charlotte Schroeder Estlow
Aksel Nielsen	Dorothy L. Retallack	Frances Z. Webster
Gladys C. Bell	Anita D. Schulenburg	Adolph "Bud" Mayer
Marion S. Gottesfeld	Kenneth W. Kindelsperger	Jack Rose
Roger D. Knight	Bernis Kindelsperger	Philip E. Gauthier
King D. Shwayder	Houston Waring	Allan O. Pfnister
Murray A. Armstrong	Anthony R. Cillo	James J. Johnston
Gene Steinke	Arthur W. Mason Jr.	Helen Pustmueller
Doris Steinke	Polly Mason	
Lewis Barbato	John R. Farquharson	

Ammi B. Hyde Award for Young Alumni Achievement

Robert D. Lazarus	Timothy P. Fox	Jeffrey S. Hopmayer
David J. Von Drehle	Angel A. Chi	

University Lecturers

1955	Fred E. D'Amour	1969	Wolfgang Yourgrau	1983	Norman Bleistein
1956	Levette J. Davidson	1970	Herbert J. Greenberg	1984	not given
1957	Vance Kirkland	1971	Gresham Sykes	1986	Frank E. X. Dance
1958	Josef Korbel	1972	Gerald W. Chapman	1987	Steve H. Carpenter
1959	Fitzhugh Carmichael	1973	Juan G. Roederer	1988	Gareth R. Eaton
1960	Ellwood Murray	1974	Wilbert Moore	1989	Stanley P. Gudder
1961	R. Russell Porter	1975	John B. Newkirk	1990	Susan Harter
1962	Essie White Cohn	1976	George Barany	1991	Karen S. Kitchener
1963	Thompson G. Marsh	1977	Gunnar Boklund	1992	Lawrence P. Tiffany
1964	W. Campton Bell	1978	David G. Murcray	1993	Toni P. Linder
1965	Harry Seligson	1979	David Bayley	1994	Donald H. Stedman
1966	John E. Williams	1980	John Horn	1995	Paul Predecki
1967	Robert L. Chasson	1981	Seymour Epstein	1996	Bruce Pennington
1968	Harold Mendelsohn	1982	Ved Nanda	1997	Peter Adler

Award Recipients

Distinguished Teaching Award

1968–69	Edith Davis	1982–83	Joel S. Cohen
	Thomas Drabek	1983–84	Herschel Neumann
	Wayne E. Shroyer	1984–85	Ronald J. Rizzuto
1969–70	George E. Bardwell	1985–86	Jere P. Surber
	Laurance C. Herold	1986–87	Anne R. Mahoney
1970–71	Stuart James	1987–88	John C. Livingston
1971–72	Allen D. Breck	1988–89	David Longbrake
1972–73	William S. Huff	1989–90	John D. Bazley
1973–74	Wilbur H. Parks	1990–91	M. E. Warlick
1974–75	Elizabeth Tuttle	1991–92	Cynthia V. Fukami
1975–76	Gerald W. Chapman	1992–93	Margaret E. Whitt
1976 77	David Anderson	1993–94	Richard N. Ball
1977–78	Ronald R. Gist	1994–95	Diane Benoit
1978–79	Luis P. Fonesca	1995–96	Jan Laitos
1979–80	Dennis Barrett	1996–97	Alvin Goldberg
1980–81	Jay Trowill		William Dorn
1981–82	Terrence Toy		

Methodist Scholar/Teacher of the Year Award

1991–82	Herbert J. Greenberg	1989 90	George W. Shepherd
1982–83	Wilbert Moore	1990–91	Robert P. McGowan
1983–84	James E. Sorensen	1991–92	James P. Gilroy
1984–85	Barry Hughes	1992 93	Janette B. Benson
1985–86	Joseph Campos	1993–94	Bernard Spilka
1986–87	Will Gravely	1994–95	Frederick Greenspahn
1987–88	Tricia S. Jones	1995–96	Richard Clemmer-Smith
1988–89	Alexandra Olsen		Sandra Eaton

Burlington Northern Foundation Awards

1984–85	J. Donald Hughes	1988–89	Sarah Nelson,
	Robert C. Schultz		Paul Colomy
1985–86	James A. LaVita,	1989 90	Ved Nanda
	Joseph S. Szyliowicz		Gregory A. Robbins
1986–87	Paul S. Dempsey,	1990–91	Donald G. Sullivan
	Charlotte F. Sanborn	1991–92	Robert N. Dores
1987–88	Aaron Goldman		
	James E. Platt		

John Evans Professorships

1990–91	Marshall Haith,	1994–95	Frank E. X. Dance
	David G. Murcray	1995–96	Sarah Nelson
1991–92	Ved Nanda	1996-97	Gareth R. Eaton
1992–93	Thomas Drabek,		Sandra Eaton
	Susan Harter		
1993–94	Donald Hughes,		
	Steve H. Carpenter		

The Women's Library Association

The Founders, 1946

Mrs. Harry Bellamy	Mrs. David Chalmers	Mrs. William Iliff
Mrs. Horace Bennett	Mrs. Dayton Denious	Mrs. Sam Levy
Mrs. Rollie Bradford	Mrs. M. Ray Gottesfeld	Mrs. Harold Webster

The Executive Chairs

1956–69	Marion S. Gottesfeld	1987–88	Emily Goodin
1969–72	Jan Pirkey	1988–89	Ann Hyde Birdsall
1972–75	Betty Carey	1989–90	Maxine Hopkins
1975–77	Betsy O'Meara	1990–91	Geraldine Wilson
1977–79	Pat Nelson	1991–92	Peggy Matsch
1979–81	Betsy Magness	1992–93	Lina Arnold
1981–83	Arlene Haley	1993–94	Patricia Vardaman
1983–84	Marie Sanborn	1994–95	Charleen Dunn
1984–85	Maggie Sahlen Brown	1995–96	Nancy Kerr
1985–86	Beulah Cherne	1996–97	Louise Rouse
1986–87	Merry C. Low		

Alumni Association

Presidents

1988–89	Nathaniel R. Goldston III	1992–93	reorganization
1989–90	William E. Mitchell	1993–95	Emmit J. McHenry
1990–91	Michael W. Fisher	1995–97	David Bailey
1991–92	Claudia M. Christie	1997–present	Richard B. Green

Secretaries and Directors

1927–32	Jane Butchert	1975–79	Anne Richardson
1932–34	William Loeffler	1979–80	Weldon Irish
1934–63	Randolph P. McDonough	1980–83	Donald W. Wilson Jr.
1963–67	James A. Cover	1983–86	Catherine Sweeney
1967–70	Jack Mumey	1986–91	Cathleen Pasquariello
1970–75	Richard Mansfield	1991–97	Sue Goss

Boettcher Foundation Lecture Series Lecturers

1989	Peter Ueberroth	1992	Helmut Schmidt	1995	Dick Cheney
1990	Elie Wiesel		Faye Wattleton	1996	Mark Shields
	Gerald Ford	1993	C. Everett Koop		Robert Novak
1991	Tom Wolfe		George Will	1997	Abba Eban
	Jeane Kirkpatrick	1994	Maya Angelou		Stephen J. Gould
	William Ruckelshaus		Carl Sagan		

Presidents of the Faculty Senate

1932–35	Frederick Maurice Hunter		1967–68	Harold Dunham
1936–40	David Shaw Duncan		1968–69	Walter O. Fischer
1941–43	Caleb F. Gates Jr.		1969–70	Paul R. Merry
1944–45	Ben Mark Cherrington		1970–71	Robert C. Amme
1946–47	Caleb F. Gates Jr.		1971–72	Stuart James
1948–49	James F. Price		1972–73	Robert D. Richardson
1950–51	Albert Charles Jacobs		1973–74	Bernard Spilka
1951–52	Levette J. Davidson		1974–75	Doris Drury
1952–53	Theodore H. Cutler		1975–76	Alton Barbour
1953–54	Byron Cohn		1976–77	David O. Franks
1954–55	John Lawson		1977–79	Ved Nanda
1955–56	Lawrence C. Miller		1979–80	Charles P. Beall
1956–57	Vance Dittman		1980–81	J. Gordon Milliken
1957–58	Earl Engle		1981–82	Robert Angell
1958–59	Alfred Clarence Nelson		1982–83	James V. Walther
1959–60	Allen D. Breck		1983–84	Howard Ancell
1960–61	Alonzo B. May		1984–86	James V. Walther
1961–62	Raymond G. Carey		1986–88	William Burford
1962–63	Wilbur H. Parks		1988–90	Joseph S. Szyliowicz
1963–64	William T. Driscoll		1990–94	Gordon von Stroh
1964–65	Jerome Kesselman		1994–96	Linda Cobb-Reiley
1965–66	J. Robert Maddox		1996–present	Keith Harrison
1966–67	Clinton Kelley			

Honorary Degrees

1882 Lilton Forbes (physician) MD

1885 Joseph C. Shattuck (educator) MA; Aaron B. Robbins (physician) MD

1886 Abner H. Lucas (minister) MA; S. Edwin Solly (physician) MD

1890 David Hastings Moore (former chancellor) LLD

1892 Robert McIntyre (minister) DD

1893 Arthur Edwards (editor) LLD

1894 John Reid Shannon (minister) DD

1897 Alva Adams (governor) MA; William Hugh Wray Boiyle (minister) DD; Lemuel Herbert Murlin (university president) DD; Horace Emory Warner (minister) DD

1900 Robert Henry Beggs (principal) MA; George Lyman Cannon (teacher) MA; John Louis Neulsen (bishop) DD

1901 Lucius W. Hoyt (law school dean) MA; William Armstrong Hunter (minister) DD; William Doughty Phifer (minister) DD

1902 Leonard Freeman (Gross Medical College) MA; James Franklin Harris (minister) DD; Samuel Henry Kirkbride (minister) DD; William Augustus Moore (law school professor) MA; Claudius Buchanan Spencer (editor) DLitt; William Russell Thomas (professor) DLitt

1903 Bethuel Thomas Vincent (former seminary professor) DD; Allison Emery Drake MS

1904   Barton Orville Aylesworth (college president), DLitt; Rulof Augustus Chase (minister) DD; Alexander Lee Doud (seminary executive committee) MA; Helen Loring Grenfell (superintendent of public instruction) MA; Benjamin Barr Lindsey (juvenile judge) MA; William Fraser McDowell (former chancellor) DLitt; Henry Moore Teller (U.S. senator) LLD

1905   Ellsworth Bethel (teacher) MA; Marquis D. Hornbeck (minister) DD; Charles James Hughes Jr. (former U.S. senator) LLD; Nathan Hugh Lee (minister) DD

1906   Richard Warren Corwin (physician) MA; John Alfred Davis (minister) DD; Frederick Alexander Hawke (minister) DD; John Francis Keating (educator) MA; William Henry Smiley (educator) MA

1907   Patrick Vincent Carlin MA; Earl Montgomery Cranston (lawyer) MA; William Henry Gabbert (judge) LLD; William Laurence Hartman (lawyer) MA; Robert Edgar Lewis (judge) LLD; Robert Wilbur Steele (judge) LLD; Edward M. Stephenson (minister) DD; John Walter Sylvester (minister) DD

1908   Charles Albert Campbell (minister) DD; Albert Howard Dunn (educator) MA; David Dryden Forsyth (minister) DD; Elijah Walker Halford (military) MA; Marvin Andrew Rader (minister) DD; Henry Lincoln Wriston (minister) DD

1909   Charles Ernest Chadsey (educator) DLitt; Horace Tool DeLong (state senator) MA; James Hamner Franklin (minister) DD; Charles Milton Hobbs (business) MA; Ammi Bradford Hyde (professor) DLitt; Bernard Jarlath O'Connell (former state senator) MA; Arthur Clermont Peck (minister) DD; Lucius Warner Hoyt (lawyer) DCL

1910   Henry Martyn Hart (Episcopal Dean) LLD; Alfred Rufus King (judge) LLD; John Bart Geijsbeek-Molenaar (educator) MCS; William O'Ryan (priest) LLD; John Albert Riner (judge) LLD; Charles Henry Schlacks (business) MLA; Henry White Warren (bishop) LLD

1911   Augustus Lincoln Chase (minister) DD; Frank Rufus Hollenback (minister) DD; Herbert Alonzo Howe (educator) LLD; Frederick Tevis Krueger (minister) DD; James Edward LeRossignol (educator) LLD; Henry Milton Mayo (minister) DD

1912   Ervin Nathaniel Edgerton (minister) DD; Charles Wesley Hurett (minister) DD; Orville Knowles Maynard (minister) DD

1913   Orrin Knowles Auman (minister) DD; Francis John MConnell (bishop) LLD; Charles Alderman Rowand (minister) DD; William Thomas Scott (minister) DD; Charles Franklin Seitter (minister) DD

1914   Mary Lindsey Barbee (teacher) MA; Eugene Marion Antrim (minister) DD; Rollin Hamlin Ayres (minister) DD; Frank Wood Bretnall (minister) DD; Sedwick Alonzo Bright (minister) DD; George Washington Downs (minister) DD; William Thomas Dumm (minister) DD; Robert Herman Forrester (minister) DD; Philip Louis Frick (minister) DD; Arthur William Trenholme Hicks (minister) DD; Charles Cotesworthy Pinckney Hiller (minister) DD; Charles William Hancher (minister) DD; Louis Jacob Hole (Minster) DD; David Ellsworth Kendall (minister) DD; John James Lace (minister) DD; Oporia Lionel Orton (minister) DD; Arthur Frederick Ragatz (minister) DD; Harris Franklin Rall (minister) DD; Henry James Talbott (minister) DD; Alfred Jocelyn Waller (minister) DD; John Henry Allen (superintendent) DLitt; Harry McWhirter Barrett (principal) DLitt; John Randolph Bell (principal) DLitt ;Edward Leroy Brown (principal) DLitt; Mary Carroll Craig Bradford (superintendent of instruction) DLitt; Anne Evans (civic leader) DLitt; Arthur John Fynn (teacher) DLitt; Chalmers Hadley (librarian) DLitt; James Francis Keating (educator) DLitt; Ida Kruse McFarlane (professor) DLitt; Daniel Edwards Phillips (professor) DLitt; George Lee Tenney (professor) DLitt; Wilbur Dwight Engle (professor) DLitt; William George Haldane (educator) ScD; Charles Alfred Lory (educator) ScD; Herbert Edwin Russell (professor) ScD; Edward Christian Schneider (professor) ScD; Frank Tappan Bayley (minister) LLD; Gertrude Harper Beggs (educator) LLD; Robert Francis Coyle (minister) LLD; Ira Mitchell DeLong (professor) LLD; Clyde Augustus Duniway (educator) LLD; Livingston Farrand (educator) LLD; Charles Clement Holbrook (judge) LLD; John Henry Houghton (minister) LLD; Frank Hunt Hurd Roberts (educator) LLD; John Wesley Lacey (judge) LLD; William Henry Smiley (educator) LLD; Benjamin Bushrod Tyler (minister) LLD; Zachariah Xenophon Snyder (educator) LLD

1915   Lawrence Cowle Phipps (scientist) MA; Milton Chase Potter (educator) LLD; Jesse Penney Martin (minister) DD; Anne McKeen Shuler (dean of women) MA; Frank Durward Slutz (educator) DLitt; Thomas Shields Young (minister) DD

1916   Carlos Merton Cole (educator) LLD; Robert Edward Dickenson (minister) DD; James Herbert Kelley (educator) DLitt; Harry Vallandingham Kepner (educator) ScD; Charles Edwin Huchingson (teacher) MA; Charles Allen Bradley (educator) ScD

1918   Samuel Alexander Lough (professor) LLD; Irving Peake Johnson(Episcopal Bishop) LLD; George Hilborn Stuntz (minister) DD; Nina McCarthy Weiss (women's clubs) MA; Frederick Johnson Chamberlin (Board of Trustees) MA

1919   Henry Justin Allen (governor of Kansas) LLD; Margaret Packard Taussig DLitt; Cyrus Ames Wright (minister) DD; Charles Odell Thibodeau (minister) DD; Guy Emmet Konkel (minister) DD; Sylvester Eldon Ellis (minister) DD

1920   George Frederick Klein (minister) DD; James William Mahood (minister) DD; James Thomas (minister) DD; Samuel Quigley DLitt; Roland J. D. Walters (dean of liberal arts) DLitt; Charles Larew Mead (minister) LLD

1922   Jesse Homer Newlon (minister) LLD

1925   Charles C. Butler (judge) LLD

1930   Archie Loyd Threlkeld (educator) LLD; James Grafton Rogers (lawyer) LLD; Lotus Delta Coffman DHL

1932   Wilbur Daniel Steele (writer) DLitt; George Cully Manly (former dean of law school) LLD; Stanley Hornbeck DHL

1933   Charles C. Mierow (professor) DHL

1934   George Norlin (educator) DHL; Charles Clinton Casey (former dean of law school) LLD

1935   Father Armand William Forstall, SJ (professor) ScD; Charles Edwin Schofield (educator) DD

1936   Thurston Jynkins Davies LLD

1938   Sam Gilbert Bratton LLD; Edmund Melville Wylie (minister) DD

1939   Anne Evans (philanthropist) DFA; Mary Dean Reed (philanthropist) DHum; Florence Rena Sabin (scientist) ScD

1941   Robert Lawrence Stearns (educator) LLD

1942   Charles Emmett Greene (educator) LLD; Mary Florence Lathrop (lawyer) LLD; Theodore Dru Alison Cockerell ScD

1943   Alta Elizabeth Dines (nursing) DHL; Clarence Addison Dykstra LLD; Wilbur Emery Hammaker (bishop) LLD; John Franklin Shafroth (lawyer) LLD

1944   Caleb Frank Gates Sr. (educator) DHL; Lowell Jackson Thomas (news commentator) DLitt; Reuben Gilbert Gustavson (educator) DHL; Mary C. Walker (military) DHL

1945   Major General Orlando Ward (military) ScD; T. Z. Koo (statesman) DHL

1946   Reverend Paul Roberts (Episcopal Dean) DHL; John Lucian Savage (engineer) ScD; Harold Stephenson Sloan (professor) LLD

1947   Clifford F. Rassweiler (business) ScD; Thomas A. Dines (lawyer) DHL; Mary Chase (writer) DLitt; Franklin D. Cogswell DHL; Hays M. Fuhr DMus; Thomas Hornsby Ferril (writer) DLitt

1948   Charles Dollard LLD; Charles Franklin Brannan (lawyer) LLD

1949   Oliver C. Carmichael (Carnegie Corp.) DHL; Fowler Berry McConnell (business) LLD; Saul Caston (musician) DMus; Burnham Hoyt (architect) DFA

1950   George Braton Pegram (educator) LLD; Robert Livingston Johnson (educator) DHL; Walter Paul Paepeke (business) LLD; Claude Kedzie Boettcher (business) DHum; William Hanson Gill (educator) LLD; Harry James Carman (educator) LLD; John Foster Symes (judge) LLD; Dwight David Eisenhower (general, educator) LLD

1951   Harold Linwood Bowen (Episcopal bishop) DD; Ralph Johnson Bunche (statesman) DPS; Charles C. Gates (business) DPS; Chester William Nimitz (military) DPS; Orie Leon Phillips (judge) LLD; Glenn Theodore Seaborg (atomic scientist) ScD; Anthony Eden (statesman) DPS; Helen Bonfils (philanthropist) DPS; Oscar Littleton Chapman (statesman) LLD; William Sharpless Jackson (judge) LLD; Robert Edmond Jones (theatrical designer) DFA; Harold Raymond Medina (judge) LLD; Arthur Hays Sulzberger (publisher) DPS

1952   Oliver Shewell Franks (ambassador) DPS; Edith Abbott (educator) DHum; Hans Albrecht Bethe (nuclear physicist) ScD; Charles Eliezer Hillel Kauvar (rabbi) DD; Quigg Newton (Denver mayor) DPS; Young Berryman Smith (educator) LLD; Robert R. Williams (philanthropist) ScD; Frank Learoyd Boyden (educator) DPS; Helen Hayes MacArthur (actress) DFA; Edward Caldwell King (educator)LLD; Irving Sands Olds (business) DPS; Harold Blake Walker (minister) DD; Albert Charles Jacobs (chancellor) DPS; Henry Knox Sherrill (Episcopal bishop) DD

1953   Ben Mark Cherrington (educator) DPS; Frank Watt Dickinson (educator) DHL; W. Maurice Ewing (scientist) ScD; William West Grant (lawyer) LLD; Loy Wesley Henderson (ambassador) DPS; Asuncion Arriola Perez (social welfare) DHum; Margaret Rogers Phipps (philanthropist) DFA; William C. Martin (bishop) DD; Robert Hugh McWilliams (professor) DPS; Clara Mitchell Van Schaack (civic leader) DHum

1954   John Gideon Gates (business) DPS; William Lee Knous (former governor) LLD; Daniel L. Marsh (educator) DHL; Donald Howard Menzel (physicist) ScD; Jesse Shwayder (business) DPS; Alfred Marshall Bailey (museum director) DPS; Samuel Miller Brownell (U.S. Commissioner of Education) LLD

1955   Otto Karl Bach (director of Denver Art Museum) DHum; Lucius Ward Bannister (lawyer) LLD; Adolph Kiesler (philanthropist) DPS; Clarence Frederick Lea (former U.S. representative) LLD; Amos Alonzo Stagg (football coach) DPS; Frederica Lefevre Bellamy (civic leader) DPS

1956   Hamlett Platt Burke (judge) LLD; Walker Van Riper (curator, Denver Art Museum) ScD; George Carl Wilsnack (scientist) ScD; Isadore Samuels (civic leader) DPS

1957   Heber Reece Harper (former DU chancellor) DPS; Edwin Carl Johnson (former Colorado governor, U.S. senator) LLD; Eugene Donald Millikin (former U.S. senator) LLD; William Edgeworth Morgan (educator) LLD; Henry Leonard Weiss (minister) DD; Wilbur McClure Alter (judge) LLD; Abraham David Hannath Kaplan (Brookings Institution) DPS; Willis McDonald Tate (former dean) LLD

Honorary Degrees

1958   Clem Wetzell Collins (educator) LLD; Morton J. May (business) LLD; Robert Wilbur Steele (judge) LLD; Alfred Hamlin Washburn (scientist) ScD; Malcolm Glenn Wyer (librarian) LLD; Florence Windsor Hutsinpillar (professor) DHL; Maurice B. Mitchell (business) LLD

1959   Emerson Buckley (music conductor) DHum; Harold Ford Carr (educator) LLD; John Arthur Chapman (drama critic) DHum; Warwick Miller Downing (lawyer) LLD; Ben Ivan Funk (military) DPS; Robert William Selig (Board of Trustees) DPS; Ina Teresa Aulls (librarian) DHL

1960   Louis Tomlinson Benezet (educator) LLD; Jean Sala Breitenstein (judge) LLD; Pyke Johnson (foundation head) DPS; Alton Ellegood Lowe (management) LLD; Aksel Nielsen (president, DU Board of Trustees) DPS; Elizabeth Lenore Fackt (professor) LLD

1961   Joseph Patterson Binns (businessman) LLD; Harold Raymond Keables (teacher) DLitt; Etienne Bernardeau Renaud (professor) LLD; John Ewart Wallace Sterling (educator) LLD; Horace Jay Wubben (educator) LLD

1962   William Henry Bernhardt (professor) LLD; Frank Harold Hanna Roberts (professor) LLD; Henry King Stanford (educator) LLD; Fred Edmund D'Amour (professor) LLD; Ruth Murray Underhill (professor) LLD

1963   Sarvepalli Radhakrishnan (president of India) LLD; Wayne Aspinall (U.S. representative) LLD; Hans Kohn (scholar and author) LLD; Father Richard F. Ryan (educator) LLD; Marcus J. Aurelius (business) LLD; Muhammed Zafrulla Khan (president of the U.N. General Assembly) LLD; John Arthur Love (governor-elect of Colorado) LLD

1964   Walter Elmer Sikes (professor) DHL; Robert Russell Porter (professor) DHL; Alfred Clarence Nelson (educator) LLD; John Evans Jr. (president, Board of Trustees) LLD; John Evans (business) LLD, W. Averell Harriman (statesman) LLD; Andrew Wellington Cordier (educator) LLD; U Thant LLD; Grayson Louis Kirk LLD; Byron Raymond White LLD; Robert Francis Goheen LLD; James Roscoe Miller LLD; Arnold Joseph Toynbee LLD

1965   John Alexander Hill (insurance) LLD; James Everett Perdue (education) LLD; Glenn Randall Phillips (bishop) LLD, Jean Chappell Cranmer (philanthropist) DHL

1966   Karl Raimund Popper (professor) LLD; Louis Wilson Menk (business) LLD; Arthur Lemoine Miller (minister) LLD; Lyndon Baines Johnson (President of the U.S.) LLD; Joseph Royall Smiley (educator) LLD; Dean Rusk LLD

1967   Chester M. Alter (retiring chancellor of DU) LLD; Charlotte Hildebrand Bradford (philanthropist) DHL; Ramsey Clark (U.S. Attorney General) LLD; Cris Dobbins (business) LLD

1968   William L. Everitt (educator) LLD; O. Otto Moore (judge) LLD; Stewart L. Udall (U.S. secretary of the interior) LLD

1969   Mark O. Hatfield (U.S. senator, Oregon) LLD; Hyman G. Rickover (military) ScD; Martin Rist (professor) LLD; Walter Orr Roberts (scientist) ScD; Donald R. Young (professor) LLD; Rosamond Gilder (author, theatre critic) DHL

1970   John H. Clarke (professor) DHL; Ian MacGregor (business) LLD; Eugene J. McCarthy (U.S. senator, Minnesota) LLD; Peter Gay (professor) DHL

1971   Ross A. MacFarland (professor) ScD; Robert H. McWilliams (judge) LLD; Hans J. Morgenthau (professor) LLD; Vernon A. Stenger (scientist) ScD; Whitney M. Young Jr. (National Urban League) LLD (posthumous)

1972 Robert O. Anderson (business) LLD; Norman Cousins (editor) DHL; Wilbur C. Miller (vice chancellor of academic affairs) LLD

1973 Howard Jenkins Jr. (National Labor Relations board) LLD; Albert Harold Rosenthal (public administration) LLD; Allen D. Breck (professor) DHL

1974 Arthur J. Goldberg (former U.S. Supreme Court justice) LLD; Archibald Cox (U.S. attorney general) LLD; Douglas Fairbanks Jr. (actor) LLD; A. Ray Chamberlain (educator) DLitt

1975 James R. Allen (superintendent, U. S. Air Force Academy) LLD; Katrina McCormick Barnes (philanthropist) DHL; Hugh B. Terry (retired Denver broadcaster) DHL; Abraham White (professor) ScD; Edward Albert Lindell (dean of arts and sciences) DHL

1976 Kurt Waldheim (U.N. secretary-general) LLD; Josef Korbel (professor) DHL; Mortimer J. Adler (writer) LLD; Fr. Theodore M. Hesburgh, CSC (educator) LLD; Joseph E. Slater (lawyer) LLD

1977 John O. Crosby (educator) DHL; Donald J. Hall (business) LLD

1978 Allan O. Pfnister (acting chancellor) LLD

1979 Edward E. Pringle (judge) LLD; Normand Lockwood (composer) DHL

1980 Jessie Whaley Maxwell (educator) DHL; Frederick Amos Praeger (publisher) DHL

1983 Willy Schaeffler (coach) DHL; Kenneth W. Thompson (educator) LLD; Malcolm Stevenson Forbes (publisher) DHL

1984 Robert Crocker Good (educator) DHL; Linus Carl Pauling (scientist) DLitt; Frank H. Ricketson Jr. (business) LLD; Francis S. Van Derbur (DU Board of Trustees) DHL; Abram Leon Sachar DHL

1985 Rexer Berndt (educator) DHEd; Hanna Holburn Gray (educator) DHum; William Lipscomb (scientist) ScD; John Naisbitt (writer) DHL

1986 Richard Lamm (governor) DHL; Franklin Lane Burns (philanthropist) DHL; Bill Daniels (business) DHL

1987 Emil Hecht (business) DHL; Elie Wiesel (writer, Nobel Peace Prize winner) DHL; Thompson G. Marsh (professor) DHL; Hugh O'Brian (Youth Foundation, actor) DPS

1988 William D. Ford (congressman) LLD; Kazuo Inamori (industrialist) ScD

1989 William Armstrong (government) DPS; Thomas Jordan (business) ScD; Thomas H. Kean (governor) DHL; Leonard v.B Sutton (judge) LLD

1990 Arthur A. Fletcher (civil rights) DPS; Helen Thompson Heath (philanthropy) DFA; William K. Hosokawa (journalism) DHL; Eugene Hughes (writer) DHL; Dwight Morrell Smith (educator) DLitt; Joyce Meskis (business) DHL; Zita L. Weinshienk (judge) LLD; Timothy E. Wirth (government) LLD

1991 Chuck Y. Gee (business) DPS; E. B. Jeppesen (business) DPS; Elizabeth Paepcke (philanthropy) DHL; Cleo Parker Robinson (artist) DFA; Bernard Weatherill (government) DHL

1992 Harold Melvin Agnew (science) DPS; Betty B. and Ferdinand C. Knoebel (business) DPS; John C. Malone (business) DHL William C. Olson (educator) DHL; Allan Phipps (business) DHL; R. E. (Ted) Turner (business) DHL

1993 John Echohawk (attorney) DHL; William C. Kurtz Jr. (business) DHL; Rachel Bassette Noel (educator) DPS; Sylvia Ortega Salazar (educator) EdD; Richard J. Watts ScD; Pete V. Domenici DPS

1994   Victor Borge (musician) DFA; Henry L. Solano (judge) LLD; John C. Welles (museum director) DHL; Duaine Wolfe (musician) DFA

1995   Carolyn Jaffe (health care) DHL; Noel Ginsburg (business) DHL; Gerald M. Levin (business) DHL; Roberta Cooper Ramo LLD

1996   Condoleezza Rice (educator) EdD; Richard C. Webb (business) ScD; Daisaku Ikeda (educator) EdD; Talbot "Sandy" D'Alemberte (educator) LLD; Clayton F. Freiheit (zoo director) DHL

1997   Norman Augustine (business) DHL; Sister Mary Luke Tobin (religion) DPS; Winfield Niblo (business) DHL; Fabio Roversi-Monaco (rector, University of Bologna) DHL; Rebecca Love Kourlis (judge) LLD; John L. Kane Jr. LLD

Endowed Chairs and Professorships

Louis D. Beaumont Chair*
Leo Block University Professor
Andrew Mellon Professor
John A. Carver Jr., Endowed Chair
Ira C. Cutler Endowed Chair in Biological Sciences
Charles W. Delaney Jr., Professor
*Denver Clearing House Association Chair
Eva and Emil Hecht Endowed Professorship
Walter Koch Endowed Chair
*Edna Biggs Kurtz Memorial Chair
Thompson G. Marsh Professorship
Brainerd Phillipson Chair
*Lawrence C. Phipps Endowed Professorship
Evelyn and Jay Piccinati Endowed Chair
*May Bonfils Stanton Chair
Transportation Law Endowed Chair
Barton Weller Endowed Chair in Science and Engineering
John C. Willemssen Endowed Distinguished Professorship
William Herschel Womble Chair

*These chairs and professorships are not currently filled but earn income for the support of faculty salaries and programs.

Table of Organization, 1997

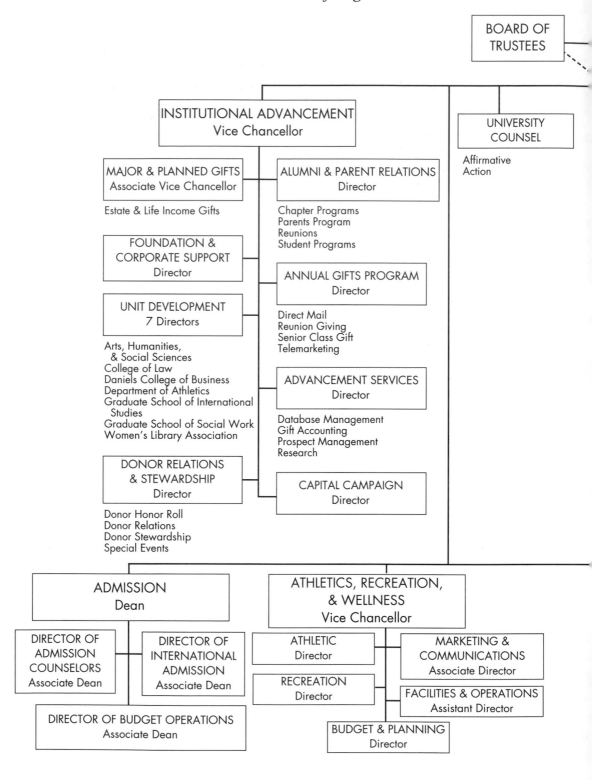

BOARD OF TRUSTEES

INSTITUTIONAL ADVANCEMENT
Vice Chancellor

UNIVERSITY COUNSEL

Affirmative Action

MAJOR & PLANNED GIFTS
Associate Vice Chancellor

Estate & Life Income Gifts

ALUMNI & PARENT RELATIONS
Director

Chapter Programs
Parents Program
Reunions
Student Programs

FOUNDATION & CORPORATE SUPPORT
Director

ANNUAL GIFTS PROGRAM
Director

Direct Mail
Reunion Giving
Senior Class Gift
Telemarketing

UNIT DEVELOPMENT
7 Directors

Arts, Humanities,
& Social Sciences
College of Law
Daniels College of Business
Department of Athletics
Graduate School of International
Studies
Graduate School of Social Work
Women's Library Association

ADVANCEMENT SERVICES
Director

Database Management
Gift Accounting
Prospect Management
Research

DONOR RELATIONS & STEWARDSHIP
Director

Donor Honor Roll
Donor Relations
Donor Stewardship
Special Events

CAPITAL CAMPAIGN
Director

ADMISSION
Dean

ATHLETICS, RECREATION, & WELLNESS
Vice Chancellor

DIRECTOR OF ADMISSION COUNSELORS
Associate Dean

DIRECTOR OF INTERNATIONAL ADMISSION
Associate Dean

ATHLETIC
Director

MARKETING & COMMUNICATIONS
Associate Director

RECREATION
Director

FACILITIES & OPERATIONS
Assistant Director

DIRECTOR OF BUDGET OPERATIONS
Associate Dean

BUDGET & PLANNING
Director

294

Table of Organization, 1997

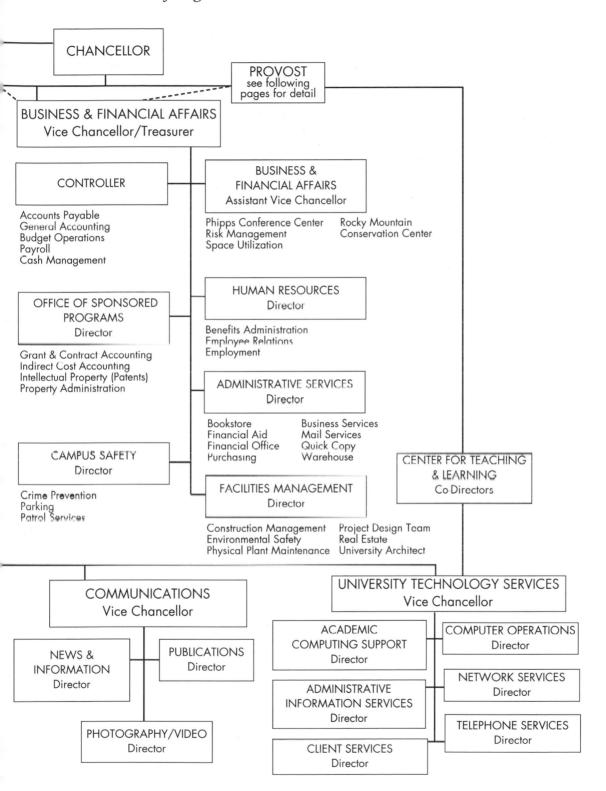

CHANCELLOR

PROVOST
see following
pages for detail

BUSINESS & FINANCIAL AFFAIRS
Vice Chancellor/Treasurer

CONTROLLER

Accounts Payable
General Accounting
Budget Operations
Payroll
Cash Management

BUSINESS & FINANCIAL AFFAIRS
Assistant Vice Chancellor

Phipps Conference Center   Rocky Mountain
Risk Management   Conservation Center
Space Utilization

OFFICE OF SPONSORED PROGRAMS
Director

Grant & Contract Accounting
Indirect Cost Accounting
Intellectual Property (Patents)
Property Administration

HUMAN RESOURCES
Director

Benefits Administration
Employee Relations
Employment

ADMINISTRATIVE SERVICES
Director

Bookstore   Business Services
Financial Aid   Mail Services
Financial Office   Quick Copy
Purchasing   Warehouse

CAMPUS SAFETY
Director

Crime Prevention
Parking
Patrol Services

FACILITIES MANAGEMENT
Director

Construction Management   Project Design Team
Environmental Safety   Real Estate
Physical Plant Maintenance University Architect

CENTER FOR TEACHING & LEARNING
Co-Directors

COMMUNICATIONS
Vice Chancellor

NEWS & INFORMATION
Director

PUBLICATIONS
Director

PHOTOGRAPHY/VIDEO
Director

UNIVERSITY TECHNOLOGY SERVICES
Vice Chancellor

ACADEMIC COMPUTING SUPPORT
Director

COMPUTER OPERATIONS
Director

ADMINISTRATIVE INFORMATION SERVICES
Director

NETWORK SERVICES
Director

CLIENT SERVICES
Director

TELEPHONE SERVICES
Director

Table of Organization, 1997

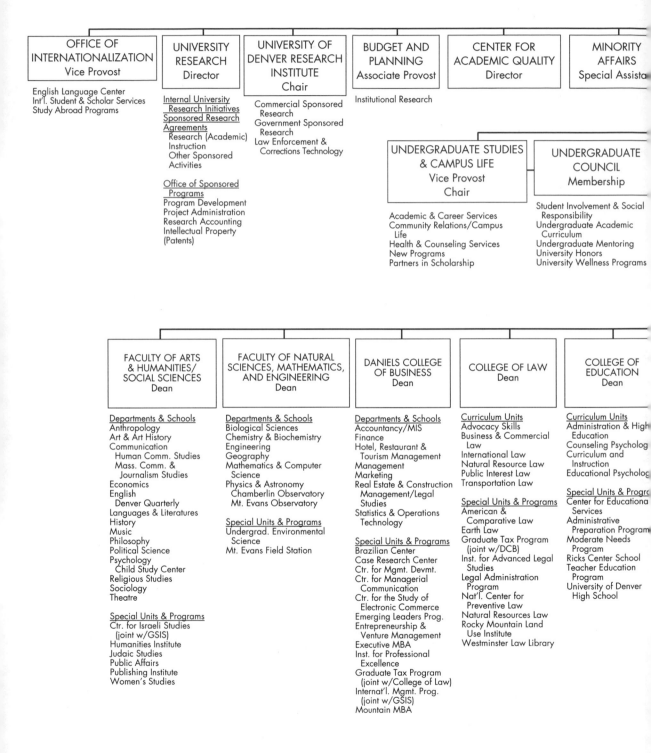

OFFICE OF INTERNATIONALIZATION
Vice Provost

English Language Center
Int'l. Student & Scholar Services
Study Abroad Programs

UNIVERSITY RESEARCH
Director

Internal University
  Research Initiatives
Sponsored Research
Agreements
  Research (Academic)
  Instruction
  Other Sponsored
  Activities

Office of Sponsored
  Programs
Program Development
Project Administration
Research Accounting
Intellectual Property
  (Patents)

UNIVERSITY OF DENVER RESEARCH INSTITUTE
Chair

Commercial Sponsored
  Research
Government Sponsored
  Research
Law Enforcement &
  Corrections Technology

BUDGET AND PLANNING
Associate Provost

Institutional Research

CENTER FOR ACADEMIC QUALITY
Director

MINORITY AFFAIRS
Special Assista

UNDERGRADUATE STUDIES & CAMPUS LIFE
Vice Provost
Chair

Academic & Career Services
Community Relations/Campus
  Life
Health & Counseling Services
New Programs
Partners in Scholarship

UNDERGRADUATE COUNCIL
Membership

Student Involvement & Social
  Responsibility
Undergraduate Academic
  Curriculum
Undergraduate Mentoring
University Honors
University Wellness Programs

FACULTY OF ARTS & HUMANITIES/ SOCIAL SCIENCES
Dean

Departments & Schools
Anthropology
Art & Art History
Communication
  Human Comm. Studies
  Mass. Comm. &
  Journalism Studies
Economics
English
  Denver Quarterly
Languages & Literatures
History
Music
Philosophy
Political Science
Psychology
  Child Study Center
Religious Studies
Sociology
Theatre

Special Units & Programs
Ctr. for Israeli Studies
  (joint w/GSIS)
Humanities Institute
Judaic Studies
Public Affairs
Publishing Institute
Women's Studies

FACULTY OF NATURAL SCIENCES, MATHEMATICS, AND ENGINEERING
Dean

Departments & Schools
Biological Sciences
Chemistry & Biochemistry
Engineering
Geography
Mathematics & Computer
  Science
Physics & Astronomy
  Chamberlin Observatory
  Mt. Evans Observatory

Special Units & Programs
Undergrad. Environmental
  Science
Mt. Evans Field Station

DANIELS COLLEGE OF BUSINESS
Dean

Departments & Schools
Accountancy/MIS
Finance
Hotel, Restaurant &
  Tourism Management
Management
Marketing
Real Estate & Construction
  Management/Legal
  Studies
Statistics & Operations
  Technology

Special Units & Programs
Brazilian Center
Case Research Center
Ctr. for Mgmt. Devmt.
Ctr. for Managerial
  Communication
Ctr. for the Study of
  Electronic Commerce
Emerging Leaders Prog.
Entrepreneurship &
  Venture Management
Executive MBA
Inst. for Professional
  Excellence
Graduate Tax Program
  (joint w/College of Law)
Internat'l. Mgmt. Prog.
  (joint w/GSIS)
Mountain MBA

COLLEGE OF LAW
Dean

Curriculum Units
Advocacy Skills
Business & Commercial
  Law
International Law
Natural Resource Law
Public Interest Law
Transportation Law

Special Units & Programs
American &
  Comparative Law
Earth Law
Graduate Tax Program
  (joint w/DCB)
Inst. for Advanced Legal
  Studies
Legal Administration
  Program
Nat'l. Center for
  Preventive Law
Natural Resources Law
Rocky Mountain Land
  Use Institute
Westminster Law Library

COLLEGE OF EDUCATION
Dean

Curriculum Units
Administration & High
  Education
Counseling Psycholog
Curriculum and
  Instruction
Educational Psycholog

Special Units & Progra
Center for Educationa
  Services
Administrative
  Preparation Program
Moderate Needs
  Program
Ricks Center School
Teacher Education
  Program
University of Denver
  High School

Table of Organization, 1997

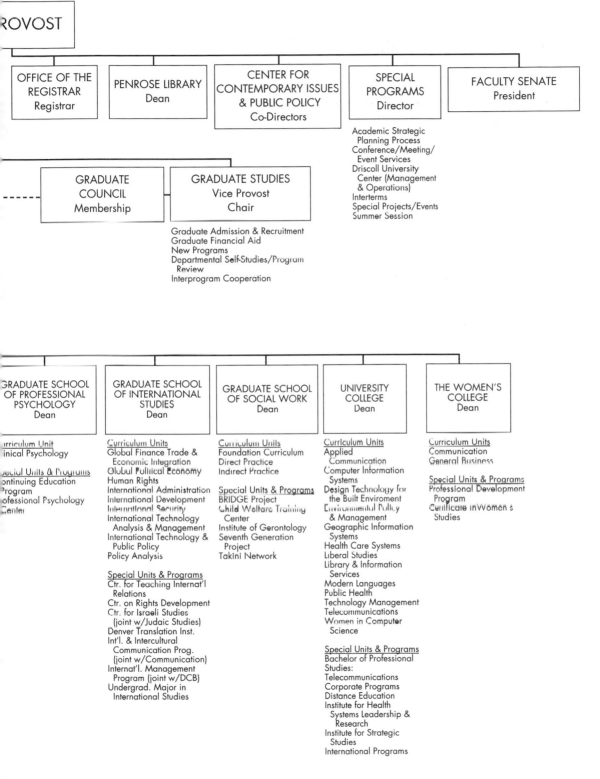

PROVOST

OFFICE OF THE REGISTRAR
Registrar

PENROSE LIBRARY
Dean

CENTER FOR CONTEMPORARY ISSUES & PUBLIC POLICY
Co-Directors

SPECIAL PROGRAMS
Director

Academic Strategic
 Planning Process
Conference/Meeting/
 Event Services
Driscoll University
 Center (Management
 & Operations)
Interterms
Special Projects/Events
Summer Session

FACULTY SENATE
President

GRADUATE COUNCIL
Membership

GRADUATE STUDIES
Vice Provost
Chair

Graduate Admission & Recruitment
Graduate Financial Aid
New Programs
Departmental Self-Studies/Program
 Review
Interprogram Cooperation

GRADUATE SCHOOL OF PROFESSIONAL PSYCHOLOGY
Dean

Curriculum Unit
Clinical Psychology

Special Units & Programs
Continuing Education
Program
Professional Psychology
Center

GRADUATE SCHOOL OF INTERNATIONAL STUDIES
Dean

Curriculum Units
Global Finance Trade &
 Economic Integration
Global Political Economy
Human Rights
International Administration
International Development
International Security
International Technology
 Analysis & Management
International Technology &
 Public Policy
Policy Analysis

Special Units & Programs
Ctr. for Teaching Internat'l
 Relations
Ctr. on Rights Development
Ctr. for Israeli Studies
 (joint w/Judaic Studies)
Denver Translation Inst.
Int'l. & Intercultural
 Communication Prog.
 (joint w/Communication)
Internat'l. Management
 Program (joint w/DCB)
Undergrad. Major in
 International Studies

GRADUATE SCHOOL OF SOCIAL WORK
Dean

Curriculum Units
Foundation Curriculum
Direct Practice
Indirect Practice

Special Units & Programs
BRIDGE Project
Child Welfare Training
 Center
Institute of Gerontology
Seventh Generation
 Project
Takini Network

UNIVERSITY COLLEGE
Dean

Curriculum Units
Applied
 Communication
Computer Information
 Systems
Design Technology for
 the Built Enviroment
Environmental Policy
 & Management
Geographic Information
 Systems
Health Care Systems
Liberal Studies
Library & Information
 Services
Modern Languages
Public Health
Technology Management
Telecommunications
Women in Computer
 Science

Special Units & Programs
Bachelor of Professional
Studies:
Telecommunications
Corporate Programs
Distance Education
Institute for Health
 Systems Leadership &
 Research
Institute for Strategic
 Studies
International Programs

THE WOMEN'S COLLEGE
Dean

Curriculum Units
Communication
General Business

Special Units & Programs
Professional Development
 Program
Certificate in Women's
 Studies

INDEX

Notes: A page number appearing in italics denotes a photograph or other graphic.

Because this is a history of the University of Denver, it is understood that the words "University of Denver" need to precede many of the entries — for example, administration, awards, faculty, endowment, mission, publications, staff, and student body.

A

A, B

B

B

C

C

D

E, F

F

F, G

G, H

H

H

I

J

K

K, L

M

N

N, O, P

P, Q

Q

R

S

T

T, U

U

V

W

W

W, Y, Z

Index prepared by Paulette Whitcomb.

University Park Campus Map, 1997

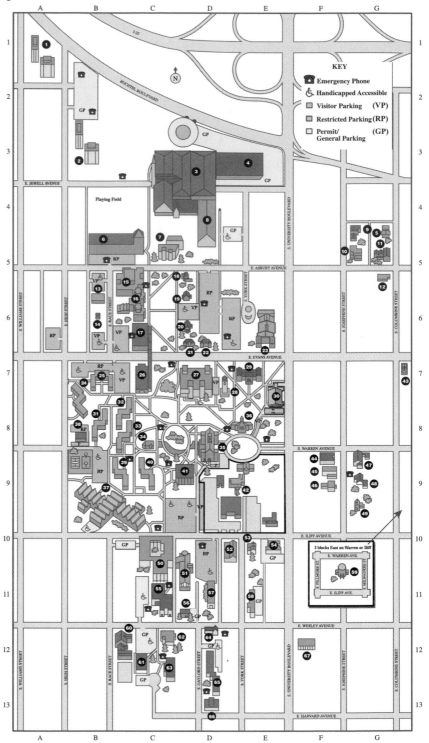

KEY

☎ Emergency Phone
♿ Handicapped Accessible
▢ Visitor Parking (VP)
▢ Restricted Parking (RP)
▢ Permit/ (GP)
General Parking

Park Hill Campus Map, 1997

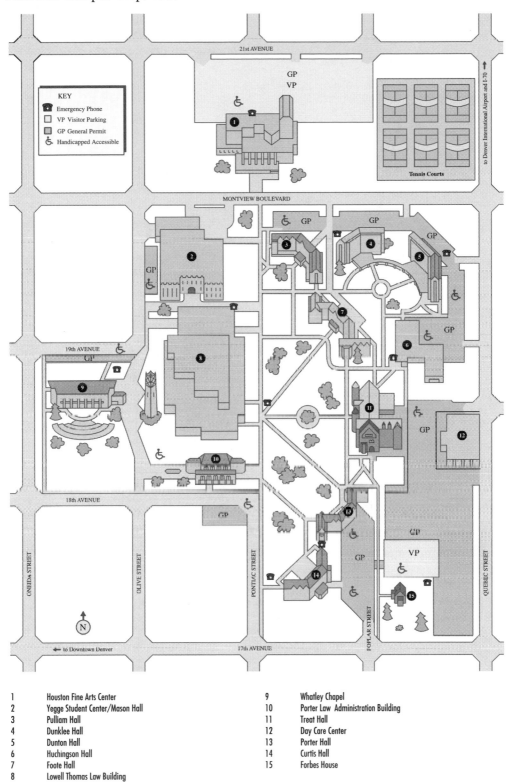

1	Houston Fine Arts Center	9	Whatley Chapel
2	Yegge Student Center/Mason Hall	10	Porter Law Administration Building
3	Pulliam Hall	11	Treat Hall
4	Dunklee Hall	12	Day Care Center
5	Dunton Hall	13	Porter Hall
6	Huchingson Hall	14	Curtis Hall
7	Foote Hall	15	Forbes House
8	Lowell Thomas Law Building		

University Hall   Mary Reed Building   F. W. Olin Hall